doing business with

Croatia

GLOBAL MARKET BRIEFINGS

doing business with
Croatia

SECOND EDITION

CONSULTANT EDITORS:
MARAT TERTEROV
VISNJA BOJANIC

Deloitte.

ZAGREB INSURANCE Co.
Confidence for a reason!

**KOGAN
PAGE**

London and Sterling, VA

Publisher's note

Every possible effort has been made to ensure that the information contained in this handbook is accurate at the time of going to press, and the publishers and authors cannot accept responsibility for any errors or omissions, however caused. No responsibility for loss or damage occasioned to any person acting, or refraining from action, as a result of the material in this publication can be accepted by the editor, the publisher or any of the authors.

First published in Great Britain and the United States in 2004 by Kogan Page Limited.

Apart from any fair dealing for the purposes of research or private study, or criticism or review, as permitted under the Copyright, Designs and Patents Act, 1988, this publication may only be reproduced, stored or transmitted, in any form, or by any means, with the prior permission in writing of the publisher, or in the case of reprographic reproduction in accordance with the terms of licences issued by the Copyright Licensing Agency. Enquiries concerning reproduction outside those terms should be sent to the publishers at the undermentioned addresses:

120 Pentonville Road
London N1 9JN
UK
www.kogan-page.co.uk

22883 Quicksilver Drive
Sterling VA 20166–2012
USA

© Kogan Page and Contributors 2004

ISBN 0 7494 4075 9

British Library Cataloguing in Publication Data

A CIP record for this book is available from the British Library

Library of Congress Cataloguing-in-Publication Data

Doing business with Croatia / consultant editor Marat Terterov.-- 1st ed.
        p. cm. -- (Global market briefings)
Includes bibliographical references and index.
   ISBN 0-7494-4075-9
   1. Croatia--Commerce--Handbooks, manuals, etc. 2. Croatia--Economic conditions--Handbooks, manuals, etc. 3. Investments, Foreign--Croatia--Handbooks, manuals, etc. I. Terterov, Marat. II. Series: Global market briefing
HF3738.Z6D65 2004
330.94972--dc22
                                        2002021971

Typeset by JS Typesetting Ltd, Wellingborough, Northants
Printed and bound in Great Britain by Thanet Press Ltd, Margate

Contents

Part Four: Business Development

Part Five: Appendices

BROTNJO DOO ZAGREB

Distributors of major
European food and
non-food brands

Agencies accepted

Tel: 00-385-1389-7740
Fax: 00-385-1389-7192

Gustava Krkleca BB
10090 Zagreb
Croatia

Foreword

Croatia is a country of abundant possibilities

In spite of all its past obstacles and difficulties Croatia has undergone a significant transformation. Here in Croatia, we are successfully building a society based on justice and a competitive market economy.

Currently, Croatia enjoys impressive macroeconomic indicators: in comparison with other countries of Eastern and Central Europe it has one of the highest rates of economic growth, an upward trend in industrial growth, low inflation and declining unemployment rates.

International institutions have positively rated Croatia's credit-worthiness, which enables it to secure favourable financing of its strategic infrastructure projects. This investment will ensure a base for future sustainable growth and development.

Furthermore, Croatia confidently sails towards full membership of the European Union. Even though membership of the EU requires numerous modifications, Croatia has shown that it is able and ready to cope with the huge task of legislative harmonization and adoption of EU standards, which will in the end facilitate and simplify doing business in Croatia and with Croatian companies.

I am confident that this publication will assist in the promotion of Croatia's business potential where international and Croatian entrepreneurs can connect together.

Ivica Racan
Prime Minister of the Republic of Croatia

Foreword

The Republic of Croatia is a country in transition, that is both mid-European and Mediterranean. It is currently undergoing dynamic changes in its economic and social structure. General political and economic stability, an effective legal system, democracy and free enterprise are the basic prerequisites for economic growth. All these will make it possible for Croatia to join in the community of modern and democratic countries along with full integration into leading economic associations in the world. It has introduced sweeping changes by signing the Stabilization and Association Agreement and by requesting to join the European Union.

Through accession to CEFTA and by signing several bilateral and multilateral free trade agreements, Croatia has liberalized foreign trade and increased its exports. It is the beginning of the most comprehensive reform process in the country to date. The main objectives are to increase industrial production, exports and investments in Croatia.

Other important objectives are a decrease in the growth of total public expenditure, acceleration of the privatization process and the continuation of restructuring in shipbuilding, the metal industry, and the energy sector. These sectors are being reformed now, which is an important step in the creation of a system that will improve preconditions for the establishment of new companies, sustainable growth and employment.

The Government of the Republic of Croatia is adopting the Investment Promotion Law, which aims to promote investments that will increase the production capacity of the country by improving the capital/labour ratio, in particular through the introduction of new technologies.

The business community can rely on a revised Company Law that has recently been adopted by the Croatian Parliament. The Company Law is in full compliance with European Union legislation – *Acquis Communitaire*. The Croatian Government has also established the Trade and Investment Promotion Agency – TIPA. The main activities of TIPA are investor facilitation, export trade promotion, investment climate improvement, investment generation, and last but not least promoting the country as a place to invest.

We invite investors to join us in the 'new Croatia' project. We welcome the capital they invest, their new ideas and technologies, their entrepreneurial spirit, their attitude to work and their 'know how'.

Ljubo Jurcic, PhD
Minister of the Economy

Foreword

The Government of the Republic of Croatia regards the rapprochement with the European Union as one of the most important objectives of its foreign policy. The Ministry for European Integration evolved from the Office for European Integration and was established on 5 February 2000, with the aim of raising the relations with the European Union to a higher level and successfully coordinating the process of European integration in Croatia. Since its establishment, the Ministry has been engaged in preparatory activities for the establishment of a system leading to the efficient adjustment of the Croatian legal and economic system to those of the European Union. Furthermore, a system has been established within the Ministry providing expert support to the negotiations for the Stabilization and Association Agreement. The mandate of the Ministry is to harmonize and coordinate the process within the state administration in order to achieve a successful and economically, socially and institutionally sustainable integration.

Its goal is to achieve the highest possible degree of integration of the Republic of Croatia into the EU, raise public awareness of the process of rapprochement with the EU, education and further training of government employees in the field of European integration, and the translation of EU legal documents required for the harmonization of the legal system.

The Ministry for European Integration has nine state officials and 133 employees with an average age of a little under 30. Among the employees, two have a PhD, 40 an MA and 71 are graduates. All of them are well educated in the fields important for Croatian integration into the EU.

Mr sc Neven Mimica
Minister for European Integration

Foreword

At a time when Croatia is facing the many challenges of globalization, we are aware that it is the development of small and medium enterprises (SMEs) that propels each country's economic development.

Globalization is a fact to be considered when making long-term economic projections. Research has shown that competition is taking place at the level of networked manufacturing and service domains. This is specifically due to the development of new technologies, new products, innovative processes, education, culture and integration processes. Current integration processes are focused on establishing links through international institutions and regional affiliations. Entrepreneurship is increasing in Croatia; it is becoming a philosophy of advancement, and entrepreneurs introducing new technologies and creating new values are creating new jobs, enabling manifold social, cultural and personal development. In a word, they are creating the welfare state and the economy.

The Ministry of Crafts, Small and Medium Enterprises encourages international networking of SMEs, as well as investments in Croatian small businesses. The Ministry's project, 'The Catalogue of Croatian Entrepreneurs' contains 300 entrepreneurial projects requiring permanent investment, funding or business cooperation. It will soon develop into a commodity exchange, an Internet offer and demand service. The Catalogue has been launched on the Web site of the Ministry, www.momsp.hr.

In addition, The Ministry has published an *Exporters' Guide* for entrepreneurs interested in exporting or investing in other countries. The book gives a detailed description of the nature of exports and international trade and includes references to sources of useful information and programmes or services that can be of assistance in entering international markets.

With great pleasure I welcome *Doing Business with Croatia*, which is aimed at increasing Croatian competitiveness and which, I am sure, will be of great help in understanding the Croatian business environment and encouraging foreign investment in new business ventures in our country.

Zeljko Pecek
Minister for Crafts, Small and Medium Enterprises

Foreword

The Republic of Croatia – a land of the future

The Republic of Croatia, situated on the border between Central Europe and the Mediterranean, encompasses 56,538 square kilometres and has a population of 4.5 million inhabitants. Its geographic configuration makes it the country with the longest border relative to its area and number of inhabitants. Croatia is a country that has been influenced by many cultures but has also actively contributed to the cultures of others. Its neighbours are Slovenia, Hungary, Serbia, Bosnia and Herzegovina, Montenegro and Italy. Croatia's geographical position has advantages but has also brought a series of problems that have determined its historical development. The war in the 1990s was only the latest in a series of misfortunes that befell the citizens of Croatia throughout a turbulent history. The devastating impact of the past war is still felt today, particularly in eastern Slavonia and Dalmatia.

Nonetheless, in a very short time Croatian development has become dynamic through restructuring and the adoption of a market economy (in the period 1990–2002, labour productivity in industry increased by a striking 5 per cent). The previous socialist system has been changed to such an extent that investors recognize their opportunity to grow in Croatia. Foreign investments started during the war in 1993 and have continued to grow: during the period 1993 to 2002, US$7.5 billion was invested directly in Croatia.

The internationalization of the Croatian economy has followed the pattern characteristic of all countries in transition. Initially, foreign investors invested in companies with which they had various forms of commercial association. This was followed by the internationalization of the financial industry. In Croatia today the financial industry operates entirely globally, with over 90 per cent of the banking system having been internationalized. It is the same situation with regard to investment banking. The share of the financial industry primarily owned by Croatian national investors is the insurance industry. In the former Yugoslavia, the Croatian insurance industry determined the entire insurance industry.

Potential food production in Slavonia and on the Adriatic coast can be determined by the need to meet the food requirements of 30 million people – an opportunity that domestic and foreign investors will not be able to resist.

Tourism is another area to which domestic and foreign investors are paying increasing attention. Shortly after the war, the Adriatic region of Central Europe, with its mild climate, became a desirable destination, attracting rising numbers of tourists from all over Europe and the rest of the world. The pristine coast, clean sea and the many islands that are a paradise for boating enthusiasts are creating a new tourism culture.

'Health tourism' is also increasing, especially in central Croatia, with its abundance of thermal waters. These are attractive to the ageing European population, another growing market.

Another factor contributing to the attractiveness of Croatia is the educational level of the workforce. On the Adriatic particular attention is paid to the development of educational centres, whose number is constantly increasing. Educational projects are being carried out in cooperation with universities of international reputation. There are also developed shipbuilding, textile, lumber, chemical, pharmaceutical and petrochemical industries, each of which represents a challenge for investors.

Croatia is a country with low inflation (0.9 per cent in 2003) and a stable rate of exchange that has remained at 7.5 Kunas per euro (pegged currency), indicating that there is no currency risk for investors. The growth rate of the Gross Domestic Product indicates that the Croatian economy is lively and that restructuring has been accelerated. The determination of the Croatian Government to adhere to the Maastricht criteria is a guarantee that it is possible to invest in Croatia with an acceptable commercial risk. The European Union is the largest investor in Croatia, while investors from the USA have recognized the positive economic environment for investment.

I invite all business people, investors and entrepreneurs to join with Croatian entrepreneurs and by extending the dimensions of their economic activity to contribute to the dynamic development of Croatia.

Welcome to Croatia!

Petra Tarle
President of the Management Board
Zagreb Insurance Company, Zagreb

MRAMOTERM – The Marble Heating Plate

In developed countries more and more thought is given to saving energy and diminishing the emissions of the carbon dioxide and the sulphur dioxide. According to the present claims for preserving the environment – by using new technological trends – a reduction of the emission of harmful materials has been planned: 20-30% until the year 2005 and 50% until 2050.

By using Energy Reports it has been estimated that about 50% of the harmful emissions are the result of the heating of living spaces. The limited resources of oil and gas and their unfavourable influence on the nature induce us to think about other sources of energy. Electricity holds a high position among them. In Western Europe the electric power is more and more used for heating, and MRAMOTERM is a simple example of a clean heating of the future.

By applying the centuries old experience of using stone structures in heating, and by progressive thinking and technology, we have created a healthy, simple, economical, environmentally and aesthetically completely solved way of heating. The MRAMOTERM heating plate is our product made of natural materials (stone, marble and granite), with high heating features, nice appearance and unlimited endurance. We can boast with thousands of our content customers in Croatia and abroad – since 1987 until today – which is proof of the high quality of our products.

Through a special process an electric heater is built into the MRAMOTERM heating plate 30 mm thick. The MRAMOTERM plate can be mounted onto any wall simply and quickly. We offer various patterns of marble, which match the aesthetic values of the room. It can be installed as a complete or partial heating. The heating plate is connected to the electric net through thermostats, which control the temperature of each room separately. After switching on, the plate heats to its working temperature of about 86°C in 30 to 40 minutes. The separation of the heat from the heater is effected through radiation, as well as by thermal convection. Just as the Sun heats every surface it illuminates, so the MRAMOTERM heating permeates the air without any movement and through a thermal radiation it heats the sold objects in the room (the walls, floors, the furniture) which become tanks of heat. The hot objects in the room diminish the exchange of the heat between the human body and the surroundings, so the human organism feels more pleasantly. This way of heating eliminates the difference of temperatures between the ceiling and the floor, and brings the circulation and drying of the air to a minimum – in the interest of your own health (especially for the asthmatic patients, and for all those who have difficulties with breathing as well as for those prone to allergy).

By keeping a pleasant temperature in a space with an average insulation the electric power consumption is only about 400-500 Wh (watt-hours) per m^2 in 24 hours, which means the saving of about 25-50% of energy – in comparison with other ways of heating. Considering the low costs of installation (2-3 times lower than with gas or crude oil heating), you does not have any expenditure either for the boiler room, the chimney, fuels tanks or maintenance and repair.

The marble heating plate does not hold any parts causing noise, vibrations, or harmful radiation, which could bring to unwanted changes in the surroundings. The protection has been made with a multilevel installation of electric wires, so there is no possibility of an electric shock or burns when touching it. The plate can be mounted even in wet paces such as bathrooms, because the MRAMOTERM plates meet all the standards of security and protection.

Due to continuous innovative work and investing in our production, and by using benefits of new technological achievements, we have improved our product. It is resistant to breakage and has an indefinite life term. We have increased security measures of our product according to all acknowledged world standards. Receiving the CE Mark of the Institute TÜV AUSTRIA and the recommendation TÜV Ostrich for product of quality (BAUMUSTER GEPRÜFT) proved that. Therefore, we have become one of the leading world producers of marble heating plates, made accordingly to the new European Standard – the EN 60 335. Our products carry the CE Mark as they comply with the European safety standards and the VDE recommendations (which are to become the new norms soon), as well. At present, we use materials of several times' better quality than those requested by New World regulations, thus proving the quality of our product and our experience.

At the end we must conclude that a purchase of various products, especially of those among which we live, should not be a result of a momentary wish or a whim – but it should be a very responsible action, firstly to your advantage. The MRAMOTERM plates make sure that you live healthier and more pleasantly with our DEFINITIVE SOLUTION of heating.

MRAMOTERM, Marinici bb , 51 216 Viskovo, CROATIA
Tel./Fax: ++385 51 257 414; ++385 51 257 161
www.mramoterm.com; e-mail: mramoterm@ri.hinet.hr

List of Contributors

Hayley Alexander is a senior manager with **Deloitte & Touche** Emerging Markets, based in Washington, DC. The Emerging Markets Group is a specialized part of Deloitte & Touche that deals exclusively with consulting engagements in emerging markets all over the world. Mr Alexander has an undergraduate degree in business (BBA) from Eastern Michigan University and a postgraduate degree (MBA) in marketing from George Washington University in Washington, DC. He spent nine years in marketing, contract administration and financial management for a privately owned Detroit area firm that manufactured and sold specialized vehicles to the US government. Then in 1994 he joined Deloitte & Touche and moved to Russia to join a business development project. Since then he has worked on long-term business consulting and institutional development projects in Egypt, Ukraine, Bosnia and Herzegovina and presently Croatia. He has worked both in project management and technical assistance capacities, the latter mainly in marketing and financial management.

Russell Aycock is Regional Director of Deloitte & Touche's Tax and Legal practice for the Adriatic Region (Slovenia, Croatia, Bosnia, Albania, Kosovo). Prior to joining the Central European and CIS practices in 1997, he was based in Deloitte New York office, where he served media clients and financial institutions.

Russell is a US Certified Public Accountant with extensive experience in international taxation, structuring of inbound and outbound investment, cross-border mergers and acquisitions, financing structures, transfer pricing, Central European corporate taxation and intellectual property taxation.

Sanja Bach has been a Spokesperson for the Ministry of Economy since 2001. In 1992 Sanja graduated from the Faculty of Political Science in Zagreb, having specialized in journalism. For over eight years she has worked as a journalist for Croatian Television (HTV), covering major economic topics including the state of the international and domestic economies, financial markets and privatization, the establishment of the EMU (European Monetary Union), and the introduction of the euro. Sanja also writes regularly for leading Croatian weekly and daily economic newspapers and magazines, thus promoting female representation in the domain of economic analyses, so far mainly reserved for men.

She recently graduated from the Diplomacy Academy in Zagreb: her thesis 'Branding Croatia', analyses the importance of diplomacy and promotion. Sanja is fluent in English and Italian. In 2001 she was given an award for her special contribution to the development of the Zagreb stock exchange.

Ms Visnja Bojanic, from Rijeka, Croatia, graduated from the Faculty of Philosophy at the University of Zagreb in 1981, and in 2002 earned a Master's Degree in European Studies at the University of Zagreb and Université Panthéon-Assas, Paris. She is fluent in English, French and Italian.

For a number of years Visnja Bojanic worked with the UN and the Croatian office of the International Helsinki Federation (IHF) where she drafted and edited reports on human rights for OSCE (Organization for Security and Cooperation in Europe), and prepared material for the International Criminal Tribunal for the Former Yugoslavia (ICTY) and other international UN organizations, as well as material for journalists.

She also took part in research on the media coverage of electoral campaigns for parliamentary and presidential elections in Croatia 1997/98 and in drafting and editing the material for 'Elections in the Media', published in 1999 in cooperation with the European Institute for the Media (EIM).

Ms Bojanic contributed to the preparation of the book *The People, Press and Politics of Croatia*, published in 2001, which addressed the evolution of the press in Croatia from Tito's period to President Tudjman's era. The book was written by Stjepan Malovic, PhD, Professor of Journalism at the University of Zagreb and Gary Selnow, Professor of Communication at San Francisco State University.

She has been a freelance journalist both during and after her studies, writing for Croatian student newspapers, several Croatian weeklies and the UN published newspapers. In the last five years she has been employed by consulting firms (PricewaterhouseCoopers and currently in Deloitte & Touche Croatia as the marketing manager). Furthermore, she is in charge of drafting and editing articles for various Deloitte publications and newspapers and also writes for *Croatia Times*, a newspaper published in English by Central Europe News, UK for the international business community in Croatia.

Radimir Cacic, Minister of Public Works, Reconstruction and Construction in the Government of the Republic of Croatia, was born in Zagreb, Croatia on May 11 1949. He has a degree in Architecture.

Prime producers since 1968 for all your plastics, cardboard packaging & furniture requirements

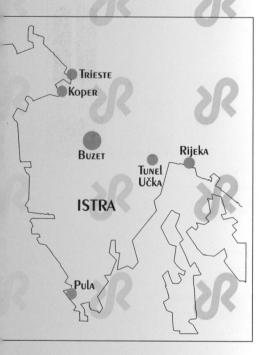

Based in Buzet

National & International

High quality

Years of expert knowledge developed through our own requirements

Tailored products to suit your requirements

Our service and products have been driven by our customers demands

Plastics

- We process 1000 tonnes of PVC a year

- Used in the construction & maritime industries

- Any miscellaneous items – we offer a bespoke service

- A variety of colours and types that have been developed in our fully equipped lab for the testing of polymer materials

Cardboard Packaging

- Developed from our own needs of packing furniture
- Specialists in transport packing
- Corrugated cardboard to small – medium sized packing boxes
- We can tailor ourselves to your needs in any area of our expertise

Furniture

- Hallways
- Bedrooms
- Specialist providers to the Tourist Industry
- We manufacture over 7000 pieces of furniture a year
- Expert area of knowledge

DRVOPLAST dd
Ivana Sancina 3
52420 Buzet
Croatia
Tel: +385-52-662-868
Fax: +385-52-662-540
e-mail: drvoplast@drvoplast.com.hr
www.drvoplast.com.hr

Between 1973 and 1977 he worked at Interpublic Zagreb, from 1978–1995 he was General Manager and co-owner of CONING Vara•din. In 1995 he became a Member of the House of Representatives of the Croatian Parliament and in 2000 he became the Minister of Public Works, Reconstruction and Construction.

He was guest lecturer in the Faculty of Civil Engineering and Harvard Business School from 1985–1990. He was one of the co-founders of the Croatian People's Party where he performed several functions.

During the war he founded the independent military unit and negotiated with JNA, he is also a holder of the Patriotic Defence War testimonial.

Maruska Cenic is junior research assistant at the Institute of Economics, Zagreb. A graduate of the Faculty of Economics, the University of Zagreb, she is now finishing her Masters degree in macroeconomics at the same faculty. Within the Institute's Department for Macroeconomic Analysis and Policy, she works at various research projects concerning different macroeconomic issues in Croatia.

The **Croatian Chamber of Economy (HGK),** which was founded 149 years ago, is a reliable source of information for all businesses in Croatia, as well as for their international partners. Also, the Chamber provides a host of services including business information on specific companies, laws and regulations related to the economy, business education and skills training, environmental protection and quality control. The door of the Croatian Chamber of Economy is open to all domestic and foreign business people. The Chamber offers business services, contacts and information within its regular activities.

The **Croatian Privatization Fund** was established to implement and complete the privatization of former socially owned enterprises, assets and legal persons in its portfolio. It transforms socially owned enterprises into public companies; privatizes shares, interests, property and rights and shares free of charge when stipulated by law; manages legal entities in which state institutions hold shares and interests, and other operations stipulated by law and the Fund's Charter; manages assets owned by the Republic of Croatia when stipulated by law or a decision of the government; and manages legal entities in which it holds shares and interests. Web site: www.hfp.hr.

Digitel d.o.o. is a core company within a group of commonly owned companies operating in the field of marketing communications. Digitel Group offers services in strategic and creative development, media planning and buying, production, realization of integrated campaigns that demand strategic thinking and planning, event management, consulting, public relations, lobbying, and the overall execution and management of communication projects. The members of the group represent international networks Lowe & Partners, Initiative Media and Weber Shandwick in Croatia and are closely cooperating with Intebrand Zinzmeyer & Lux. **Lowe Digitel**, a full service advertising agency, is ranked as the number one full-advertising agency in Croatia. Lowe Digitel has the biggest production output and is ranked 137 on the list of 400 most successful Croatian companies in 2001 (source: *Privredni Vjesnik*). **Digitel Medijski Servisi**, representing Initiative Media for Croatia, is the biggest media buying agency in Croatia. **Premisa**, a PR company within Digitel Group, representing Weber Shandwick, is the leading PR agency in Croatia.

Renata Djuricic is Senior Associate in the Public Information Office, and Assistant in the Ministry of Craft, Small and Medium Enterprises. Renata graduated from the Faculty of Political Sciences in Zagreb. She first worked in the Ministry of Economy, in the scope of the Government program of the promotion of the enterprise sector in Croatia. In 2001 she moved to the Ministry of Craft and SMEs where she focused on the SME sector in Croatia, and participated in creating measures, conceived by the Ministry, aimed at enhancing and supporting entrepreneurial spirit in Croatia. She continuously broadens her expertise in the field; she attended the seminar on techniques of presentation and communication and techniques of moderations, organized by Die Deutsche Gesselschaft fur Technische Zussamenarbeit.

Her primary responsibilities as an expert associate of the Cabinet of the Minister lie in the development of external communications with the public, ie to inform the public on all activities and achievements in the SME sector.

Renata also took an active part in the organization of an International conference on small and medium economy, held in Zagreb this year. She also contributes to various publications issued by the Ministry.

In 2001 and 2002, a legal framework was set for energy business activities and privatization of energy companies, respectively. In mid-2002, **HEP** began the process of restructuring its vertically organized utility, and was reorganized to form **HEP Group**, which consists of a parent company and subsidiary companies set up to perform core electric activities and auxiliary businesses. This is the first step in the change process aimed at preparing HEP for participation in an open energy market in conformity with EU legislation.

INA is a vertically integrated oil and gas company operating in oil and gas exploration and production, refining and marketing of oil products. Its subsidiaries are engaged in LPG business, natural gas transportation and providing integrated oilfield services. INA is a medium-sized European oil company and a significant regional player. For the time being it is owned by the Republic of Croatia but privatization plans are under way. **Biserka Cimesa** is a business secretary and translator at INA.

The **Institute of Economics, Zagreb** is a scientific and research institution whose basic goal is economic research and the application of modern economic science, with the aim of promoting the overall progress of the Republic of Croatia. The Institute has a long tradition in scientific and applied research projects in the economic field, which goes back to 1939. Through research projects, the Institute significantly contributes to theoretical understanding of economic processes and practical solutions in market economy conditions. To achieve this, the Institute has built up its human resources for research in Croatia, while at the same time developing scientific cooperation with similar institutions abroad.

Ljubo Jurcic DSc is a senior lecturer at the Faculty of Economics at the University of Zagreb. In 1981 he worked for the Factory of Electrical Equipment and from there went on to become a foreign trade counsellor for Progres, and a part-time lecturer at the university. By 1987 he was manager of the Factory and in 1990 was in permanent employment with the university.

Drawing on 30 years of injection moulding experience, **Kaplast** provides new ideas for plastic packaging and other products. The Kaplast team specializes in finding solutions geared to meet exact requirements. They produce crates with a modern look, which are strong and easy to handle.

Ms Sanja Kos is the Government Spokeswoman and Head of the Media and Public Relations Office as of 2000.

In 1998 Sanja graduated from the Faculty of Law at the University of Zagreb. While still a student she entered the world of journalism where she rapidly climbed the ladder of success: from being a freelancer she soon became the editor or the economic section of the largest Croatian daily, *Vjesnik*. From 1994 to 1996 she assumed the role of the main columnist-commentator and soon introduced the new supplement of the daily *Vjesnik*, 'The Financial Market', of which she became editor. Combining her expertise both in law and economy she elaborated the most salient topics in the Croatian economy, focusing particularly on entry of Croatian companies into the international capital markets. In 1997 she took the position of Head of Public and Media Relations Office in Zagrebanka banka d.d., the biggest bank in Croatia, and, during her 3 years mandate, the bank was three times nominated as the shareholders' company with the best public relations person. She continuously works on her education in public relations, attending specialized seminars both in country (Diplomatic Academy) and abroad (Management Centre Europe, London). Sanja speaks fluent English, German and Italian.

Josip Kregar is a professor of law at the University of Zagreb. He teaches sociology and sociology of law and has been director of the postgraduate seminar 'Economy and Democracy' (IUC) since 1996. He was the president of Transparency International Croatia between 1998 and 2002 and was appointed as a commissioner for the city of Zagreb in 2000.

Zoran Markovic and **Miroslav Pliso** established their respective law offices in 1987. Initially, the offices dealt with cases related to general civil law, but in the following years they started focusing more on advising. During 1989 new legislation allowed the establishment of private enterprises, so their legal practice began offering its services to numerous clients in the field of corporate law, legal consulting, and representation before courts and other state authorities. This work soon represented 80 per cent of the matters handled by the office and such corporate focus continues today. In the spring of 1995 they formally founded the law firm **Markovic & Pliso** in Zagreb at Smiciklasova 21, which currently employs 18 jurists, nine of whom are attorneys at law, two legal advisors, seven legal trainees, six executive secretaries, a translator/court interpreter (for English and German languages) and two paralegals. Their law firm enjoys an ongoing cooperation with Radovan Pavelic, attorney from New York (licensed to practise law in New York, Washington, DC, and Connecticut), as their special advisor for common law. In addition to their regular work, the law firm is also engaged in privatization proceedings and offers legal advice on securities, construction, taxes, financing, denationalization and similar matters.

At the head of the Ministry for European Integration is **Neven Mimica**, who gained his Masters degree at the Faculty of Economics at the University of Zagreb with the thesis 'Elements of the Croatian Export Strategy'. At the moment he is preparing his doctoral thesis. His early career revolved around the economy and diplomacy. He served with the Croatian embassies in Cairo and Ankara, and he filled several posts in the Ministry of Economy. As the Assistant Minister for Economy he was the Chief Negotiator for Croatia's accession to the WTO. Later on he occupied the post of the Deputy Minister of Economy. In November 2000 the Croatian Government appointed him as the Chief Negotiator for the Stabilization and Association Agreement.

The **Ministry of Crafts and SMEs** has developed several key documents for SMEs, which conform to the norms of the European Union. The objective of these documents is to improve the system within the framework of which crafts, cooperatives and SMEs operate. The Small Business Development Programme 2000–2004 includes numerous development incentives. The Small Business Encouragement Act identifies key people, development objectives and programmes, incentives and programme promoters and anticipates the establishment of the Croatian Agency for SMEs (HAMAG) to implement the incentives.

Changes and amendments to the Craftsmen Act have defined simpler framework conditions for crafts, making it possible to be engaged in crafts seasonally, opening crafts to foreign citizens on the same basis as those for the citizens of the Republic of Croatia, and improving the vocational education system. The Law on Changes and Amendments to the Cooperatives Act has introduced the system of cooperative organizing within the umbrella organization of the Croatian Association of Cooperatives and it has improved the means for supporting and organizing cooperatives. They persist in their endeavours to provide even more favourable loan terms and conditions for entrepreneurs, organize training programmes, encourage competition, support authentic local products and assist entrepreneurs when entering foreign markets.

The **Ministry of Environmental Protection and Physical Planning** was constituted by virtue of the Law on Amendments to the Law on Structure and Competence of Ministries and State Government Organisations (*Official Gazette* No 15/2000), which came into force on 5 February 2000. The newly established Ministry of Environmental Protection and Physical Planning took over the tasks and responsibilities of the former Ministry of Zoning, Construction and Housing in the section related to physical planning, site-permits, building permits and operation permits, urban planning and building inspection, and the corresponding legal and administrative matters, as well as the tasks and responsibilities of the former State Directorate for the Protection of Nature and the Environment.

The **Ministry for European Integration**, evolved from the Office for European Integration, was formally established on 5 February 2000, highlighting the improvement of relations with the European Union. Its core mission is coordination of the process of European integration in the Republic of Croatia. Since its establishment, the Ministry has been engaged in preparatory activities for the establishment of a system leading to the efficient adjustment of the Croatian institutional, social, legal and economic system to those of the European Union. In this respect, the Ministry is mandated with coordination of the implementation of the Stabilization and Association Agreement and Interim Agreement, coordination of the process of harmonization of the Croatian legal system with EU law, coordination of EU assistance programmes, analytical support to the process of European integration, raising public awareness for the process of rapprochement with the EU, training of civil servants in the field of European integration as well as the establishment and coordination of the system for translation of EU legal documents. The staff of the Ministry for European Integration numbers nine state officials and 125 employees with an average age a little below 30. There are two employees with Doctorates, 40 of them have Masters degrees and 71 of them are graduates. All of them have received proper training and educated in the fields important for Croatian integration into the EU.

The **Ministry of Tourism of Croatia**, which contributed an article to this publication, acts wholeheartedly to encourage tourism in the Republic of Croatia due to its recognition of the positive impact that tourism has on the domestic economy.

Dr Zarko Primorac was born in 1937 in Krucevici (Citluk), Bosnia and Herzegovina. In 1976 he obtained a PhD degree in Economics at the University of Sarajevo. He has over 35 years of experience in industry, finance, banking and consultancy. He worked for more than 25 years in Energoinvest, one of the biggest industrial companies in former Yugoslavia, where he held a number of senior management positions. Dr Primorac was the President of the Chamber of Commerce in Sarajevo for few years, and also Minister of Finance in Bosnia and Herzegovina. For more than 15 years he lectured at the Faculty of Economy at the University of Sarajevo. Since the beginning of the 1990s he has lived in Zagreb. Prior to joining Deloitte & Touche as the Regional Chairman, Dr Primorac was the director of PricewaterhouseCoopers. He is also an active participant in professional organizations and state institutions. He has published more than 100 articles in different Croatian and international economic reviews and two books: *Investment Spending as a Development Factor in Bosnia and Herzegovina,* Institute for Economics, Sarajevo, and *Business*, Oslobodenje, Sarajevo. Dr Primorac prepared the *Croatian Financial Guide* for 1995, 1998 and 2002. He is also editor of special issues of *Privredni vjesnik – Ranking of Croatian Banks, Business Expectations in 400 Best Croatian Companies.* Dr Primorac actively participates in economic, financial and business conferences.

Ivana Prohic graduated from the Faculty of Philosophy at the University of Zagreb, specializing in Phonetics and Croatian studies. Between 1976 and 2000 she worked as a presenter/journalist at Croatian

Television. For 5 years she worked as a teacher in a secondary school in Zagreb. Since 2000 she has been working as Adviser to the Minister – Spokesperson in the Public Relations department of the **Ministry of Public Works, Reconstruction and Construction**.

She attended the International Broadcasting Bureau Voice of America Seminar in Washington, USA.

In 1994 the 117-year old Raiffeisen banking group from Austria decided to invest in Croatia and founded **Raiffeisenbank Austria d.d. Zagreb (RBA).** Now headquartered in Zagreb, Petrinjska 59, it was the first foreign-owned bank in Croatia. Today, RBA holds third place by volume of its assets, employs over 1,100 people and operates through a dense business network covering 15 Croatian towns and cities. RBA's success is based entirely on organic growth and investment in the training of its staff as well as continuous development of the products and services it offers.

In addition to offering retail and corporate customers as well as small businesses a broad range of products and services, RBA is well known for its sophisticated e-banking solutions. An important contribution to RBA becoming a household name has been its macroeconomic and financial research unit. For several years now RBA has been issuing a series of publications that have become an important and often-quoted source of information in both professional circles and the media. The periodicals published in Croatian are *Daily News* (a daily financial report), *RBA Info Spot, Raiffeisen Weekly Report, Raiffeisen Research Report* (published quarterly) and the most recent addition, *Commercial Papers,* while *CEE Weekly Bond Markets Outlook* (published in coopera-tion with RZB), *RBA Croatia Weekly Report, CEE Equity Weekly* (also published in cooperation with RZB) and *Raiffeisen Research Report* are published in English. All publications are available at RBA's home page, www.rba.hr, or can be obtained via e-mail, while the quarterly reports are available in print.

RBA is a member of the global Raiffeisen banking group (RBG), the largest Austrian privately owned banking group, comprising roughly one-quarter of the Austrian banking industry. The group's central unit is the Vienna-based Raiffeisen Zentralbank Osterreich AG (RZB).

Mrs Pave Zupan Ruskovic is the foremost businesswoman of Croatia in the tourism sector. She was appointed the Minister of Tourism of the Republic of Croatia in 2000, leaving her position as the President of ATLAS Travel Agency, one of the largest travel companies in Croatia, with its head office in Dubrovnik.

Mrs Ruskovic had served as the President of ATLAS since 1982, and she was also the President of the Association of Croatian Travel Agencies (UPHA) and the Association of the American Travel Agencies, ASTA.

Mrs Ruskovic was the recipient of ASTA prestigious International Travel Agent of the Year award in 1999, and the same year the World Travel Market awarded her with the 'Tribute 21' award which was granted to twenty-one professionals from the tourism sector for their outstanding accomplishments in the field. She was also awarded the 'King Hussein Peace Award 2000' by his majesty King Hussein of Jordan in the same year, for her exceptional contribution to peace and promotion of the city of Dubrovnik as a tourist destination during the war. In 2002, Ruskovic was recognized by the Travelling Times, Inc as one of the few individuals that have made an indelible impact on the world of travel and for her endurable contribution to the industry she was awarded 'Onore de Amerigo Vespucci', in the spirit of the great explorer who ventured into the world with courage and optimism. She was appointed at the same time with life-long membership of the association.

Mrs Pave Zupan Ruskovic was born in 1947 in Dubrovnik. She graduated from the Faculty of Economy of the University of Zagreb with a Master's Degree in economy in tourism.

Professor Petar Turkovic is a psychologist, psychotherapist and cybernetician. He recently founded a new company, Explora, to focus on intra- and interpersonal communciation as well as processes of change in organizations. Formerly with experience in mental health, management consultancy and the management of NGOs and social welfare organizations, Petar has advised numerous individuals and organizations on communication, change and strategic planning issues, and directed national institutions for the rehabilitation of the blind, and numerous sports organizations, including the national Olympic Committee. In 1999 he was one of the founders, and elected chairman of the first Croatian think tank, **Foundation 2020**, for which in 2001/2002 he directed the civic scenario project in cooperation with Swedish company Nextwork.

Miroslav Vajagić, is the Tax and Legal Department Manager at Deloitte &Touche Croatia. In 1997 Miroslav graduated from the Faculty of Law at the University of Zagreb. Immediately after graduation, Miroslav joined Coopers & Lybrand, and later PriceWaterhouseCoopers as a senior consultant. Miroslav has over five years of working experience in tax advisory services and, as a lawyer, has comprehensive experience in legal advisory services. As a manager, Miroslav has been involved in many of the complex services provided to the clients operating in Croatia, from legal and tax due diligence, cross border transactions to merger & acquisitions. He is also an expert in issues related to labour law, company law, VAT issues as well as foreign exchange business operations performed for the biggest domestic and international companies. Miroslav joined Deloitte in 2000 and thanks to his extensive experience and expertise he soon became a manager within the Croatian Tax and Legal Practice. He is fully responsible for the quality of tax and legal consulting within the Adriatic cluster for both domestic and international companies. He speaks English fluently.

The Zagreb Insurance Company (Osiguranje Zagreb d.d.) of Zagreb is the oldest private insurance company in Croatia. In keen market competition, the Zagreb Insurance Company maintains a high fourth place, in that its portfolio structure is increasingly similar to that of the same type of company in the European Union. According to these criteria, the Zagreb Insurance Company is a leading Croatian insurance company.

Roland Zuvanic, Minister of Maritime Affairs, Transport and Communications, graduated from the Faculty of Civil Engineering of the University of Zagreb and worked for a construction company, Hidroelektra, in Zagreb. Since 1984 he has worked as a representative for National Oilwell, Baroid and Dreco in Eastern Europe, gaining expert training in the oil industry in London and Houston at National Oilwell. Since 1987 he has owned a significant share of a German commerce company, RMN GmbH, founded in Munich with branches in Graz and Zagreb. He came back to Croatia at the end of 1997 and worked in Boric-Zuvanic Construction. He is a permanent court expert for civil engineering and also a member of the Rotary Club, Zagreb, and LIBRA.

Tehnomont Shipyard "Pula" Ltd, a sector of the Tehnomont Empire has been involved with the Shipping Industry since 1905. Based in Pula, we have branch offices in Rijeka, Split, Trogir and internationally in Germany, Netherlands and Italy. With a workforce of over 650 we have built up specialist knowledge and work on a variety of highly skilled and sophisticated projects. From this we have earned a much envied reputation world wide for our first class products and services.

- **Shipbuilding** – Patrol Boats, Turistic Boats, Sandcarriers, Fishing Boats
- **Steel Constructions** – Stuttgart Airport, Water Pipelines, Railway Bridges, Water Towers, Herlitz Berlin, 45ft Port Cranes, Turbine Plants
- **Solar Equipment** – Solar Boilers, Solar Collectors

TEHNOMONT SHIPYARD – PULA Ltd.
Fizela 7, 52100 PULA, R. of CROATIA

Tel: 00-385-52-386-923
Fax: 00-385-52-386-328

tehnomont@tehnomont.hr
www.tehnomont.hr

Acknowledgements

I would like to acknowledge the invaluable assistance provided to me during the compilation of this book by Visnja Bojanic, who provided endless reserves of energy while both recommending and recruiting some of the finest business authors available in the Republic of Croatia. It was with her able assistance that we were able to secure their editorial contributions for this publication.

Marat Terterov
Oxford, England

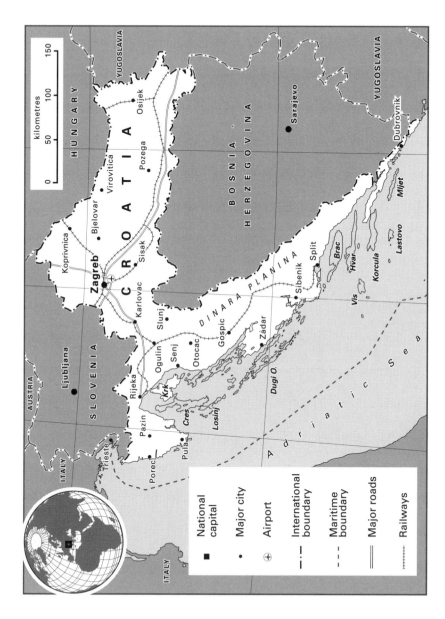

Map 1 Croatia and its neighbours

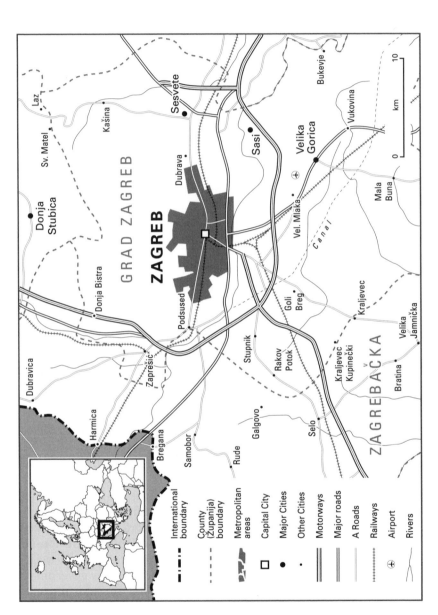

Map 2 Zagreb and the surrounding area

Introduction

Dr Zarko Primorac, Regional Chairman, Deloitte & Touche

The Croatian economy is on an upturn. In 2002, a 5.2 per cent rise of the GDP was recorded compared to 2001, industrial output rose by 5.4 per cent, and tourism grew at a rate of 6 per cent pa. In the same year, a high level of stability in local prices was achieved (the inflation rate was around 2 per cent), the exchange rate of the Croatian Kuna indicated a constant trend in the long run, the foreign currency reserves of the central bank were growing, and the chronically high unemployment rate was declining.

The most significant underlying factor for such a dynamic GDP growth was local demand, resulting from the construction of motorways and other forms of public spending. In 2003 a record 137 kilometres of modern highways were opened, connecting the central part of the country with the Adriatic coast. Important highway sections between Croatia's capital, Zagreb, and the biggest Croatian port, Rijeka, as well as between Zagreb and Split, the centre of Dalmatia, the biggest Adriatic region in Croatia, have been completed.

Despite certain downsides resulting from such a dynamic economic growth, primarily in terms of a large increase in imports, a significant trade deficit and increased foreign debt, the Croatian economy has been achieving strong economic growth on the whole. This has been supported by positive trends in the ratings by international financial institutions and rating agencies. Fitch has recently increased Croatia's credit rating from BBB– to BBB+. Certain unfavourable developments in foreign economic relations will have to be corrected by means of a more active economic policy. This will probably be a priority for the new government following the parliamentary elections expected to take place in November 2003.

Such a powerful economic recovery is a positive sign that Croatia has finally managed to overcome the aftermath of the past 10 to 12 years. Following the decision of 1991 to abandon the former common state, Yugoslavia, Croatia entered into a very painful period of gaining and defending its independence: a war and occupation of a large portion of its national territory, accompanied by losing a large number of vital industrial corporations, huge war damage and devastation, taking in refugees and displaced persons, spending enormous funds on defence, a non-transparent privatization, etc. Fortunately, all these painful and disadvantageous processes now belong to the past.

Today, Croatia is consolidated as a state; democratic processes in all spheres of life have made significant progress; a modern legal system based on the Central European tradition has been established; transition processes in other sectors are accelerating; all the legal and economic institutions have been set up; most enterprises, or 60 per cent of the total social capital, has been privatized; the privatization of the infrastructure has commenced (Croatian Telecom was sold to Deutsche Telecom, and 25 per cent plus one share of INA, Croatia's largest oil corporation, were recently sold to Hungarian MOL); foreign direct investments in the Croatian economy are high (over US$8 billion in total); capital markets are functioning; and Croatia's financial and banking system is among the most developed of the transition countries. Further, Croatia is member of the WTO and the CEFTA, and has signed the Stabilization and Association Agreement with the European Union, and applied for full membership. In 2004 the European Union is expected to enter into official negotiations with Croatia regarding its full membership. The intense preparations that are under way, as well as solid assessments by the EU of the harmonization of processes with the EU, allow for optimism that Croatia will be accepted as a full member of the EU in 2007 or 2008 at the latest, together with Romania and Bulgaria.

Croatia has enormous development potential. Its geographic position and natural resources embody prerequisites for developing tourism, travel, services and other sectors, in addition to manufacturing. The development potential of tourism deserves special mention. With more than a thousand islands and islets, only 67 of which are inhabited, and over 5,000 kilometres of an extremely indented coastline, with a rich cultural heritage along the Adriatic Coast – from Dubrovnik, through Split, all the way to the Istrian Peninsula and the Briuni Islands – the Croatian part of the Adriatic Coast is one of the most attractive tourist destinations in Europe. The spas and rich thermal water springs, health tourism and hunting add to the potential.

Manufacturing has traditionally been key to development. Croatia had the most developed industrial economy in the former Yugoslavia. However, some of the key industries, such as metal and wood processing, while others lost their traditional markets and became technologically outdated because of the war, such as the pharmaceutical, electronic and food processing industries, made significant progress modernizing their production capacities to the extent that they are now the basis for the regional expansion of Croatia's industry. Since the manufacturing and processing industries have traditionally been the leading sectors in Croatia, they offer much room for revival. Croatia possesses other key prerequisites: a young population with a solid educational background and computer literacy, favourable living conditions, and an incentivized economic system for investment in new industrial and manufacturing projects.

This overview of Croatia's potential must include its geographic position as a comparative advantage for the development of traffic, trade and related activities, specifically in the area of business, finance, storage and other services. In this segment, free zones – 17 altogether – represent an extremely favourable form for developing modern industries, such as electronics, communications and other technologically demanding industries. The agricultural sector, in addition to existing well-known brand names, such as Podravka, Agrokor, Kras, Franck, Vindija and Dukat, also offers huge development potential.

In short, Croatia is facing a new, challenging development stage in all economic sectors. There is no doubt that the preparations for joining the EU will spur institutional and structural reforms. Institutional reforms are already in full swing, while structural change is more time-consuming and requires significant investment.

In the next decade, thanks to its potential and traditions, Croatia will become a highly attractive destination, not only for foreign tourists but also for serious investors. We hope that the information contained in this book will help them to become acquainted with an attractive and challenging country for doing business.

About this book

Doing Business with Croatia is designed for anyone contemplating Croatia as a market in which to do business. Part One contains general background information on the Croatian market, including political and economic overviews, privatization, foreign trade patterns and the foreign investment climate. The financial sector – banking, securities markets, and foreign exchange regulations – and the increasingly topical issue of Croatia's accession to the European Union – are discussed.

In Part Two, we take an in-depth look at the diversified Croatian economy from a sectoral perspective. This part of the book will prove to be of major interest to foreign investors not deeply familiar with the structure of Croatia's economy. Our authors not only cover the country's renowned industries, such as food and beverages, tourism, textiles and garments, but also newly expanding sectors, such as telecoms, insurance and pharmaceuticals. We also cover energy sector regulation, the power sector, and advertising and marketing, and present a case study of the business experience of a well established manufacturing enterprise in the city of Karlovac, Kaplast.

In Part Three, Deloitte & Touche give extensive coverage to topics pertaining to Croatian commercial legislation, taxation, auditing and accounting. In Part Four, our authors give detailed attention to practical and operational topics relevant to business development in Croatia, including real estate, work permits and employment law, intellectual property, dispute resolution, corruption, and the small and medium-sized enterprises sector. There is also a 'Final thought' discussing several hypothetical socio-economic models of development that Croatia may be embarking upon in the not too distant future.

Finally there are appendices elaborating on the Croatian transport sector, Croatian business organizations, useful Web sites and author contact details.

Part One

Background to the Market

Political Profile

Ivana Norsic, PM Cabinet

> *If you wish to come somewhere and reach some destination, nobody will make a trip instead of you. You have to do it on your own. We will either find the way – or make one.* (Hannibal)

The Government of the Republic of Croatia is based on a coalition of five parties – (SDP (Social Democratic Party), HSS (Croatian Peasants' Party), HNS (Croatian People's Party), LS (Liberal Party) and LIBRA (Liberal Democrats' Party) – which concluded an agreement and adopted a joint programme on strategic goals and priority objectives. This programme is the backbone of their joint activities and governs their decision-making.

It is important to stress that the Croatian Government sees membership of the European Union as its strategic objective and an issue of national interest. Back in 2000, in its Operating Programme for the period 2000–2004, the Government emphasized that the Stabilization and Association Agreement (SAA) would be the most important step towards full membership of the EU, as it implies the fulfilment of a series of conditions and criteria pertaining to the economy, democracy, civil society, and regional stability and cooperation. Therefore the Agreement and the Government's activities aimed at its implementation clearly indicate our commitment and dedication to the achievement of this strategic objective.

Croatia's decision to submit a formal application for EU membership in February 2003 was based on a high degree of public unity and support for Croatia's accession to the EU (78.6 per cent of the population). This is also reflected in the parliamentary Resolution on Croatia's Accession to the EU, which all parliamentary political parties unanimously endorsed. By this Resolution the Parliament instructed the Government to submit an application for membership by the end of February 2003. This decision was also based on the progress Croatia has made in meeting the Copenhagen criteria, particularly in relation to political conditions, as well as the fact that Croatia has already met more than 50 per cent of the obligations laid down by the SAA in the course of one year. The Government has also adopted the National Programme for EU Accession (2003).

When one looks at current conditions in Croatia, one sees a general improvement in economic and financial indicators resulting from the implementation of Government policies. Croatia's per capita GDP of €5,140.00 is far above the average (€2,026.00) of other countries covered by the stabilization and association process. The process of economic stabilization has been largely finalized, macroeconomic stability has been maintained (2.2 per cent inflation, low interest rates, substantial gross foreign exchange reserves), the growth rate exceeds 5 per cent, and major steps have been taken in balancing the central budget. In addition, over the last year unemployment has been in constant decline. Cooperation with the IMF and the World Bank is exceptionally good, so much so that officials in both institutions state that in their opinion Croatia represents a positive and valuable example. Another important argument is that Croatia is and continues to be committed to implementing numerous reforms in labour law, higher education and science, the judiciary, public administration, defence, etc.

In 2003 the Government adopted the National Programme for EU Accession precisely in order to facilitate the most effective and fastest possible adaptation to EU standards. This is a document that provides a broad platform for comprehensive reform of the economic and political systems and the progress that must be made on the way to EU accession. These reforms and the thorough adaptation to the legal, economic and political standards of the EU demand both individual and joint engagement by all people and institutions in Croatia. Based on the need to adjust to EU standards, this year the Government will propose 42 new laws and the amendment of 36 existing laws.

By enacting the Ethnic Minority Rights Act, Croatia has elevated the status of ethnic minorities to a level guaranteed by few other countries in the world. It should be pointed out that the protection of minorities and the advancement of their position are vital to the establishment of mutual trust as a crucial element of democratic stability.

With reference to the return of displaced people and refugees, the Government's active policies and its considerable financial investments in the last three years have encouraged a high number of displaced people and refugees to return home, especially Croatian Serbs. In 2000 we removed all legal, administrative and security barriers to the return of all Croatian citizens. Particularly good progress has been made in the restitution of property, which is one of the key factors for return, and the protection of fundamental human rights, especially the right of individuals to freely dispose of their property, as well as the normalization of life in multi-ethnic communities. Since the start of the return process in 1995, approximately 300,000 displaced people and refugees have returned, including 100,000 Croatian Serbs. There are still around 15,000 people who have yet to return to their homes. The Government's strategic goal is to secure sustainable conditions for all those who want to return, and in this manner finally bring closure to the issue of the consequences of war in Croatia. Conditions for the sustainable return and reintegration of those who still have not done so are being secured through several programmes currently being implemented. Finally, by the end of 2004 this task will have been completed in full. The basic problem is the sizeable financial requirement, and in 2003 the Government earmarked €300 million for this purpose.

Considering corruption a threat to democratic development and the rule of law, the Government has undertaken a series of legislative and institutional measures with the goal of fighting corruption – a problem that otherwise besets various segments of society. The National Programme and Action Plan to Combat Corruption has been adopted and further measures will be taken for effective implementation of this Programme. Croatia has ratified the Agreement on the establishment of the 'Group of States Against Corruption' (GRECO) and the Criminal Law Convention on Corruption from Strasbourg. These are the two most important instruments, accompanied by the corresponding legislation and preventive measures, directed at the protection of societies against corruption. Croatia is also involved in numerous activities that have been under way in Europe for years and are aimed at achieving the Council of Europe Programme of Action against Corruption. Croatian representatives in the Council of Europe Multidisciplinary Group on Corruption have been working on the development of the GMC's legal instruments since its foundation.

Enhancing regional stability and cooperation, in terms of our efforts and the support of neighbouring countries, will be one of priorities of the Croatian government. Our contribution to the stability of our neighbours and the entire region is vital to Croatia's stability. However, while Croatia will continue to subscribe to regional cooperation, we will not allow our country's fate to be exclusively tied to the region. In evaluating the convergence with the EU, Croatia will persist in the view that each country of the region must be judged on its own merits.

One of the strategic goals of the Government of Croatia is to process war crimes in cooperation with the International Criminal Tribunal for the former Yugoslavia (ICTY), as well as to prosecute perpetrators before national courts. The Government of Croatia continues to fully cooperate with the ICTY not only because of its duty to meet its obligations under international law, but primarily because it considers such cooperation to be an important factor in the normalization of relations in the region and the achievement of justice and a lasting peace.

Croatia intends to secure its own stability and well-being through membership of the EU and NATO, and to contribute to the achievement and maintenance of stability and well-being in the region and throughout Europe.

A priority for Croatia is to prove that it is capable of joining the other candidate countries slated to become EU members in the second round of enlargement. Of crucial importance to the achievement of this objective is that all concerned parties recognize and accept their role in this process. We have already made several steps down the path to Europe, but we are aware that there are many more to follow.

Finally, it is important to stress that this Government has taken major steps in the democratization of society, and a consensus has been reached between all political parties on the most vital political issues. Much has been done to improve the general political culture, so that it can be stated that all conditions for the country's political stability have been secured.

Today Croatia knows what it wants and how to achieve it.

1.2

Economic Overview

Maruska Cenic, Institute of Economics, Zagreb

History and the nature of transition

Through most of the 20th century Croatia was a part of Yugoslavia. Once Croatia declared its independence in 1991, war broke out and Croatia faced a multitude of economic challenges. As well as the ongoing transition crisis and hyperinflation inherited from the previous system, the country had to deal with serious supply shocks caused by the war and the occupation of its territory. After a thriving stabilization effort started in late 1993, the economic situation began to deteriorate in 1997 (due to a combination of factors: a tightening of monetary policy, mounting structural problems, a crisis in the banking industry, increases in taxes and administrative prices, the Kosovo crisis), and the country found itself in a recession, which started in the last quarter of 1998 and continued through the first three quarters of 1999.

From the end of 1999 the macroeconomic situation started to improve. A rebound in household consumption, improved exports and the very good performance of the tourism sector in 2000 meant that GDP started to grow again in the last quarter of 1999, albeit at modest levels, with a rate of 3.7 per cent in 2000, while price inflation remained subdued. Industrial output recovered only moderately in 2000, with an output growth of 1.7 per cent over the previous year, but strengthened in the first months of 2001.

Throughout the last eight years the Croatian economy showed a 4.2 per cent real GDP growth rate on average, while real private consumption and real government consumption grew 2.4 per cent and 0.7 per cent respectively. The 1993 stabilization programme managed to retain the low price level, with 4.0 per cent average retail price change, but at the cost of sluggish average investment (3.5 per cent) and average industrial output (2.8 per cent) growth. Unemployment has grown steadily since Croatia's independence (caused by the recession, slow progress in restructuring and modernizing the economy, and wage increases above productivity gains), reaching an average rate of 21.6 per cent in November 2002, according to official figures, although this official rate is likely to overstate the actual situation.

During the first 10 years of democracy, the political scene was dominated by the rule of the conservative Croatian Democratic Union. On 13 January 2000, the coalition of six political parties won the elections and formed a new pro-reform government. That date was a major turning point not only for the future political direction of the country, but also for economic policy questions. After three years in office progress in several areas is evident. New policy makers successfully managed to lower the general government deficit and expenditure ratios. Progress was also being made in restructuring and privatizing the economy, especially in the banking sector, which suffered three severe banking crisis during the 1990s. However, the public debt ratio has continued to climb, the labour market remains inflexible and several large public enterprises are a drag on the economy. Against this backdrop, the government programme promised further substantial progress in future years, although this will have to be followed by more adjustments and reforms. Since new parliamentary elections are likely to be held at the end of 2003, it is questionable whether there would be any room for further reforms, which the current government had promised. It is more probable that planned reforms and adjustments will be delayed until after the election in order to please various interest groups.

The main economic indicators for 1995 to 2002 are shown in Table 1.2.1 and details of GDP in the first quarter of 2003 are shown in Figure 1.2.1 and 1.2.2..

Overall health and recent performance of the economy

(This part of the text is based on *Croatian Economic Outlook Quarterly*, Numbers 13, 14 and 15, issued by the Institute of Economics, Zagreb.)

The year 2002 will be remembered as the first year in which policy measures introduced by the new government gave a noticeable result.

Overall activity began to accelerate in first quarter of 2002, fuelled by rising domestic demand, thus boosting the Croatian economy by 5.2 per cent in 2002, the highest rate of growth since 1997. Personal consumption and gross capital formation led such rapid expansion, while government consumption stagnated. After the banking sector increased its credit potential thanks to the inflow of foreign currency during the Euro conversion, credit expansion and lower interest rates enabled strong personal consumption.

In the first quarter of 2003, GDP growth reached 4.9 per cent year-on-year. The trend was again backed up by strong personal consumption

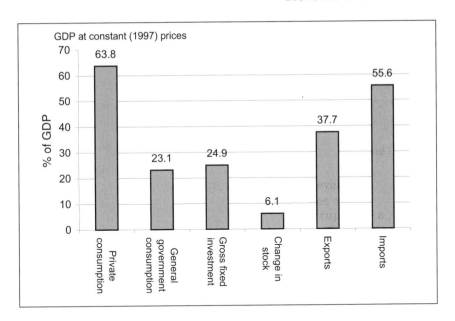

Source: Croatian National Bank, Special Data Dissemination Standards, June 2003

Figure 1.2.1 Components of gross domestic product for the first quarter of 2003

and an upswing in investments, which brought about a further expansion in imports. Personal consumption rose 4.9 per cent year-on-year in the first quarter of 2003. Its persistent upward trend has been fuelled by modest real disposable income growth and relatively low borrowing costs.

The track of positive developments has been confirmed by the April and May 2003 figures, which show rising employment, industrial output and retail sales. Thus, the economic outlook for the near future remains favourable.

An unexpectedly strong 16.2 per cent year-on-year increase in gross fixed capital formation in the first quarter of 2003 can only be explained by an expansion of highway construction works, undertaken by the Government. Besides, it should be noted that a strong and stable upward trend has characterized overall investment activities for the last three years, suggesting a general improvement in the business environment.

Furthermore, investment by private companies accounts for more than a half of all investment, indicating widespread recovery and generally improved business confidence. More easily accessible and favourable credit lines were an important factor behind the investment rebound. Nevertheless, generally favourable economic conditions have

Table 1.2.1 Main economic indicators

	1995	1996	1997	1998	1999	2000	2001	2002
Economic activity								
Real GDP (% change)	6.8	5.9	6.8	2.5	-0.4	3.7	3.8	5.2
Real private consumption (% change)	na	na	na	-0.6	-2.7	4.1	4.6	6.6
Real government consumption (% change)	na	na	na	2.3	0.8	-0.7	-4.3	-1.8
Real investment (% change)	na	na	na	2.5	-1.1	-3.5	9.7	10.1
Industrial output (% change)	0.3	3.1	6.8	3.7	-1.4	1.7	6.0	5.4
Unemployment rate (registered, %, pa)	14.5[+]	16.4[+]	17.5[+]	17.2	19.4	21.3	22.0	22.3
Nominal GDP (US$ million)	18,811	19,872	20,109	21,628	20,064	19,031	19,536	22,436
GDP per capita (US$)	4,029	4,422	4,398	4,805	4,371	4,153	4,403	5,057
Prices, wages and exchange rates								
Implicit GDP deflator (% change)	na	na	na	8.4	4.1	6.4	3.0	2.9
Retail prices (% change, pa)	2.0	3.5	3.6	5.7	4.2	6.2	4.9	2.2
Producer prices (% change, pa)	0.8	1.4	2.3	-1.2	2.6	9.7	3.6	-0.4
Average gross wage (% change, pa)	na	12.2	13.1	12.6	10.2	7.0	3.9	6.0
Net wage bill (% change, pa)	42.8	7.8	16.4	11.5	7.8	8.3	na	na
Exchange rate, HRK/DM/EUR (pa)	3.65	3.61	3.56	3.62	3.88	3.90	7.47	7.41
Exchange rate, HRK/US$ (pa)	5.23	5.43	6.16	6.36	7.11	8.28	8.34	7.86
Foreign trade and capital flows								
Exports of goods (US$ million)	4,517	4,643	3,981	4,517	4,302	4,432	4,666	4,899
Imports of goods (US$ million)	7,352	7,784	9,101	8,276	7,799	7,887	9,147	10,713
Current account balance (US$ million)	-1,407	-995	-2,512	-1,453	-1,397	-549	-725	1,587
Current account balance (% of GDP)	-7.5	-4.8	-12.5	-6.7	-7.0	-2.4	-3.7	-7.1
Gross foreign direct investment (US$ million)	114	511	533	932	1,479	852	1,561	980
Foreign exchange reserves (US$ million, eop)	1,895	2,314	2,539	2,816	3,025	3,525	4,704	5,886
Foreign debt (US$ million, eop)	3,809	5,308	7,452	9,586	9,872	10,840	11,316	15,337

Government finance

Conventional central govt deficit (HRK million)	-715	-134	-1,160	1,257	-2,522	-6,108	-3,758	-3,872
Conventional central govt deficit (% of GDP)	-0.7	-0.1	-0.9	0.9	-1.8	-3.9	-2.3	-2.2
Primary central govt deficit (HRK million)	677	1,084	577	3,208	-423	-3,509	-779	-658
Primary central govt deficit (% of GDP)	0.7	1.0	0.5	2.3	-0.3	-2.2	-0.5	-0.4
Privatization proceeds (HRK million)	594	1,123	461	1,789	6,311	3,101	4,543	219
Domestic public debt (US$ million, eop)	3,337	3,116	2,465	2,409	2,191	2,617	2,569	3,462
Foreign public debt (US$ million, eop)	241	2,397	2,906	3,395	3,973	4,753	5,133	6,356
Total public debt (% of GDP)	19.0	27.7	26.7	26.8	30.7	38.7	39.2	39.5

Monetary indicators

Narrow money, M1 (% change, eop)*	24.0	38.1	20.8	-1.5	2.4	30.1	31.5	30.2
Broad money, M4 (% change, eop)*	39.3	49.1	38.3	13.0	-1.1	29.3	45.2	9.5
Total domestic credit (% change, eop)*	18.6	3.1	44.4	22.4	-6.6	9.0	23.0	30.0
DMBs credit to households (% change, eop)*	35.4	39.5	93.5	38.4	8.6	21.0	29.3	43.0
DMBs credit to enterprises (% change, eop)*	21.2	2.6	35.6	17.1	-14.5	0.9	21.3	22.7
Money market interest rate (%, pa)	21.1	19.3	10.2	14.5	13.7	8.9	3.9	1.7

Notes

HRK/DM until 31.12.2000, HRK/€ from 01.01.2001, plus non-military.

* Inter-temporal comparisons including 1999 are impeded because banks in which bankruptcy procedures have started were excluded from monetary statistics, while certain items of the Privredna Banka Zagreb balance sheet were cleared during its privatization.

Conventional abbreviations: na –not available, pa – period average, eop – end of period, govt – government, HRK – Croatian Kuna, DM – German mark, US$ – US dollar, € – Euro, DMB – deposit money bank.

Sources: Central Bureau of Statistics, Croatian National Bank, Ministry of Finance, Payment Transfer Agency

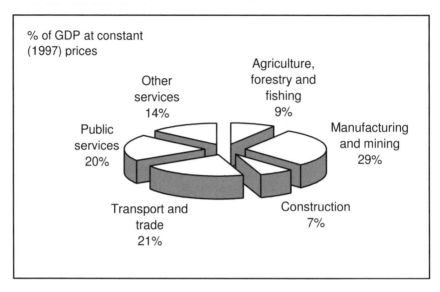

Source: Croatian National Bank, Special Data Dissemination Standards, June 2003

Figure 1.2.2 Origins of gross domestic product for the first quarter of 2003

been slow in spilling over to the labour market, although seasonally adjusted data indicate that a long-term contraction in employment has been halted.

Following the introduction of new registration procedures for unemployed people by the Croatian Employment Service, the seasonally adjusted figure for official unemployment has fallen for the past 14 months. In May 2003, the Employment Service counted a total of 330,882 unemployed people, which gives an unemployment rate of 19.6 per cent. Notwithstanding the methodological issues, there are important political implications of this statistical figure in the pre-election period. The last time the unemployment rate was below 20 per cent was in October 1999, during the previous Government. Since one of the important election issues then was unemployment, the current Government has still a little time to substantiate its ability to meet one of the key goals of its mandate.

The results of a Labour Force Survey reveal less pronounced changes in the Croatian labour market compared to the administrative sources. During 2001 and 2002, there were increases in both the activity rates and the employment rates. According to the Labour Force Survey, the unemployment rate for women and men in the second half of 2002 amounted to 15.8 and 13.3 per cent, respectively.

The ways to resolve the unemployment problem in Croatia are perceived quite differently by different partners. The Government is trying to introduce more flexibility on the supply side – in terms of easier dismissal procedures, stricter rules for unemployment benefit applications and through the introduction of sponsored education programmes. At the same time, trade unions believe that the unemployment issue can be resolved without any reduction of the workers rights, ie through job creation that would result from stronger economic activity.

An acceleration of overall activity is also apparent on the real economy front. Throughout 2002, industrial output exhibited increasing year-on-year growth rates and hit 9.2 per cent in the fourth quarter of 2002. It increased by 5.4 per cent for the year as a whole. Industrial output increased by a cumulative 5.8 per cent in the first five months of 2003 on a year-on-year basis. As suggested by the seasonally adjusted figures, after a volatile start to the year, industrial activity had a strong upward push in April, followed by a slight further rise in May. In the environment of intensified construction activity, this sector has experienced the highest growth rates.

For the third year in a row, the government succeeded in reducing its consumption in real terms. After a strong 4.3 per cent decrease in 2001, 2002 brought a 1.8 per cent decline. Nonetheless, it should be noted that this downward trend almost ceased at the very end of 2002 and there was a rise in the first quarter of 2003. This accords with the assumption that there is little room for further reductions in government spending, at least in the current political environment with parliamentary elections looming. Incentives to reform and consolidate the public sector, especially with regard to the number of employees, are now much weaker than before. At the same time, the Government is facing increasing pressures from various interest groups aimed at delaying reforms or obtaining certain benefits. Rising expenditure seems a tempting response in such a situation.

According to the official data (Croatian National Bank, *CNB Bulletin*, No 83, June 2003), the consolidated central government deficit reached 5.5 per cent of GDP in 2002. Fortunately, local government performed much better than central government in 2002, ending the year with a surplus equal to 0.7 per cent of GDP. The combined deficits of all government units thus reached 4.7 per cent of GDP. Although still considerable, the deficit was surprisingly small compared to the 6.2 per cent of GDP that appeared in the official and IMF estimates. In terms of GDP, the general government deficit was reduced from 6.8 per cent in 2001 to 4.7 per cent in 2002.

In May 2003, the Government placed its first issue of long-term Kuna-denominated bonds, bearing a 6.125 per cent coupon. The HRK 1 billion issue was applauded by investors for its relatively attractive yield, and also by the corporate sector, which lacked a benchmark for similar issues in the longer end of the yield curve.

The export of goods in 2002 did not show any notable shift from its long-running stagnating trend. The underperformance of the export sector had a significant impact on a widening current account deficit. According to the national accounts data, the volume of exports and imports increased strongly in the first quarter of 2003. Goods and services exports increased by 14.3 per cent over the same period last year, while the imports of goods and services expanded by 10.3 per cent. The elasticity of imports with respect to GDP is high. This level of imports, coupled with a slow export growth, has put a severe strain on the external balance of the country, as confirmed by the goods and services deficit, which reached 10 per cent of GDP in 2002.

The presence of twin deficits reveals a side-effect of strong economic activity. Strong domestic demand has pulled in ever-increasing imports. Coupled with sluggish export of goods, it has resulted in a deterioration in the trade balance. Nevertheless, growth driven by domestic demand makes the Croatian economy resilient to a sluggish recovery of the global economy and its poor near-term prospects.

Turning to monetary developments, their main characteristic in 2002 may be summarized as strong credit growth, which was not induced by the expansion of broad money so much as by the growth of commercial banks' foreign liabilities. The broad money M4 year-on-year growth rate broke the threshold of 40 per cent during the months when the euro cash rollout took place. However, a portion of the foreign currency deposits made during that time was later withdrawn from banks.

In the first half of 2003, the growth of monetary aggregates slowed down. In May, total liquid assets (M4) were 2.6 per cent higher than in December, indicating that the major sources of a rapid deposit growth in 2002 had been exhausted.

In 2002, due to the strong liquidity, interest rates declined, while the Kuna exchange rate fluctuated mildly. The Kuna began to appreciate very early on in the second quarter of 2003. At the end of June 2003, it was 2.4 per cent stronger than at the end of March. The appreciation was driven by seasonal factors (tourism inflows around Easter and in June, when the tourist season begins), and capital inflows associated with loans syndicated to some of the major Croatian banks.

Measures introduced early in 2003 by the Croatian National Bank (CNB) to curb credit growth have started to deliver results, despite the fact that commercial banks' lending activity remains strong. Total domestic credits expanded 7.6 per cent in the first five months of 2003, a slower rate than in the same period a year before, indicating that the banks are making efforts to comply with the maximum 4 per cent lending increase quarter-on-quarter that the monetary authority has set. Bank lending to households has remained the most dynamic part of total domestic credits, rising 12.9 per cent in the first five months of 2003. In more stringent conditions, commercial banks are obviously focusing more on retail lending, where profits are higher and risks lower than in corporate lending.

Given relatively favourable developments with the oil prices in the aftermath of the war in Iraq and a weaker US dollar, inflation calmed down to stay close to historical lows. While producer prices were 1.7 per cent higher in June 2003 than in June 2002, the retail price index indicated no more than a 1.1 per cent increase.

The exchange rate has once again proved to be the main factor behind inflation movements in Croatia. A fairly stable exchange rate against the Euro provided for a stable business environment, which helped keep inflation low.

Structural reforms and government policy

For every country in transition there is an urgent need to conduct serious structural reforms. The gradual implementation of such reforms is often the toughest challenge for the government of a country in transition, since structural reforms often have great social impact. While reform efforts are being made in Croatia, there are still many areas left unaddressed. The European Bank for Reconstruction and Development (EBRD) in its Transition Report for 2001 praises notable progress being made in following areas: the privatization of state-held enterprises and banks, the liberalization of capital account transactions, the reduction of consolidated central government deficit, the reduction of the total number of arrears in economy, the consolidation of the banking system, and social reform (the launch of a privately managed second-pillar pension system in January 2002).

According to the Government's Memorandum of Economic and Financial Policy, sent on 11 February 2003 to the IMF, during 2003 the Government is committed to reform some crucial aspects of the fiscal sector. The new budget law, which was approved jointly with the 2003 budget framework execution law, requires the submission of an updated three-year budgetary framework with each annual budget, the presentation of all budget data on a consolidated general Government basis, and the regular publication of consolidated general Government data (all three issues were frequently criticized by Croatian fiscal policy experts). It also strengthens the enforcement of penalties for overspending budget limits. Four new funds and agencies have been created under the 2003 budget (the environmental protection fund, the agency for small and medium-sized enterprises (SMEs), the agency for investment and export promotion and the state aid agency). This year's emphasis on promoting the growth of SMEs was designed to help meet the Government's goal of fostering sustainable development within the framework of a market-oriented, stable and predictable business environment.

A new foreign exchange law was created in order to induce reforms in the financial sector. It will be consistent with EU standards and it will empower the CNB to introduce temporary restrictions on short-term capital inflows. It also requires that foreign securities that are eligible for outward portfolio investment by residents satisfy minimum ratings from international rating agencies. Also, several bylaws (on classification of claims, calculation of capital-asset ratios, supervision methodology, auditing decisions, consolidated supervision, management of liquidity risk and operation of subsidiaries) to implement the new banking law have been prepared by the CNB for application from 1 January 2004 at the latest.

Progress is being made in the public enterprise sector as well. The government is committed to divesting virtually all public enterprises and to keep a minority share in only some of them. The privatization fund (HFP) expects to reduce its portfolio of some 1,100 companies by about one-half by the end of 2003. Outside HFP's portfolio, the government continues to pursue the restructuring and privatization of most large state enterprises. The binding tender for 25 per cent plus one share of the oil and gas company (INA) is expected to be resolved. The electricity company (HEP) will complete its split into separate power generation, transmission and distribution companies during 2003, for possible privatization of power plants in 2004. Finally, 7 per cent of shares in the telecommunication company HT will be sold to its employees in the second quarter of 2003. The selling of stakes in large public enterprises (HT and possible INA privatization) and banks to foreign enterprises and banks has raised a lot of attention among the general public. Some politicians and economic analysts feel that Croatian public enterprises that are vital for the sound functioning of the economy and infrastructure should not have been sold off as readily as they were. Also they are opposing any further selling of state stakes in public enterprises to foreign capital holders.

The Government is also preparing a new company, competition and labour law that would enhance the functioning of markets and encourage the growth of employment. Also, a new bankruptcy law aimed at accelerating bankruptcy procedures and allowing payoffs to creditors before the completion of all procedures is expected to be approved.

Within the limits of its tight financial recourses, the Government plans to develop a more active employment policy to alleviate the acute unemployment problem. Particular emphasis is placed on bundling the retraining and re-employment measures for workers affected by the privatization of state-owned enterprises and public sector redundancies. Also, measures that aim to rationalize social welfare policies and to establish a new labour rights legislative framework are being undertaken. Trade unions strongly oppose the new labour policies, claiming that they leave the workers less protected.

The European Commission in its Country Strategy Paper for Croatia, 2002–2006, suggests that both the size and the role of the state in Croatia are still very large and there is therefore a need not only to reduce Government expenditure, but also to increase the efficiency of public administration. This can be done through decentralization, which would strengthen local administration and self-governing units, so regional development has to be taken more seriously. There are two principal goals in regional development: a) to reduce the development imbalances, in particular promoting the prospects for sustainable development of war-affected areas, rural areas and islands, and b) decentralization, territorial reorganization and strengthening of local authorities. The effects of an inefficient state administration have clear economic impacts since both foreign and domestic investors face a variety of administrative barriers to investment.

The Croatian health system is at a critical and unstable point, with its finances in major deficit. The health sector, therefore, represents a major fiscal problem, but it is also a sensitive social issue that needs to be addressed very carefully. Some reforms have been made, but they were insufficient to bring about more effective health spending.

Role of foreign direct investments

According to the latest figures from the Croatian National Bank and Ministry of Foreign Affairs, from 1993 until the end of the first quarter of 2003, foreign direct investments totalled US$7,710 million (see Figure 1.2.3). It is important to note that until 1996 only ownership investments were registered, while from 1997 total investment included reinvested profits and other non-ownership arrangements.

The first notable foreign investments in Croatia took place after 1995 and the completion of the successful military liberation, while the notable privatization of the large state enterprises and banks in 1999, currently the most representative form of foreign investment, were a record. Direct foreign investment in 2001 reached US$1,55 billion, the highest yearly amount.

In the period 1993–2002, direct foreign equity investment in Croatia was realized through a number of sectors (see Figure 1.2.4). Due to the privatization of Croatian Telecommunications, large Croatian banks and the sale of shares in Pliva (the Croatian pharmaceutical company) on European markets, 62 per cent of total foreign investment was concentrated in the telecommunications, banking and pharmaceutical industry sectors. These were followed by investments in cement production, hotels, motels and restaurants, the extraction of crude oil and natural gas, and so on.

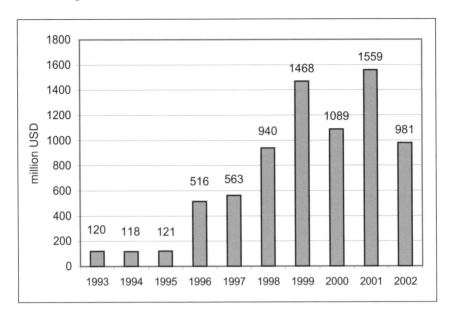

Source: Croatian National Bank

Figure 1.2.3 Direct foreign investment in Croatia per year

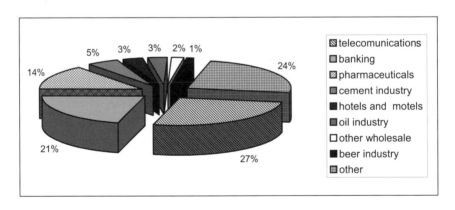

Source: Croatian National Bank

Figure 1.2.4 Direct foreign equity investment in Croatia, 1993–2002, by sectors

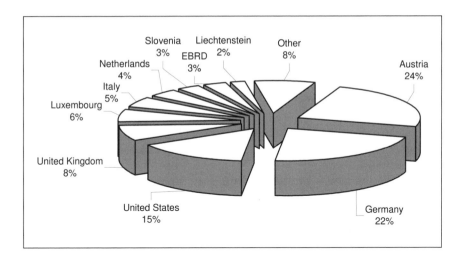

Source: Croatian National Bank

Figure 1.2.5 Direct foreign investment in Croatia, 1993 to first quarter, 2003, by country of origin

According to investments by country of origin, the largest single investor in Croatia during the period 1993 to the first quarter of 2003 was Austria (see Figure 1.2.5), when Austrian investments made up 24 per cent of total foreign investment.

The second largest investor was Germany with almost 22 per cent, whilst the USA was third with 15 per cent. They were followed by the UK, Luxembourg, Italy, the Netherlands, Slovenia, EBRD and Liechtenstein. Over 70 per cent of total foreign investments up to the first quarter of 2003 came from member states of the European Union.

The total direct foreign investments for the period 1993–2002 has reached over 30 per cent of GDP or about US$1,500 per capita, which places Croatia amongst the more successful transition countries as far as attracting investment is concerned. The privatization of some large public enterprises such as INA, HEP and HZ could noticeably change the look and structure of foreign investment in Croatia.

Relationship with international institutions and donors

In October 2001 Croatia signed the Stabilization and Association Agreement (SAA) with the European Union, which was then ratified by the Croatian Parliament and the European Parliament. Having signed the SAA, Croatia made an important step forward in institutionalizing its relations with the European Union and started a comprehensive process of fulfilling its assumed obligations to bring its political, economic, legal and institutional systems in line with European standards. Croatia's application for EU membership in Athens on 21 February 2003 gave further impetus to continued membership negotiations.

By a consensus of all Croatian parliamentary parties (111 votes to one abstention), at its session on 18 December 2002 the Croatian Parliament adopted the Resolution on Croatia's Integration into the European Union. By applying for EU membership, Croatia contributed to the stability of the wider region of South-East Europe and demonstrated to the SAP countries the desirability of carrying out the required reforms, making their prospects of EU membership more real.

Croatian CEFTA membership took effect on 1 March 2003. A free trade agreement with the Federal Republic of Yugoslavia was initiated in November 2002 and is expected to come into effect soon. Other free trade agreements are being negotiated with Estonia, Latvia and Moldova.

Croatia has been a member of the IMF since 1992 and has benefited from the IMF's technical assistance in key monetary, fiscal and public administration areas. After the new Government was elected, negotiations on a stand-by credit started in March 2000 and resulted in the agreement of a 14-month stand-by credit for SDR (Special Drawing Rights, an IMF currency) 200 million. Two steps further were taken on 19 March 2001 and 3 February 2003, with the approval of stand-by arrangements that provide the Government with a framework for economic policy-making and monitoring.

According to the figures from European Commission Country Strategy Paper 2002–2006, as of September 2001, the World Bank Group has committed a total of US$930 million for 26 projects. Its focus for assistance has been shifted from post-war reconstruction to capital market developments, and reform of the financial, health, agriculture and forestry sectors. Also Croatia has developed relationships with donors such as EBRD (its cumulative commitment of €745 million, classified as private sector operations), USAID (assistance to local government, political parties, labour unions and the media) and CEB (engaged in health, education, refugee return and cultural heritage projects).

1.3

Privatization

Croatian Privatization Fund (HFP)

The privatization process in Croatia started in the early 1990s, at the same time as in other countries of Central and Eastern Europe. Privatization in Croatia differs from that in other transition countries by virtue of the system of 'social ownership' that existed in former Yugoslavia.

At the beginning of the transition process, Croatian enterprises already enjoyed a considerable degree of economic openness and independence from the government. Unlike centrally planned economies, ex-Yugoslavia's economic system did give a role to markets. Therefore, the relative price structure was much less distorted and, even more important, both enterprises (managers) and households had the opportunity to learn about market behaviour. Superior human capital and more efficient physical capital than in other CEECs resulted from the higher degree of economic and political openness in the country, and relatively better education. The existence of a private sector and an important (and in part temporary) emigration of Croatian workers abroad also contributed to relatively high efficiency. The standard of living was substantially higher than in other CEECs, except Slovenia.

However, in the aftermath of the collapse of former Yugoslavia in 1991, Croatia was not able to capitalize on its relative advantages. Due to the war on its soil at the beginning of the 1990s, Croatia experienced a more pronounced initial transition slump (1991–1993) than other transition countries. These initial years of transition were also characterized by macroeconomic instability. Then, after successful stabilization at the end of 1993, Croatia was quick to regain ground as one of the top performers in Central and Eastern Europe. The average growth rate has been very good since 1994 compared to the peer group of countries.

Enterprises in Croatia were to a certain extent privatized even before the collapse of socialism, since Croatian enterprises were not government owned and had been 'self-managed' since the 1950s. That system assured them a much greater degree of independence and autonomy in all spheres, particularly in how to organize and manage their business activities.

As a result, privatization of Croatian enterprises was to a great extent under the influence of the enterprises themselves. The first proposals on how to structure the privatization of Croatian enterprises were designed to come from the enterprises themselves and not from the State. As a consequence, many present and former employees of these enterprises, as well as other citizens, could purchase shares up to a certain amount in the privatization process of almost all Croatian enterprises. Shares that were above the permitted limit were transferred in certain percentages into the portfolio of the Governmental Croatian Privatization Fund (CPF) and into the two social funds (state agricultural and pension funds). The sales of the shares from the CPF's portfolio are organized from time to time by the CPF through public tenders. On the basis of their holdings of shares, the CPF and the other two funds are today shareholders in respective enterprises and participate in their management.

The first comprehensive rules on privatization were contained in the Law on Transformation of Social Enterprises (*Narodne novine* 19/91, 23 April 1991). This law was amended several times and in its present form was consolidated in 1996, with the Law on Privatization (*NN* 21, 14 March 1996 with amendments *NN* 71/97 and 73/00). The CPF, established in 1993, is in charge of the privatization process. In 1995, the Ministry of Privatization was also established to assist in the final stages of privatization, ie in the privatization of major public utilities and in a mass privatization voucher programme. The Ministry was later abolished. The CPF has, in the privatization process, acquired shares in numerous enterprises and the Law states that the Fund must strive to sell the shares in the nominated public enterprises.

Today, the CPF is responsible for the privatization of shares owned by various government institutions like Pension Funds, Health Services, the Governmental Agency for Recovery, public enterprises, etc. Only the Government can decide which shares the CPF may continue to hold. The privatization portfolio consisted of about 3,000 formerly socially owned enterprises. These firms, along with 50,000 originally private small firms and a small number of large state trade companies and public utilities represented the entire Croatian economy.

In 1991 the appraised value of equity that was privatized amounted to Kuna 86 billion (approximately €11.5 billion). The privatization process covered less than 10 per cent of the companies in the economy, but these companies in value terms accounted for approximately 80 per cent of the Croatian economy.

In the period 2000–2001, 647 companies were privatized, out of which 392 were privatized in the bankruptcy process, 112 by settlement of capital outlays, 98 by public auction, 26 by public tendering and 112 by free charge distribution. About one-third of the original privatization portfolio still remains in state hands, and intensive preparations are under way for the privatization of public utilities. The total nominal value of the state portfolio available for privatization amounts to €2.99 billion. Shares of 832 companies, in which the value of the state portfolio does not exceed 50 per cent of equity, are privatized at Stock Exchange auctions. The value of this portfolio amounts to €0.62 billion.

The CPF sells the shares of the companies in which it holds minority stakes through public auction on the Zagreb Stock Exchange. Foreign and domestic legal and natural persons may acquire share ownership if they are represented by a registered member of the Zagreb Stock Exchange. Prices ranges from HRK1 for companies facing bankruptcy to the nominal value of the appraised equity for more successful companies. Shares are paid for exclusively in cash, with a payment period of up to 7 days from the transaction date on the Stock Exchange. A list of brokerage houses registered on the Zagreb Stock Exchange can be acquired from Zagrebacka burza (www.zse.hr).

The purchase on the Stock Exchange does not in any way obligate the future owner except in terms of the offered price. The portfolio of 173 enterprises where the share of the state capital is above 50 per cent, with significant managerial influence, is being privatized by public tender; 85 of these companies are considered to be of strategic importance. The priority in their privatization will be given to strategic partners. In selecting the winning bidder, the key criterion is not only the offer price, but also the proposals of the purchaser to develop and make further investments in the company and to assume the liabilities to employees and creditors. The current state portfolio also includes 1,400 individual objects and real estate for industry and tourism, and 10 major coastal real estate properties. More detailed information can be acquired from the CPF (www.hfp.hr). The most significant part of the portfolio that is privatized by public tender relates to agriculture, tourism and the processing industry. The survival and development of these enterprises are of strategic importance to Croatia.

Due to the financial situation and the fact that it acts as both owner and vendor, the State is ready to negotiate various privatization options in order to fulfil its own and investors' expectations relating to the future of privatized companies. This partnership does not mean the State intends to interfere in the activities of the new owner, but it seeks the willingness of the investor to negotiate and participate in the solution of inherited financial problems. Especially valued is the willingness of the purchaser to invest in new technologies, modern market-oriented organizational structures, and retaining the existing workforce or preparing a redundancy programme in compliance with Croatian law.

The intentions of the purchaser must be backed by firm guarantees, primarily a bank guarantee payable upon the first request, or a corporate guarantee. Regarding the terms of the invitation to tender, given that the vendor is in principle the largest creditor of the company, consultations with the bidders are desirable so as to define the most acceptable privatization model.

In Croatia there are about 10 major state-owned enterprises engaged in the utility and energy sectors. The Law on Privatization lists several major legal entities still in public ownership in the oil, gas, electricity, postal communications, radio and television, public roads and forestry sectors. The Law provides that these enterprises will be privatized on the basis of separate laws to be enacted by the Government. It also sets up a procedure for establishing the commercial value of specific public enterprises before their privatization.

The general model of privatization of public enterprises was outlined in the Law on Privatization (*Narodne novine* 21/96 and 71/97). The privatization programme provides for restructuring of the enterprises in order to determine the true value of their share capital (ie the difference between the total assets and total liabilities, including preference shares). The intention of the Government is to privatize each of the largest enterprises individually on the basis of special decrees, tailored for each company. The individual programmes will be prepared by the Ministry of Economy in cooperation with the ministries in charge of the companies. The intention is to initially privatize 25 per cent of each company, while 30 per cent would be transferred to the Pension Fund. Privatization could evolve through the sale of assets, offerings to strategic investors, offerings to the public, and flotation on the local and foreign stock exchanges.

The process of privatizing public enterprises started in 1999 and continued in 2001 with important sales in the telecommunication sector. Other important public enterprises like INA (oil and gas), the biggest insurance company Croatia, Hrvatska Elektroprivreda (electricity) and some others are making serious efforts to be ready for privatization.

Since the privatization process in Croatia was marred by certain irregularities, the Croatian Parliament (Sabor) enacted the Law on the Revision of the Transformation and Privatization (*NN*, 44/2001). A special state office was established for the purposes of the revision.

The Croatian Privatization Fund (HFP)

The HFP was established to implement and complete the privatization of assets. The Fund engages in the following professional and administrative operations:

- transformation of socially owned enterprises into state-owned companies;
- privatization of shares, property and rights and the transfer of shares free of charge when stipulated by law;

- management of companies in which state institutions hold shares, and other operations stipulated by law and the Fund's Articles of Association:

- management of assets owned by the Republic of Croatia when stipulated by law or a decision of the Government;

- management of companies in which the Fund holds shares, and other operations stipulated by law and the Fund's Articles of Association.

Foreign Trade – A Major Development Potential

Dr Zarko Primorac, Regional Chairman, Deloitte & Touche

Foreign trade has traditionally formed a significant portion of Croatia's economy. Commodity import and export, ie the visible trade balance, accounts for about 55 to 60 per cent of GDP, while the export of goods is substantially lower, representing about 22 per cent of GDP. If services and other 'invisible' transactions are included, the participation of Croatia in the global economy is significantly higher.

Income from tourist and traffic services has a notable share in the total economic performance. The tourist trade accounts for 8 to 12 per cent of GDP, with the highest figures recorded during the summer months.

Foreign trade, in particular commodity export and import, tourism, and especially traffic, ie transport services, were seriously affected by the war in the 1990s. The transition processes, as well as the inadequate privatization concept applied to exports, have had an additional adverse effect on the development of foreign trade relations. Privatization in certain sectors, especially in the tourist trade, is still in progress. Unfortunately, a major share of export potential has been lost as a result of privatization in the manufacturing sector, mostly affecting metal processing, wood processing, chemicals and other industries. At a time when the industries in other, more advanced countries in transition were being converted to the market economy, along with the modernization of their economic structures, primarily by attracting foreign investors, the Croatian economy was still suffering from the consequences of the war, followed by delayed restructuring and failed privatization.

However, foreign trade activities in the Croatian economy have been rapidly recovering. The effects of the processes that have been taking place in the past few years in the various areas of foreign trade are different. Unfortunately, commodity imports are still stagnant, as shown in Table 1.4.1.

Table 1.4.1 Exports, imports and current account balance (US$)

	1995	1996	1997	1998	1999	2000	2001	2002
Exports	4633	4512	4171	4541	4280	4432	4666	4899
Imports	7510	7788	9104	8383	7799	7887	9147	10713
Trade deficit	−3228.0	−3488.0	−5383.2	−4071.5	−3298.6	−3203.8	−4101.3	−5279.3
Services balance	1047.0	1580.0	2024.2	2076.7	1625.2	2267.9	2927.0	3118.1
Current Account Balance	−1407.0	−1091.3	−2512.1	−1452.8	−1397.2	−459.4	−725.1	−1546.7

Source: Croatian Chamber of Commerce and WIIW

The stagnation of export performance is a result of several factors, the most important being the loss of traditional markets, slow modernization of industry and non-competitive prices, the latter partly due to an extremely rigid foreign exchange rate policy. Since 1994 the Croatian National Bank has been enforcing a policy of a relatively fixed exchange rate, ensuring internal price stability and maintaining a low-inflation level, which 'pushes' industry and exporters towards a faster restructuring and a reduction in input costs.

On the other hand, commodity imports show a rapid rise, as clearly indicated in Table 1.4.1. The long-term policy of applying a relatively fixed exchange rate has permanently ensured a certain premium for importers, so that the position of imports in the total trade balance has been rapidly increasing. From 1994 to 2002, Croatian imports recorded a real growth of more than 65 per cent, whereas cumulatively, exports rose by only a few percentage points.

Such a diverging trend, in the exports and imports, generated high deficits. Thus, the data presented reveal a large increase in the trade deficit, especially in 2002. Foreign trade deficits were compensated for by increased revenues in the services sector – tourism, transport services, and funds remitted from abroad. As a result, the current balance reveals no dramatic deficit, although even this figure worsened in the last year of the period: the negative current balance for 2002 exceeds 6.8 per cent of GDP, representing a weighty load for an economic stabilization policy.

Apart from the stagnant export performance, the export commodity structure is another weak point in foreign trade. Croatia's export commodities comprise mostly traditional products, with textiles, footwear, clothing, rubber, chemical fertilizers and fuels being predominant.

There are only few commodities that are based on modern technologies. The metal processing industry, which should be using modern technologies, has lost a good share of its traditional markets. Transport vehicles, specifically vessels, represent the most significant export item in the metal processing industry. The export commodity structure is shown in Figure 1.4.1.

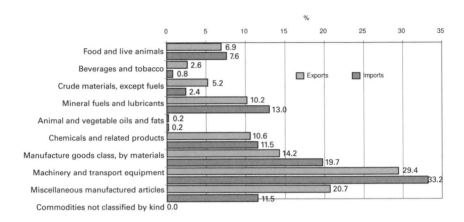

Source: WIIW

Figure 1.4.1 Imports and exports by commodity group (2001)

Not even the regional structure of foreign trade activities is capable of satisfying the ambitions of a modern and dynamic economy. True, most of Croatia's present economic activities are oriented towards the EU countries, with approximately 55 per cent in terms of total exports, and 56 per cent of total imports. Croatia's traditional economic partners have remained dominant, with Italy and Germany being the leading ones.

Although Croatia's share of trade with the EU countries is relatively high (see Table 1.4.2), it is still significantly lower than the leading transition countries and, particularly important, it has been gradually shrinking. The EU market is very demanding, both in terms of its size and quality, and the diminishing Croatian share warns of a gradual, although slow, decline in the competitiveness of Croatian exports.

Other major foreign trade partners include countries in the region, first of all those that emerged after the disintegration of the former Yugoslavia, which is natural given that the economies of the former Yugoslav republics were very much complementary.

Croatia should invest a lot of effort in its foreign trade strategy, and there are numerous opportunities to restore intense regional economic

Table 1.4.2 Exports and imports by destination and origin, 2002 (%)

	Country	Exports	Imports
1.	Italy	22.7	17.1
2.	Germany	13.9	15.8
3.	Bosnia and Herzegovina	12.5	...
4.	Slovenia	8.7	8.0
5.	Austria	7.9	6.6
6.	Yugoslavia	3.3	...
7.	France	3.0	5.2
8.	Russia	1.7	6.6
9.	Hungary	1.5	2.7
10.	Belgium	1.5	...
	Other countries	23.5	31.5

Source: Croatian Chamber of Commerce

relations. We believe that this is a sound direction to take, considering the many favourable circumstances and common features of the economic structures and the relative size of the market.

Croatian exports and imports by region are illustrated in Figures 1.4.2 and 1.4.3. Once again, one should bear in mind the warning fact that the relative share of foreign trade with the EU countries has been decreasing in relative terms – the share in imports dropped from 62.1 per cent in 1995 to 56 per cent in 2001, and the share in exports declined from 57.6 per cent to 54.7 per cent in the same period.

Such a trend is not at all satisfactory. The EU market is of crucial strategic importance for Croatia's economy. The Croatian economy has to make efforts to come as close as possible to the EU countries in terms of market size, the quality of market competitors, business standards, tourist destinations and all other elements. In 2001, Croatia signed the Stabilization and Association Agreement, and the preparations for admission to the European Union in 2007 or 2008, together with Romania and Bulgaria, are under way, which represents another very strong 'pressure' to intensify efforts to restore and increase the level of foreign trade with the EU countries.

Apart from certain unfavourable developments in the Croatian foreign trade sector, the overall trends should not be seen as discouraging.

When speaking of commodities, Croatia has traditionally been an exporting country. Economic paralysis brought about by the war and the effects of the untypical transition have been gradually overcome. Coming closer to the European Union, combined with the measures taken by the Croatian Government to encourage exports, in particular research and development in the economic sector, are a positive impetus, which should result in innovating and modernizing export production

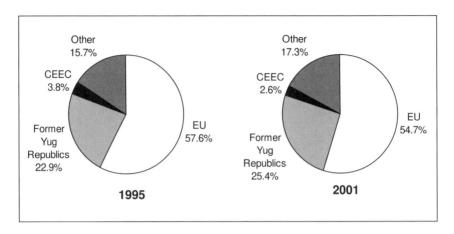

Figure 1.4.2 Exports by region

by introducing new products based on know-how and high technologies. Positive examples can be found in the pharmaceuticals sector, among certain export-oriented agricultural producers and in the food processing sector. There are already several large companies with regional ambitions and they will certainly 'pull' Croatian imports, particularly in certain areas.

Croatia has distinct advantages in boosting its exports in the services sector, including its geographic position, tourism potential, traffic and travel position, etc, which even at present ensure a high growth of inflows from the services sector.

Imports, which are currently at the highest level ever recorded, should not be constrained by any quantitative restrictions (see Figure 1.4.3). On the contrary, the Croatian economy has been opening itself more and more, offering everyone equal opportunities in fair market competition. Still, Croatia has to gradually give up importing those commodities and services that can be competitively produced at home and even exported. This is particularly true of agricultural products and other 'traditional' products.

Foreign direct investments give a significant impetus to Croatian exports. Croatia has a relatively high level of foreign direct investment – a total of over US$8.4 billion since 1994. The problem lies in the structure of these investments, most of which are portfolio investments in the financial, telecoms and other monopolistic economic sectors.

In order to improve the structure of foreign direct investments, a strategy involving tax and other incentives for investing in manufacturing is being prepared. According to estimates, intensified foreign direct investments in the manufacturing sector would rapidly modernize the

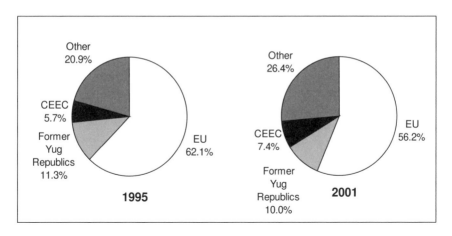

Figure 1.4.3 Imports by region

existing industry by creating new 'export' production. Naturally, this implies taking several measures to enhance the efficiency of the legal system, to improve tax treatment, to create a more flexible labour market, and others.

Finally, the basis for Croatia's foreign trade strategy is to achieve the highest possible level of participation in international economic trends. This assumes increasing exports and imports, as well as enhancing other forms of international economic cooperation. Undoubtedly, such a strategy will be successfully implemented, considering Croatia's potential, the decisiveness underlying the economic policy and the efficiency of measures implemented in the country. We believe that the expected accession to the European Union in 2007, together with Romania and Bulgaria, or in 2008 at the latest, will be a special, decisive drive for this strategy.

1.5

Foreign Direct Investment in Croatia

Hrvoje Dolenec and Zvonimir Savic,
Raiffeisenbank Austria d.d. Zagreb

Methodology

Many Eastern European countries try to comply with the IMF's definitions when processing foreign direct investment (FDI) data. The basic problem is how to cover all investment types. Although all CEE (Central and Eastern Europe) countries try to comply with the IMF's definitions and methodological guidelines, in reality there are numerous difficulties because national methodologies are often not clearly defined and are prone to changes. Still, data are improving both in accuracy and in coverage.

Calculation of the levels of international investments in Croatia is made in accordance with the recommendations of the IMF (*Balance of Payments Manual*, Fifth Edition, 1993). Data sources include reports from banks, enterprises, the CNB (Croatian National Bank) and the Zagreb Stock Exchange. Data on foreign direct and portfolio investments are taken from the CNB's statistical research. Foreign investments in the Republic of Croatia are shown in US dollars.

One of the most important challenges for transition economies, in the medium term, will be maintaining a stable FDI inflow both to cover the external deficit and to raise competitiveness. A reduction in the growth of the global economy could negatively influence the expansion of multinational companies and consequently FDI. Over recent years there has been a notable increase in the FDI inflow into CEE countries attracted mostly by lower production costs, the proximity of the European Union and improvement in the business environment. In the beginning, FDI inflow was connected to mass privatization, especially within the banking and telecommunication sectors; Croatia was no exception in the last decade.

Table 1.5.1 Foreign direct investments in Croatia (in million US$)

	Equity investments		Reinvested earnings	Debt securities		Other capital		Total
	Claims	Liabilities		Claims	Liabilities	Claims	Liabilities	
1993	0.00	120.33	n/a	n/a	n/a	n/a	n/a	120.33
1994	0.00	117.93	n/a	n/a	n/a	n/a	n/a	117.93
1995	0.00	120.81	n/a	n/a	n/a	n/a	n/a	120.81
1996	0.00	515.86	n/a	n/a	n/a	n/a	n/a	515.86
1997	0.00	370.00	57.61	0.00	2.65	−7.95	140.99	563.30
1998	0.00	640.59	70.84	0.00	0.00	−14.65	243.23	940.01
1999	0.00	1,283.68	47.08	0.00	0.36	−0.61	137.07	1,467.58
2000	0.00	711.38	93.91	0.00	0.01	−0.00	283.34	1,088.64
2001	0.00	814.97	153.00	0.00	−1.63	−0.13	593.22	1,559.43
2002	0.00	502.84	169.86	0.00	0.00	−0.30	308.11	980.51
2003 Q1	0.00	0.25	21.89	0.00	0.00	0.10	214.30	236.54
Total	**0.00**	**5,198.64**	**614.19**	**0.00**	**1.39**	**−23.54**	**1,920.26**	**7,710.94**

Source: Croatian National Bank

FDI by economic activities

From the significant privatization accomplishments in recent years in Croatia we can single out the privatization of Croatian telecommunications (HT), (US$859 million for a 35 per cent stake in 1999 and another €500 million for an additional 16 per cent stake in 2001).

In the banking sector we can list numerous examples of privatization. According to the last available data from the CNB, 89.9 per cent of domestic banking assets were under foreign ownership. Last year, the Government sold a 25 per cent stake in Privredna Banka Zagreb to IntesaBci and EBRD (for US$140 million, in addition to the sale of the first stake of the bank in 2000 for US$300 million). Additionally, Rijecka Banka was sold to Erste Bank. HVB bought Splitska Banka from Unicredito and Charlemagne Ltd became the owner of Nova Banka and Dubrovacka Banka, in 2002.

Since 1999 FDI in Croatia has regularly exceeded US$1 billion, but last year this trend was not continued, which was in line with expectations. After the release of 2002 data, there has been a correction of results for previous periods, so 1999, when FDI totalled US$1.48 billion, prompted by the sale of a 35 per cent stake in HT, is no longer considered to be a record year. According to the latest data from the CNB, in 2002 FDI in Croatia was US$980.5 million, while a record high was recorded in 2001 at US$1.53 billion. In 2002 FDI did not reach even two-thirds of that amount. Although the end of 2002 saw the sale of the remaining state-held stake in one of Croatia's leading banks, FDI failed to reach record levels due to a delay in the privatization of the state insurer Croatia osiguranje and the state oil and gas company INA. Analysis of economic activity showed that 2002 was dominated by the item 'other money business', which accounted for 63.75 per cent of total FDI. It was followed by 'hotels and motels, with restaurants' (9.62 per cent) and 'non-specialized wholesale of food, beverages and tobacco' (3.47 per cent), 'business and management consultancy activities' (2.73 per cent), 'manufacture of pharmaceutical preparations' (2.37 per cent), 'collection, purification and distribution of water' (2.27 per cent), 'other wholesale' (2.21 per cent), 'extraction of crude petroleum and natural gas' (1.65 per cent), 'manufacture of beer' (1.59 per cent), and 'management activities of holding companies' (1.25 per cent). Almost two-thirds of 2002's FDI came from Austria (28.59 per cent) and Italy (22.75 per cent), which together with Luxembourg (6.53 per cent) accounted for more than three-quarters (76.96 per cent) of the total FDI, followed by the European Bank for Reconstruction and Development (9.56 per cent), France (6.09 per cent), Germany (5.07 per cent) and the Netherlands (4.12 per cent).

Until 1999, FDI never exceed US$1 billion. In 1993 it recorded a modest US$120 million, followed by US$118 million in 1994 and US$121 million in 1995. The years that followed recorded significantly higher figures, but still far below the US$1 billion level. In 1996, FDI reached US$ 516 million and it rose to US$563 million in 1997. Previous numbers for 1998 suggested FDI over US$1 billion, but they were revised downwards to US$940 million. In 1999, FDI rose sharply to US$1.47 billion largely due to the privatization of Croatian telecommunications (HT). FDI of US$1.1 billion was realized in 2000, followed by US$1.56 billion in 2001.

Cumulatively, in the period from 1993 to 2002 FDI totalled US$7.47 billion, out of which 'telecommunications' accounts for roughly one-quarter (26.25 per cent), followed by 'other monetary intermediation' (21.35 per cent), 'manufacture of pharmaceutical preparations' (13.99 per cent), 'manufacture of cement' (4.49 per cent), 'hotels and motels, with restaurants' (3.31 per cent), 'extraction of crude petroleum and natural gas' (2.93 per cent), 'other wholesale' (1.70 per cent), 'manufacture of beer' (1.35 per cent), 'manufacture of bricks, tiles and construction products' (1.19 per cent), and 'other retail sale in non-specialized stores' (1.06 per cent). In 2003, it is expected that FDI will reach around US$1.5 billion largely from planned privatization income, eg the sale of the insurer Croatia osiguranje and the state oil and gas company INA.

Austria and Germany are among Croatia's most important trading partners, with a total 21.8 per cent share in the foreign trade of goods in 2002. The USA accounted for a 14.69 per cent share in FDI for the period 1993–2002, Luxembourg follows with 6.53 per cent and Italy with 4.36 per cent. Italy is an important trading partner, accounting for 20 per cent of the total trade of goods in 2002. The high position of

Luxembourg on the list of FDIs is very interesting but one should bear in mind that foreign companies often use their subsidiaries located in tax havens. Such was the case with an Italian bank making payments with Luxembourg, resulting in a relatively low recorded FDI percentage from Italy. If we analyse the value of Croatia's foreign trade with developed countries over the last few years, we come to the conclusion that there is a connection between the proximity of the market and intensity of the FDI. Germany invested the most in telecommunications and other monetary intermediation. Austria placed the majority of its FDIs in money business, production of instruments and apparatus for measurement and control, production of bricks and roofing-tiles, etc, while Italy largely specialized in investments in monetary intermediation.

Economic and political environment

An overview of Croatia's main indicators, which are an integral part of the package when considering an investment in a country, reflect that in comparison to other Central European countries in transition Croatia shows moderate competitiveness: a small country by number of inhabitants, with high unemployment, low inflation and positive GDP growth rates over the last few years.

There are signs of positive movements in trade and product distribution to third markets – tariff protection of Croatia's market was reduced by the country's admission to the WTO, and in March 2003 the Republic of Croatia became the eighth CEFTA Member Country.

The Agreement on CEFTA membership is expected to raise the level of overall trade exchange, ie to enable Croatian companies to export significantly more to CEFTA member countries. When this agreement came into force, it replaced all prior agreements on free trade signed with CEFTA member countries – Slovenia, Hungary, the Czech Republic, Poland and Bulgaria

Just a short while before, on 21 February 2003, the application for Croatia's membership of the European Union was formally submitted in Athens. This was a crucial step on Croatia's participation in the second wave of EU enlargement. Croatia hopes to complete EU accession talks in 2006 and to join the Union in 2007 or soon thereafter. But, in order to make membership by 2007 a realistic goal, negotiations will need to progress fast. Croatia's entry into the EU is a strategic task for this or any other government and needs to be pursued seriously, regardless of the forthcoming election .

Furthermore, at the end of March, an annual report of the European Commission on Stabilization and Association Agreement in Croatia showed that the political situation is stable, the economic situation continues to improve and the overall situation in the country is satisfactory. So, Croatia has continued increasing its presence in neighbouring markets and its attractiveness to investors.

Inefficiencies in institutions and administration are the main cause of the country's bad image. After the election in early 2000 the country's isolation from the international community became less prominent, and by signing the stand-by arrangement with the IMF its development chances improved.

The large coalition government, inexperienced at running a country, had problems with implementing its economic policy, and differences among its members subsequently led to the reduction of a six-party coalition to a four-party coalition. The problems it has faced are a relatively high external debt, a rising foreign trade deficit (US$5.8 billion in 2002), a high balance of payments current account deficit (6.9 per cent in 2002), company restructuring, and delays in privatizing large companies such as the state oil and gas company, INA, and the insurer Croatia osiguranje.

Among the country's most important natural resources are the Mediterranean climate combined with 5,800 km of shoreline laced with over 1,100 islands. In such an environment tourism is a fast-developing sector of the economy; Croatia is the nearest destination for tourists from East European countries as well as Germany, Austria and Italy.

Motorway construction gained momentum over the last year, providing further ground for optimism regarding tourism development. Profit-driven future investors will most certainly press for the prolongation of the currently short tourist season, which will impact on the entire economic microenvironment, including local state institutions, regional suppliers and small and medium-sized entrepreneurs.

Despite large-scale state investment in road construction, the infrastructure has still not reached the level necessary for the complete and normal functioning of the economy. Problems are most pronounced in rail transport. Difficulties are created by legal complexities and bureaucracy in establishing new companies, not to mention the fact that local governments do not have a unified mechanism for regulating land and utility fees.

The Act on stimulating investments

The Act on stimulating investments has been in force since the beginning of 2000. A person is considered an investor if he or she invested at least HRK4 million.

Those who invested HRK4–10 million (approximately €0.53–1.33 million) can count on incentives (for employment or staff retraining) as well as tax-free equipment imports.

The Act contains fiscal and non-fiscal aspects. The fiscal aspects encompass gradual income tax exemption (partial or overall) and import benefits for new equipment and machinery. Income tax relief on investment of HRK10 million (€1.33 million) and employment of at least 30 people would amount to a minimum of 28 percentage points; on investments exceeding HRK20 million (€1.66 million) and employment of at least 50 people it would amount to 32 percentage points, and on investments of HRK60 million (€8 million) and employment of at least 75 people the relief would amount to 35 per cent, that is, all of the income tax due. The tax relief remains valid over a long period of time – 10 years – which ensures continuity but also involves high costs for the state. The non-fiscal aspect, in addition to employment and staff retraining incentives, includes handing over land and real estate to investors.

The Act stipulates employment as the primary goal of investment stimulation. Many provisions of this Act contain the phrase 'may approve', which gives plenty of room for discretionary decisions and thus an increase in administrative costs and a decrease in transparency.

These incentives are only part of the package foreign investments depend on, and a superficial comparison with neighbouring countries shows that Croatia has reacted faster than Slovenia in implementing stimulative financial measures. In comparison with Hungary, Croatia has defined a lower level of investment capital under which an investor qualifies for state stimulation benefits. The tax benefits period of 10 years has probably been copied from other countries in transition in order for Croatia to be competitive. It is important to stress that a general improvement in investment conditions is a substantially bigger incentive to foreign and domestic investors than immediate subsidies. In this respect, Croatia is trying to push ahead strongly, especially within the framework of European integration.

A shortcoming Croatia must gradually overcome is a lack of knowledge of the workings of a market economy, as well as business management and organization. This problem could be alleviated by foreign investments and the know-how that foreign investors are expected to bring, encouraging competition, as has been the case in the telecommunications and banking sectors. This could lead to more efficient domestic companies, through implementing new products and technologies, resulting in a faster restructuring of the country's economy.

Conclusion

An advantageous territorial structure and friendly legislation, a diverse land attractive to both businesses and tourists, a large number of independent commercial entities on the market, and a strong transit location at the hub of east–west and north–south routes are factors that create a favourable environment for investors. The Government actively encourages foreign direct investment to stimulate the economy, with a number of multinationals already established in the Croatian market. Croatia has accelerated integration into Western institutions and increased the prospects of regional political stability. (Croatia has joined NATO's Partnership for Peace, become a member of the WTO and European Free Trade Association, concluded the Stabilization and Association Agreement with the EU, and submitted an application for full EU membership.) Foreign investors are entitled to special tax exemptions, depending on the nature of the investment and the activities they carry out in Croatia. As an opportunity for investment, tourism can be singled out: the rapid re-emergence of tourism provides investors with an opportunity to invest in a dynamic and growing sector.

Table 1.5.2 Foreign direct investments in Croatia (In million US$)

| | Equity investments | | Reinvested | Debt securities | | Other capital | | Total |
	Claims	Liabilities	earnings	Claims	Liabilities	Claims	Liabilities	
1993	0.00	120.33	n/a	n/a	n/a	n/a	n/a	120.33
1994	0.00	117.93	n/a	n/a	n/a	n/a	n/a	117.93
1995	0.00	120.81	n/a	n/a	n/a	n/a	n/a	120.81
1996	0.00	515.86	n/a	n/a	n/a	n/a	n/a	515.86
1997	0.00	370.00	57.61	0.00	2.65	−7.95	140.99	563.30
1998	0.00	640.59	70.84	0.00	0.00	−14.65	243.23	940.01
1999	0.00	1,283.68	47.08	0.00	0.36	−0.61	137.07	1,467.58
2000	0.00	711.38	93.91	0.00	0.01	−0.00	283.34	1,088.64
2001	0.00	814.97	153.00	0.00	−1.63	−0.13	593.22	1,559.43
2002	0.00	502.84	169.86	0.00	0.00	−0.30	308.11	980.51
2003 Q1	0.00	0.25	21.89	0.00	0.00	0.10	214.30	236.54
Total	0.00	5,198.64	614.19	0.00	1.39	−23.54	1,920.26	7,710.94

Source: Croatian National Bank

The Banking System and Capital Markets

Hrvoje Dolenec, Raiffeisenbank Austria d.d. Zagreb

Outline of the banking system

Croatia has a two-tier banking system in which the Croatian National Bank (CNB) acts as a central bank but does not engage in commercial banking. There are 46 banks operating in Croatia. Foreign banks may operate in Croatia and currently there are 23 majority foreign-owned banks in the country, which control around 90 per cent of total banking assets. Most of the foreign owners are from Italy (the two largest banks) and Austria (the next five largest banks). Only two banks are state owned, with a 4 per cent stake in total banking assets. The rest are small domestic private banks.

The Croatian National Bank

The CNB became the central bank of Croatia on 23 December 1991, when the Croatian dinar was introduced as legal tender.

Its role as a central bank was defined by the Act on the Croatian National Bank, passed on 4 November 1992 (CNB Act). Article 53 of the Croatian Constitution and the CNB Act established the CNB's independence and specified its relations with Parliament. The Governor of the CNB and members of its Board of Governors are appointed by Parliament for six-year terms and can only be removed by Parliament in extraordinary circumstances defined by the CNB Act.

A new law regulating the policies and powers of the CNB was enacted on 5 April 2001 (the 2001 CNB Act). This Act, which is modelled on the rules governing the European Central Bank, grants the CNB further independence and allows it new powers of self-governance. For example, the new CNB Act prohibits the Government from borrowing directly

Small Bank with big **potential**

 Banka **SONIC** d.d.

Banka **SONIC** d.d.

Bank branch office network

ZAGREB
Republike Austrije 5
Tel.:01/3701-507 ili 01/3773-274
Vukovarska 23
Tel.:01/3094-662 ili 01/3094-663
Martićeva 14b
Tel.:01/4614-313 ili 01/4615-143
Savska 161
Tel.:01/6345-630 ili 6345-628

OSIJEK
Trg Slobode 2
Tel.:031/213-192 ili 031/200-181
Radićeva 28
Tel.:031/200-559 ili 031/200-560
Trg Bana Jelačića 17
Tel.:031/502-484 ili 031/502-485
Županijska 7
Tel.:031/203-390 ili 031/204-390

SLATINA
Trg Sv. Josipa 1
Tel.:033/553-780 ili 033/550-818

SLAVONSKI BROD
Pilareva 28
Tel.:035/411-162 ili 035/411-163

VUKOVAR
Štrosmajerova 14 a
Tel.:032/450-663 ili 032/450-664

VARAŽDIN
Kratka ulica 2
Tel.:042/301-490 ili 042/301-491

SPLIT
Kneza Višeslava 6
Tel.:021/360-732 ili 021/360-733

PULA
Ul. Sergijevaca 16
Tel.:052/217-005 ili 052/215-166

RIJEKA
Užarska bb
Tel.:051/211-353 ili 021/333-612
Štrosmajerova 8a
Tel.:051/377-062 ili 021/377-063

 info centar 062 27 27 27

from the CNB, and allows the CNB to trade only in government short- and long-term securities in the secondary market. Also, the new CNB Act specifies that the CNB's main goal is price stability, while retaining the CNB's responsibility for banking supervision and monitoring of the payments system.

The Croatian banking system

Banks in Croatia are mostly structured as universal banks. They are authorized to carry out wholesale and retail banking activities, and 37 of them have licences to operate internationally. The four largest banks (Zagrebacka Banka, Privredna Banka Zagreb, Splitska Banka, and Raiffeisenbank Austria) accounted for around 59 per cent of all banking assets in 2002. At the end of 2002, the two largest banks held 36 per cent of total capital and the four largest banks held 49 per cent of total capital, while the two largest banks also held 44 per cent of the total banking assets. The banking system may be described as oligopolistic with a significant concentration of the power among the largest banks. Business indicators have been improving the rehabilitation and consolidation process.

In 1999, four housing savings banks were established, three of which are foreign-owned. After a merger of two savings banks in mid-2002, three still operate. They are permitted to collect deposits from their customers, who must maintain their deposits for at least two years before they may be granted a housing loan. After this period, customers may be granted a housing loan proportionate to their savings, which are dependent on the duration of their deposits. Interest rates on such loans are 6 per cent per annum with 10 to 15 year maturities.

During 1998 and 1999, some of Croatia's small and medium-sized banks encountered severe difficulties. Between January 1999 and February 2001 10 banks were declared bankrupt and two were rehabilitated through a process of government receivership. In addition, in 2000 and early 2001, there were several mergers and bank liquidations. That reduced the number of banks from 60 in December 1997 to the current 46, and increased the soundness of the whole system.

Bank regulation and prudential standards

Since 1992, the CNB has set prudential guidelines for all Croatian banks. The current system of prudential standards includes a minimum 10 per cent risk weighted capital adequacy ratio calculated in accordance with BIS (Bank for International Settlements) recommendations and international authorities' standards, daily monitoring of liquidity levels, classification of the quality of bank assets, provision of reserves with respect to problem loans, and limits on foreign exchange positions.

Individual loans or the total of all loans to a single borrower cannot exceed 25 per cent of the so-called liable capital (defined as tier-one plus a portion of tier-two capital).

Banks must provide security for their operations, and therefore are required to set aside provisions. In addition to general provisions for covering unidentified potential loan losses, banks must set aside specific provisions against identified potential losses from doubtful credits, investments and a portion of off-balance sheet items. Annual reports of banks must be checked and evaluated by an authorized external auditor. Large banks usually have their annual reports audited by internationally recognized auditing firms.

Banks are independent in their business activities from the Government and the CNB, and operate as joint stock companies with management being responsible to the shareholders. Banks may be established by one or more legal or natural persons, resident or non-resident. The minimum equity capital requirement is set at HRK40 million. Both new banks and savings banks must obtain a licence from the CNB. Licence applications must include, among other documents, proof of the capital required, qualified managers and business plans for two years. Under certain conditions the licence can be revoked if the bank does not comply with the regulations.

Major legal changes occurred in 2002 when Parliament approved the 2002 Banking Act. The new Act has introduced a legal framework for banks' operation during accession to the EU, it has further strengthened the CNB supervisory power, and it has introduced consolidated supervision. Under the new Act, all bylaws and regulations were enacted by January 2003, while the Act itself came into effect immediately, except for certain provisions that can only be applied once Croatia joins the EU.

The Act on the State Agency for Deposit Insurance and Bank Rehabilitation (which came into force on 11 June 1994, and was amended in 1998, 1999 and 2000) provides for a scheme of bank-funded deposit insurance for all banks. The Act creates a special account with full coverage for savings deposits of individuals in kuna or foreign currency up to a level determined by the Minister of Finance. This level is HRK100,000 at the moment. The deposit insurance scheme started functioning in mid-1997, so depositors who held their money in the banks that failed during the 1998–1999 period received payment from the State Agency up to the HRK100,000 limit. These payments were all made by the end of 2000.

The Bank Rehabilitation programme

Since achieving independence, Croatian banks have suffered both from high levels of bad debt and from liquidity problems.

Nava was a majestic sailing-ship, built during the 17th and 18th centuries, representing the most prosperous part of Croatian maritime heritage. Like the ship gliding across the ocean, Nava Bank is committed to being the best at serving its client's requirements.

The Bank was founded in 1995 as a completely private bank. Its aim is to perform and deliver clear solutions for its clients based predominantly on commercial banking whilst our professional caring staff readily available to assist with all their banking needs.

Our further development focuses on areas for stable growth, market efficiency and our area of expertise based on small and medium-sized entrepreneurship and private banking products.

The Bank is always aiming to contribute to the growth of economic activities and further the development of the financial market.

NAVA BANKA DD
TRATINSKA 27
10000 ZAGREB, CROATIA
TEL: +385 1/36 56 711, 36 57 777
FAX: +385 1/36 56 700, 36 56 701
SWIFT: NAVBHR22
E-MAIL: navabanka@navabanka.hr

NAVA BANKA d.d. Zagreb

REPORT OF THE MANAGEMENT BOARD

We are pleased to report that in the year 2002 the Bank continued to operate successfully.

The year 2002 is characterised by the slightly recovery of Croatian economy and by the increase of industrial production, investment and gross domestic product particularly. The basic characteristics could be described as follows: unresolved structural problems in the economy; gradual growth of industrial production; increase of gross national product; uncertain development strategy; budget deficit; deficit in balance of payments and extremely high rate of unemployment.

Banking operations were performing in more favourable circumstances than in the year 2001. The consolidation process of Croatian banking sector is almost finished. The wholesale placements were growing slightly, while the retail placements obtained exceptionally high growth. The competition in banking industry became significantly strong, influencing the decreasing trend of interest rates and interest spread. Financial markets remains still undeveloped with a poor choice of financial instruments.

As at 31 December 2002, the balance sheet of the Bank recorded HRK 267,879 thousand representing the 21.7% growth. The Bank has been primarily focused on the stability and safety of its operation, development of new technologies and implementation of new products and service. The cash and cash equivalent assets remained stable, while the placements to the customers have significantly increased as well as total assets accordingly. Household savings recorded HRK 95,234 thousand and represent 44% of all the Bank's liabilities. The growth of savings is confirming that the Bank is keeping the confidence of depositors and the image of safe and stable private bank.

The shareholders' capital remains mostly unchanged. At the end of the year the Bank has 31 shareholders: 11 Croatian private companies and 20 Croatian citizens.

The Bank organised its foreign payment's transactions in co-operation with other authorised banks. During the year 2002 the Bank has arranged the settlement of 1,525 foreign payment transactions for its customers, in amount of EUR 40 million approximately.

Net interest income remains the same compared to the last year and it does not follow the Bank's assets growth. This is a consequence of stronger competition in the banking market and significant decrease of interest rates. The Banks incomes and expenses are the result of the business policies applied, of the Bank's market position and the structure placements and liabilities. Management ahs adopted the competitive credit and interest policies, with respect to the predominant prices on the financial markets, the valid conditions for drawing of deposits, including also the premium from currency and credit risk exposure.

From the point of expenditure control, currency risk control and risk exposure, as well as regarding the operative efficiency obtained, the year 2002 could be assessed as successful.

The total income in amount of HRK 11,666 thousand is 15.2% lower compared to the last year. The profit before taxation in amount of HRK 3,393 represents the 143.2% growth, due to effective control of expenses and the decrease in provisions. New profit for the year 2002 in amount of HRK 2,752 thousand is almost twice higher compared to the last year.

During the year 2003 we will continue to run the banking transactions by tailoring the adequate measure and business policies for efficient risk management, providing the successful current operating of the Bank and its clients. The most significant element of the business policy remains respecting the principles of safety and liquidity, honouring the very high level of customer's confidence with the quality of services and market efficiency continuously.

We are planning the Bank's assets growth of 21% return on assets 2% or higher and return on equity 10% or higher, keeping the similar structure of asset and liability's portfolio.

At the beginning of the year 2002 the Bank has successfully adopted the domestic payment system settlement and transferred the significant portion of these transactions during the year into its own Internet banking – NavaNET. At the beginning of the year 2003 the Bank obtained the approval for complete range of banking activities, including all sorts of security dealing and international operations. In the year 2003 we are planning to improve the further technological development and competitive strength of the Bank, innovation of products and services and to maintain high level of productivity and quality of relations with the customers.

STATEMENT OF THE
MANAGEMENT BOARD'S RESPONSIBILITY

Pursuant to the Croatian Accounting Low (Official Gazette 90/92), the Management Board is responsible for ensuring that financial statements are prepared for each financial year, which give a true and fair view of the state of affairs on the Bank and of the Profit and Loss Account of the Bank for that period, in accordance with International Financial Reporting Standards (IFRS).

In preparing those financial statements, the Management Board is required to:

- Select suitable accounting policies and than applied them consistently;
- Make judgements and estimates that are reasonable and prudent;
- State whether applicable accounting standards have been followed, subject to any material departures disclosed and explained in the financial statements; and
- Prepare the financial statements on the going concern basis.

The Management Board is responsible for keeping proper accounting records, which disclose with reasonable accuracy at any time the financial position of the Bank, enabling them to ensure that the financial statements are in compliance with the Croation Accounting Low. The Management Board has a general responsibility for taking any reasonable step open to them to safeguard the assets of the Bank and for the prevention and detection of frauds and other irregularities.

We would like to express our gratitude to all the Bank's clients and shareholders, especially to Supervisory Board members and employees for their continued support, commitment and responsible acting and great contribution to the success of our operations.

Zagreb, 14 March 2003-10-17

The Management Board:

Stipan Pamukovic, President & CEO

Zeljko Skalec, Vice-president & CEO

Ante Samodol, Member & CEO

Stipan Pamukovic, President & CEO

Shortly after Croatia's declaration of independence on 25 June 1991, the National Bank of Yugoslavia (NBY) froze all the foreign exchange deposits of Croatian banks that it held. For Croatian banks this amounted to approximately US$3 billion. Frozen foreign exchange deposits on the banks' balance sheets were subsequently converted into Government bonds with a maturity of 10 years, with repayment linked to the DMark and bearing interest of 5 per cent per annum.

In an attempt to recapitalize banks suffering from high levels of bad debt and to aid indebted enterprises, in 1991 and 1992 the Government issued bonds under the so-called 'Big Bonds Scheme'. The proportion of claims on the Government is declining. At the end of 1993, 39.4 per cent of the total assets of deposit money banks were net claims on the Government; this ratio had fallen to 9.9 per cent by end of 2002.

Rehabilitation programme and the privatization of banks

The legislative structure for the new rehabilitation programme was set out in the Act on Bank Rehabilitation and Restructuring, which came into force on 11 June 1994 (the Act on Rehabilitation). The Act was revoked in 2000, after the Government privatized most of the restructured banks. In late 1995 the Government began implementing this new rehabilitation programme for the banking system. The objectives of the programme included changing bank ownership structures, ensuring additional capitalization of banks that are suitably qualified to operate successfully, and excluding bank debtors from the management of the banks. Rehabilitation was being implemented on a case-by-case basis. The CNB was responsible for appraisal of the economic feasibility of rehabilitation in particular instances. A new state agency, the State Agency for Deposit Insurance and Bank Rehabilitation (the 'Agency for Rehabilitation'), was established to implement certain aspects of bank rehabilitation.

The bank rehabilitation process had three phases:

1. a financial restructuring designed to recapitalize the bank, restore its liquidity and transfer its non-performing assets to the Agency for Rehabilitation;

2. an institutional reform process, designed to install new governance, controls and policies, and to focus the business strategy and operations of the bank on new and growing markets;

3. return of the bank to the private sector as the rehabilitation process is completed, by the Agency for Rehabilitation selling its shares to qualified investors (ie investors who are not also major debtors of the bank).

Six banks have entered the rehabilitation process and Slavonska Banka Splitska Banka, were successfully privatized in 1999 and 2000. Slavonska

Banka was sold to the European Bank for Reconstruction and Development (EBRD), and Klagenfurt-based Hypo Alpe-Adria Bank in 1999. On 17 December 1999, the State Agency for Deposit Insurance and Bank Rehabilitation (the DAB) announced that it had signed an agreement to sell 66.3 per cent of the shares in Privredna Banka Zagreb d.d. (PBZ) for €300 million to Banca Commerciale Italiana SpA (BCI). The DAB sold the remaining stake of 25 per cent plus two shares in December 2002. In the first quarter of 2000, Rijecka Banka was sold to strategic partner Bayerische Landesbank for US$41 million. This was subsequently followed by a strategic sale of Splitska Banka to Unicredito ltaliano for €48 million.

In 2001, Unicredito Italiano sought approval from the CNB for the acquisition of a majority shareholding in Zagrebacka Banka, Croatia's largest bank. CNB approved the acquisition subject to Unicredito Italiano selling its interest in Splitska Banka to HVB Bank. Both transactions were completed in April 2002.

In March 2002, Rijecka Banka announced heavy losses in foreign exchange trading activities resulting from internal fraud. Due to a successful agreement between its two major shareholders, Bayerische Landesbank and the Croatian Government, the crisis was quickly brought under control. Bayerische Landesbank withdrew from the bank by returning its shares to the Croatian Government, and in April 2002 the Government sold an 85 per cent interest in the bank to Erste and Steiermarkische Bank for €55 million with an obligation to inject a further €100 million into the bank as capital.

In March 2002, Dubrovacka Banka was acquired by Dalmatinska Banka for €24 million. The privatization of Croatia Banka is expected to be completed in 2003.

The securities market

The Croatian securities market is predominantly a debt market despite a few issues of securities. Almost 80 per cent of total turnover on the Zagreb Stock Exchange in 2002 was accounted for by bond trading. In the first quarter of 2003, bond turnover was more than half of the total bond turnover in 2002. A negligible portion of turnover is made up by three existing issues of corporate bonds (US$9 million). Turnover of government and government-guaranteed bonds (total issue of €1,452 million) comprised almost the total bond turnover. There are four banks acting as market makers in the bond market. The main investors are institutional, such as pension funds, insurance companies and growing investment funds.

Bond prices on the local market grew constantly in 2002 as a result of growing demand from domestic institutional investors and favourable price developments on international markets (both world bonds and Croatian international issues). However, a global fall in prices hit the local market in March 2003, along with exchange rate movements. Positive influences are coming from Croatian Eurobonds spread developments and emerging market debt.

Domestic markets consist of two stock exchanges, the Zagreb Stock Exchange and the Varazdin Stock Exchange. Most shares are listed in a semi-regulated market segment. The most famous share listed in the domestic market is Pliva, which comprises most of the turnover and also the largest market capitalization.

The Zagreb Stock Exchange

In general, the Croatian equity market is dominated by small investors who have become shareholders through the process of privatization. There are an estimated 600,000 private shareholders and a few institutional shareholders. The pension and health funds, which have also received parcels of shares as part of the privatization process, have not yet sought to manage their portfolios. The leading players in the market are the commercial banks and private brokerage houses that are members of the exchange. The Croatian Privatization Fund is active on the market, though only as a seller as it seeks to dispose of its holdings. A new Securities Act came into force on 1 January 1996 which instituted primary and secondary market procedures and regulations along standard Western lines and set up a Croatian Securities and Exchange Commission (CROSEC) with supervisory powers over the primary and secondary markets.

The liquidity in Croatia's capital markets is improving. Currently, the market has 41 members. CROSEC will support Croatia's capital markets by establishing laws and regulations to protect the rights of market participants, as well as developing its technical infrastructure.

The Zagreb Stock Exchange (ZSE) was founded in 1918 but was disbanded in 1946 by the communist authorities. In June 1991, the ZSE was incorporated as a joint stock company and reopened by 25 commercial banks and insurance companies. Today, the ZSE has 43 shareholders.

Trading at the ZSE may take place either on the official market (the ZSE's principal market) or through the ZSE's second-tier market. There are only three companies that are presently listed on the official market, although approximately 61 companies have a second-tier listing. Companies can be also listed in 'JDD' (public shareholding companies) quotation, with three companies on the ZSE and one on the VSE. Creating this kind of quotation, the Government and CROSEC sought to give a stimulus to a greater level of public listings.

Trading is now executed through MOSTich, a new fully electronic distributed trading system, developed in-house by the ZSE. All trading in equity and fixed income instruments must be executed through ZSE members. There are no restrictions on foreign direct investments in Croatia; the same rules apply as for domestic investors.

Last year was the best yet for the ZSE in terms of turnover value. Total turnover amounted to US$823 million of which US$64 million was made by shares and US$654 million by bonds.

The Croatian Central Depository Agency (SDA), which commenced its operation in April 1999, has implemented a new clearing and settlement process (NKS). The NKS started its operations on 5 February 2001, replacing the manual trade-for-trade environment between counter-party brokers.

The Varazdin Stock Exchange

In July 2002 the over-the-counter market in Varazdin became the Varazdin Stock Exchange. Varazdin OTC started to operate in 1993. Currently, there are 386 different securities listed on the VSE in six different quotations, with the first quotation introduced in autumn 2002. The VSE has 32 members. Total turnover in 2002 was around US$240 million, which was the best trading result since it began operating on the Croatian market.

In 2002 the VSE introduced a new trading system, BTS, which allows networking of regional stock exchanges. In this context, in early 2003 the VSE signed a cooperation and data-exchange agreement with the Ljubljana Stock Exchange.

1.7

Foreign Exchange Regulations in Croatia

S Miroslav, Deloitte & Touche

With Croatia's strategic commitment to becoming a full member of the European Union, extensive work on reconciling legal regulations with EU criteria and practices is currently under way in the Republic. One of the areas requiring in-depth revisions is the foreign exchange system, ie the Effective Law on the Foreign Exchange System, Foreign Exchange Operations and Gold Transactions. Because the existing law is not compliant, a new foreign exchange operations law is going through Parliament, which should bring about liberalization of individual segments of the capital account and capital transactions, in accordance with the EU guidelines.

Residency

The underlying criterion for the definition of residency under the new law is 'centre of economic interest', except for those temporarily residing in Croatia, to which the criterion of 'temporary residence' applies. Thus, those temporarily resident in the Republic of Croatia, on the basis of a work permit, whose centre of economic interest is abroad are classified as residents.

Also, under the new law, subsidiaries of foreign companies registered abroad are considered resident, whereas representative offices of foreign founders, whose status is not defined under the current law, are regarded as non-residents.

Residents for the purpose of the new law are:

- legal entities headquartered in the Republic of Croatia, except for their subsidiaries abroad;

- subsidiaries of foreign companies and sole traders entered in the register kept by the competent state authority or administration in the Republic of Croatia;

- sole-traders, craftsmen and other persons headquartered or resident in the Republic of Croatia, who carry out independently the economic activity for which they have been registered;

- persons resident in the Republic of Croatia;

- persons residing in the Republic of Croatia for a minimum of 183 days on the basis of a valid work permit;

- diplomatic, consular and other representatives of the Republic of Croatia abroad financed from the state budget, and Croatian citizens employed by such representative offices and their family members.

Direct investments

The new law defines direct investments as a sub-category of capital transactions in accordance with the Directive of the Council of the European Communities No 88/361/EEC.

The new law gives a precise definition of direct investments, which comprise the following:

- initial capital investment in a new company, or in the share capital of an existing company fully owned by a foreign investor; establishment of a subsidiary, or acquisition of an existing company fully owned by the investor; or investments in the business of a sole entrepreneur;

- investment in a new or an existing company if the investor acquires a 10 per cent or higher proportion of the share capital of a company, or acquires 10 per cent of votes;

- subordinate or hybrid loans for a period of five years or more to establish permanent economic relations;

- reinvestments of profit, ie a share of a direct investor in the profit of a company not distributable as a dividend or similar;

- debt transactions between a direct investor and an investee (the company), including debt securities, commercial loans, untied loans and other creditor/debtor relationships.

Additionally, direct investments of residents made abroad will be unrestricted, according to the final proposal of the new foreign exchange operations law.

Real estate investments

Under existing regulations, Croatian residents are not permitted to transfer capital abroad for the purpose of acquiring real estate.

The new law has, in this respect, been reconciled with the relevant EU regulations, enabling residents to freely transfer funds abroad to acquire real estate, provided that the obligations, ie taxes and other duties payable in Croatia as defined by law, have been settled.

Resident investments in securities abroad

The major innovation in the new foreign exchange operations legislation is that residents will be allowed to make investments in securities abroad: this is currently not permitted.

However, the final proposal of the new law on foreign exchange operations distinguishes several categories of residents in terms of free transfer of capital for the purpose of portfolio investments. Capital transfer by resident financial institutions for the purpose of portfolio investments abroad will no longer be subject to the restrictions provided by the Law on the Foreign Exchange Operations. Other residents abroad will be allowed to make unrestricted investments only in securities issued by the OECD countries, international financial institutions (EBRD, the World Bank, the European Investment Bank, etc).

To implement the legal norm described above, the Croatian National Bank will initially issue a regulation under which only securities assigned an A rating or better by reputable international investment agencies FitchIBCA, Standard & Poor's and Moody's, will be eligible for investment.

The new legal solution will for the first time enable Croatian residents to invest in securities of foreign issuers, which will provide the legal basis for the implementation of stock option plans for Croatian employees of companies established by foreign founders and multinational corporations.

Lending activities

The regulations governing lending operations as a part of the foreign exchange regime are a novelty in Croatian legislation. The implementation of legal norms in the area of lending operations will be facilitated once lending activities are incorporated in the new Law on the Foreign Exchange Operations, and the Law on Foreign Lending Operations is revoked.

Under the legislation, Croatian legal entities are to collect and transfer to Croatia foreign currency receivables from foreign transactions within 150 days, with an option of a one-off extension of 60 days.

The final proposal of the new foreign exchange operations law considers deferred payments and advance payments to be commercial credits, and will abolish the obligation of Croatian legal entities to provide evidence of having transferred foreign currencies to Croatia within the specified period.

The rules governing the receivables and liabilities from foreign operations will also be significantly liberalized. In other words, cessions, assignments, acquisitions and debt assumption transactions will no longer require prior approval by the Croatian National Bank, which, in practice, has been very difficult to obtain.

As opposed to the current legislation, under which approval of loans to non-residents is conditioned on the legal status of the majority shareholder or the founder of the company, the new foreign exchange operations legislation will enable unrestricted approval of long-term loans (over one year) to non-residents.

Liberalization of short-term loans is expected at the end of the four-year period from the effective date of the Stabilization and Association Agreement with the EU.

Croatia and the EU – A Progress Report on Entry

The Ministry for European Integration

Opening word from HE Neven Mimica, Minister for European Integration

Over the past several years the relations between Croatia and the European Union have greatly improved, especially in the wake of the signing of the Stabilization and Association Agreement in October 2001. The activities initiated by the Croatian Government towards its implementation testify to Croatia's dedication and determination to reach its strategic goal – first associated, then full EU membership. With EU membership Croatia would like to achieve and sustain its own stability and prosperity, as well as help ensure and maintain stability and prosperity in the region and across Europe. Consequently, on 21 February 2003 in Athens, Croatia formally embarked upon the accession path, with its membership application being presented to the Greek Presidency of the European Union. We expect that Croatia could become the next candidate for membership of the EU by the summer of 2004.

Croatia believes in 'enlargement after enlargement'. As far as Croatia is concerned, there is only one choice: EU membership. The Croatian Government is firmly determined to be ready to assume the obligations arising from EU membership by the end of 2006 and to function as a 'virtual member' from 1 January 2007, as the actual membership depends not only on Croatia's determination and preparedness, but also on the willingness and preparedness of the EU to accept new members after the large-scale enlargement in 2004.

We know exactly how much daring reform effort it takes, and how difficult are the comprehensive and coordinated tasks we have to fulfil on that road. With these reforms, we are creating a better life in a better Croatia, and membership of the EU comes as a by-product of these activities. I am confident that the goal of the Croatian Government can be achieved, provided that the present dynamics of meeting the European Union membership criteria are maintained.

Besides the remaining political preconditions, we have to continue reforming our legislation by bringing it in line with the European *Acquis*, thus creating a familiar and reliable legal framework for foreign investors. And then there is economic performance, where Croatia can already show a very good track record. Macroeconomic stability is a long-lasting trend in Croatia's economy. Major macroeconomic indicators place Croatia far in the lead of all Stabilization and Association Process countries, but also in the mid-range of countries currently acceding to the EU. The Government is exerting additional efforts to translate the existing macroeconomic stability into sustainable development of the economy, especially faster progress in structural reforms and privatization. The Government's economic and financial policy is being supported and endorsed by the World Bank and IMF arrangements. Croatia's overall economic performance represents a proper basis for the European Commission to positively evaluate it as a functioning market economy.

Finally, I would like to emphasize that the business community should start to regard Croatia as a definite future EU member state. This will formally happen within a mid-term period. Therefore, now is the right time to contemplate all the benefits and advantages that an early decision to start business and investment in a potential new EU market could bring to those that are ready to recognize the facts early enough. Doing business in Croatia today means that businesses are able to take advantage of liberalized trade and economic relations with the EU. But it also means that they can benefit from the fact that Croatia is regaining its position of economic leader and political model in the economic area of South-East Europe.

Introduction

Full membership of the European Union is the most important strategic foreign policy goal of Croatia and the values underlying the European democracies are the principal guidelines in the internal development of Croatia. Hence the tasks to be carried out towards these ultimate objectives occupy a central place in the Croatian Government's programme. Croatia is both realistic and ambitious when declaring its wish to become a new EU candidate country and begin accession negotiations in 2004. Croatia is also confident of its ability to reach the appropriate level of readiness for EU membership by the end of 2006. Substantial evidence exists to show that Croatia is capable of fulfilling its obligations arising from the Stabilization and Association Agreement (SAA), enabling the EU to honour its proclaimed 'individual' merits, 'differentiation' and 'catching-up' principles and allow Croatia to embark upon the next stage of rapprochement with the EU. Candidate country status would certainly encourage and motivate Croatia to successfully continue the reform processes and meet in full the Copenhagen criteria.[1]

There is strong public support in Croatia for integrating into the EU. All the public opinion surveys that have been carried out since 2000, on a six-monthly basis, have shown support for integration at about 75 per cent. However, it is reasonable to expect the support to decrease as Croatia makes progress in the process.

Development of Croatia–EU relations

On 15 January 1992 the EU recognized the Republic of Croatia as an independent and sovereign state.

The EU General Affairs Council adopted the Regional Approach in April 1997, establishing political and economic conditionality for the development of bilateral relations with the five countries of South-East Europe, among which is the Republic of Croatia.

In May 1999 the Commission, seeking to provide a more coherent framework for relations with Croatia, the former Republic of Yugoslavia, Bosnia and Herzegovina, Albania and the former Yugoslav Republic of Macedonia, and to build on the regional approach, proposed a new Stabilization and Association Process (SAP). This proposal was put forward following the conclusions of the General Affairs Council of 26 April 1999 and against the background of preparations for the Stability Pact for South-East Europe.

At the beginning of 1999, the Government of the Republic of Croatia decided to commence a process of voluntary assessment of the harmonization of legislation with the *Acquis Communautaire* in the Plan of Integration Activities. The basis for the assessment was the White Paper on the preparation of Central and Eastern European countries for integration into the internal market of the EU. The document was sent to the European Commission in October 1999.

---

[1] In June 1993, the Copenhagen European Council recognized the right of the countries of Central and Eastern Europe to join the European Union when they have fulfilled three criteria: a) political: stable institutions guaranteeing democracy, the rule of law, human rights and respect for minorities; b) economic: a functioning market economy and the ability to cope with the competitive pressure of internal markets; c) incorporation of the Community *Acquis*: adherence to the various political, economic and monetary aims of the European Union.

These accession criteria were confirmed in December 1995 by the Madrid European Council, which also stressed the importance of adapting the applicant countries' administrative structures to create the conditions for a gradual, harmonious integration. (Source: www.europa.eu.int).

At the beginning of 2000, as a preparatory step towards the institutionalization of relations between Croatia and the EU, four meetings of the Joint Consultative Working Group of Croatia and the EU were held with the European Commission in order to commence concrete professional and technical discussions. Joint Recommendations of the Joint Consultative Working Group, which identified the areas in which Croatia committed itself through concrete steps to approach EU standards, followed each of the meetings.

A 'fact finding mission' was sent to Croatia to collect the data necessary for the preparation of the Study on the Feasibility of Negotiations on the SAA (the Feasibility Study). By preparing and adopting the Feasibility Study in June 2000, the European Commission gave a recommendation to the Council of Ministers of the EU to commence the SAA negotiations.

The Zagreb Summit brought together heads of state and government of the EU member states and of the SAP countries on 24 November 2000. It was the most important international political gathering ever held in Zagreb. The event marked a new beginning for the Stabilization and Association Process. For Croatia this prospect took shape in the formal opening of the SAA negotiations.

The SAA was negotiated during Autumn 2000 and Spring 2001 and signed on 29 October 2001. The Interim Agreement on Trade and Trade Related Matters has applied since 1 January 2002, while the SAA is still to be ratified by several member states. Being aware that only a successful implementation of the SAA will ensure continuous progress towards the negotiations for full membership, the Government adopted the Implementation Plan for the SAA on 18 October 2001. The Implementation Plan defines measures, deadlines and responsibilities for implementing the SAA for the period 2002 to 2006, mirroring the goal to become ready for membership by the end of 2006. The Implementation Plan has been continuously updated. Regular monthly reports show that the execution of the Implementation Plan has been successful and that delays are minimal. The Ministry for European Integration has also prepared the Interactive Implementation Plan for the Stabilization and Association Agreement. Its principal aim is to simplify and expedite access to information on the implementation process and make it completely transparent to the wider public.[2] Further, the Parliament adopted the National Programme for the Integration of the Republic of Croatia into the European Union – 2003 on 18 December 2002.[3]

Croatia submitted its application for membership of the EU to the Greek Presidency in Athens on 21 February 2003. The decision of the Government of the Republic of Croatia to submit an application was

[2] See at www.mei.hr/ippssp.
[3] See page 64, Legal framework of the harmonization of legislation.

based on the Government's assessment that Croatia has made substantial progress in fulfilling the necessary political, economic, legal and institutional commitments undertaken in the SAA, as well as on the Government's firm determination to be ready to assume the obligations arising from EU membership by the end of 2006. This assessment is most notably confirmed by the existence in Croatia of the highest regional level of constitutional and political stability; the functioning of a political, state and democratic system together with related institutions; the steady growth of democracy; the strengthening of the rule of law; improvements in the protection of human rights; and constantly improving economic performance. The Parliamentary Resolution on the Accession of the Republic of Croatia to the European Union supporting the application was adopted by consensus on 18 December 2003, underlining the strong commitment of all parliamentary parties to the strategic goal of membership of the EU and the far-reaching reforms required.

On 14 April 2003 the Council of Ministers mandated the European Commission to start preparing the *avis* on Croatia's membership application. During his visit to Croatia on 10 July 2003, the President of the European Commission handed over the *Questionnaire*. The *Questionnaire* is a document that contains several thousand questions addressing criteria for membership: political, economic and the ability to assume the obligations of membership. An applicant country is requested to provide the European Commission with all the necessary information within 3 months. On 9 October 2003 the Croatian Prime Minister presented the President of the European Commission with the information provided by the Croatian Government.

Economic adjustment

Together with earlier economic reforms, the implementation of the SAA has significantly contributed to progress on meeting the Copenhagen economic criteria. They include a functioning market economy and the ability to cope with the competitive pressures of the EU. Having in mind the present level of economic development, macroeconomic stability, the level of liberalization of trade and prices, the progress in setting up a regulatory framework related to the internal market, as well as development of the financial sector, Croatia could relatively soon be considered as a functioning market economy, but it still does not fulfil the second economic criterion, due to the present level of competitiveness.

The general assessment of the current economic situation in the Republic of Croatia indicates that the general, economic and financial conditions have improved over the last few years and that the Government's policies have achieved significant positive results. Macroeconomic stability is a continuing trend in Croatia's economy. However, the transition reforms in other areas are either ongoing or still to be undertaken. Major macroeconomic indicators place Croatia at the forefront of all SAPP countries, as already discussed. More comparative economic data is available online at www.mei.hr – Re:member Croatia – the CD-ROM that accompanied Croatia's application for membership.

In 2002, Croatia was for the first time included in the study of global competitiveness by the World Economic Forum. Croatia ranked 58th out of 80 countries listed as regards the growth competitiveness index and 52nd as regards the microeconomic competitiveness index. This study positioned Croatia behind the accession countries but in front of the remaining candidate countries for membership of the EU.

In its last Stabilization and Association Progress Report for Croatia (presented in April 2003), the European Commission recognized that the economic situation was continuing to improve and that the Government had adopted an ambitious programme for the integration of Croatia into the EU. It underlined that the implementation of the SAA is being coordinated in a highly efficient and professional way, so the EC's outlook for Croatia remained positive.

This was also underlined by the EU report, 'The Western Balkans in Transition' (*European Economy,* January 2003). However, the continuation of structural reforms remains a priority, including speeding-up of privatization, fiscal consolidation, enterprise restructuring, and judiciary and public administration reform as well as reforms in education, health and other priority areas.

Mechanisms of legal harmonization

In order to create the preconditions that will enable the smooth conclusion of the SAA, the adjustment of the legislation of the Republic of Croatia to the *Acquis Communautaire* and the implementation of all measures necessary for further rapprochement with the EU, the Government of the Republic of Croatia passed a number of decisions on 15 February 2001. These confirmed the intention of the Republic of Croatia to invest maximum efforts for the purpose of promptly signing the SAA, and expressed its wish that key progress in attaining the necessary level of readiness for membership of the EU should be achieved by the end of 2004, with a view to being ready for attaining EU membership by the end of 2006.

All the Ministries and state administration organizations committed themselves to undertake without delay preparations to modify the legislation, which the Republic of Croatia will have to harmonize with the *Acquis Communautaire*, to take into consideration the provisions of the *Acquis Communautaire* when preparing new Acts, and to provide information about the level of harmonization in the explanation of the Acts.

Recognizing the importance of the process of harmonizing the legislation, on the basis of the Rules of Procedure of the Government of the

Republic of Croatia (*Official Gazette* No 107/2000), the Government adopted a novel procedure whereby the opinion of the Ministry for European Integration has to be attached, *inter alia*, to the draft proposals on Acts and other regulations. The same applies to reports, information and similar materials, if they contain proposals on conclusions determining the obligations of state administration bodies or if they create financial liabilities. Also, through the amendments to the Rules of Procedure of the Croatian Parliament (*Official Gazette* No 117/01), a proposal on an Act which is harmonized with the EU regulations bears a special mark, namely 'P.Z.E. no...'. At the request of the proposer, an Act that is harmonized with EU regulations may be enacted by a speedy procedure, which combines the first and second readings of the Act. The Committee for European Integration of the Croatian Parliament has a key role in this legislative process since, among other things, it monitors the harmonization of the legal system of the Republic of Croatia with the legal system of the EU.

Given that the improvement of the level of know-how and competence of staff is an absolute precondition for the success of the European integration processes, the Government of the Republic of Croatia requested from all state administration bodies an analysis of the status and expertise of staff for this process, which was carried out during March 2001. On the basis of this analysis, a programme is being prepared for the training of staff to fulfil basic functions and to apply nomothetic skills in the preparation of legislative proposals adjusted to the standards of the EU.

In order for the harmonization of legislation to be carried out as effectively as possible, on 19 July 2001 the Government of the Republic of Croatia adopted a Decision on the Measures in the Procedure of Harmonization of the Legislation of the Republic of Croatia with the *Acquis Communautaire*, the obligatory application of which started on 1 December 2001. In keeping with the Decision, state administration bodies, in the preparation of legislative documents which harmonize the legislation of the Republic of Croatia with the *Acquis* pursuant to Article 69 of the SAA, are obliged to submit with the legislative Act a statement on harmonization and a review of the conformity of the provisions of the proposed Act to the provisions of the relevant regulations of the EU. Both instruments, together with the proposal on the act, are submitted to the Ministry for European Integration for verification and confirmation. A draft proposal on an Act harmonizing the legislation of the Republic of Croatia with the relevant *Acquis* that is not accompanied by both instruments is returned to the competent authority for refinement and is not submitted to further legislative procedure. As this is a new Government procedure, the Ministry for European Integration provides to the state administration bodies all the necessary technical and expert support in completing these instruments. Also, competent authorities are required to involve the Ministry for European Integration as early as the first stage in the preparation of a relevant Act. This helps significantly in the final evaluation of the harmonization of such an Act with the *Acquis* and also enables an exchange of knowledge at the sectoral level and at the level of the Ministry for European Integration, as the body in charge of coordinating the process of harmonizing legislation.

Institutional mechanisms to support legislative harmonization

In order to connect departments more closely with the European integration process, the Government of the Republic of Croatia has entrusted the Ministers to appoint Assistant Ministers as coordinators responsible for the overall functioning of the Ministries in the process of adjustment to the EU. The Conclusions also specify that the Government would appoint a National Coordinator for technical assistance provided from the funds of the EU and its members. In addition, all Ministries were obliged to establish units dealing exclusively with this segment of cooperation with the EU, in accordance with the Decision of the Government of the Republic of Croatia dated 18 October 2001. In line with the commitments in the Agreement, the Ministry for European Integration was entrusted with the continuation of the activities in the preparation of the National Programme for the integration of the Republic of Croatia into the EU.

On 19 September 2002 the Government of the Republic of Croatia passed a Decision on the Establishment of Working Groups for the Harmonization of the Legislation of the Republic of Croatia with the *Acquis Communautaire*. The Group's tasks are as follows:

- monitoring the measures included in the Agreement Implementation Plan, proposing new measures in the Plan, and proposing measures necessary for the preparation of draft proposals;

- participation in the harmonization of legislation by monitoring the dynamics of the harmonization of legislation, assessing the harmonization of a specific legal regulation in the scope of authority of the competent Working Group prior to submission to the Government procedure, and providing recommendations in terms of better quality legal regulations;

- participation in the annual cycle of the preparation of the National Programme;

- assessment of the part of the programme relating to the competent Working Group;

- assessment of the parts of the CARDS projects relating to the scope of authority of the competent Working Group;

- assessment of the draft standpoint for the meeting of the Interim Committee and, after the entry into force of the SAA, for the needs of the Stabilization and Association Council.

Working Groups have been established pursuant to Chapter 31 of the *Acquis*. At this stage, 14 working groups have been established, encompassing all the 13 priority areas in the obligatory harmonization of legislation: electronic commerce, competition and state aid, intellectual, industrial and commercial property, public procurement, technical legislation, financial services, accounting law, company law, consumer protection, land transport, health and safety at work, equal opportunities and protection of databases, as well as the judiciary and internal affairs.

The work of the Working Groups is important in resolving numerous preliminary issues related to the harmonization of the legislation of the Republic of Croatia with the *Acquis*, which currently emerge only when specific proposals on regulations are already in train. Based on the commitments of the Republic of Croatia assumed by the Agreement and also on the experiences of the candidate countries for membership in the EU, the work of the Working Groups will greatly contribute to the process of the harmonization of legislation, assuming common standpoints in resolving essential issues, and will considerably accelerate legislative procedures on the level of the Government of the Republic of Croatia.

In order to exchange experience and knowledge between state administration bodies, the Ministry for European Integration has launched a national twinning initiative – an exchange of lawyers of state administration bodies and lawyers employed in the Ministry for European Integration. Given the Ministry for European Integration's role as a coordinating body, this approach allows for an exchange of knowledge among experts about specific sectors on one hand, and the European regulations relevant for harmonization in those sectors on the other. Almost all employees in the Directorate for the Harmonization of Legislation participate or have participated in the work of other state administration bodies on legal issues in their area of competence: in the Ministry of Finance, the Ministry of Justice, Administration, and Local Self-government, the Ministry of Environmental Protection and Physical Planning, the Ministry of the Economy, the Ministry of Maritime Affairs, Transport, and Communications, and the Ministry of Health.

Legal framework of the harmonization of legislation

(Article 69 of the SAA: Public procurement, intellectual property, competition and state aid, consumer protection and technical legislation)
The process of harmonizing legislation, commenced on the day of the signing of the Agreement, is being further developed over the six-year

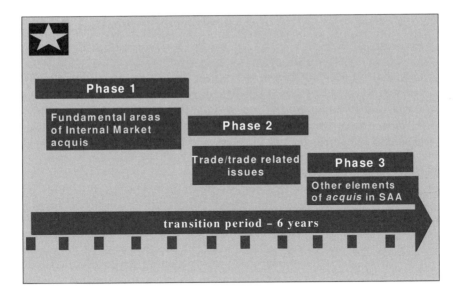

Figure 1.8.1 Phasing and timing of harmonization of legislation

transition period. The gradual nature of this process is reflected both in the time frame and in the approach; see Figure 1.8.1. The first phase of the harmonization of legislation encompasses the basic elements of the internal market, trade and trade-related areas and, finally, other elements of the *Acquis* referred to in the Agreement.

The initial phase of the harmonization of legislation includes five priority areas: competition and state aid, public procurement, technical legislation, consumer protection and intellectual property, and industrial and commercial property.

The Government of the Republic of Croatia is striving to fulfil the commitments assumed by the Agreement before the deadlines through increased legislative activities. A framework law regulating the public procurement area was enacted in December 2001 and entered into force on 1 January 2002. It is expected that 2003 will see the enactment of a legislative package regulating the five priority areas.

Competition/state aid

In order to fulfil the obligation stemming from Article 70 of the Stabilization and Association Agreement, an Act on the protection of market competition and the State Aid Act have been adopted, fully compliant with all relevant *Acquis*.

Intellectual, industrial and commercial property

According to Article 71, SAA, an analysis of compatibility of copyright and other related rights as well as industrial property has been prepared.

In 2003, the following will be enacted: Draft Proposal on the Copyright and Related Rights Act, Draft Proposal on Industrial Property Rights Act, Draft Proposal on the Act on Legal Protection of Topographies of Semiconductor Products, and the Regulation on the Implementation of Customs Measures for the Protection of Intellectual Property Rights.

Public procurement

Article 72, SSP-a regulates the harmonization of Croatian public procurement legislation. The harmonization has two stages. The Public Procurement Act was adopted before the SAA deadline and has been in force since 1 January 2002; it marks the first stage of harmonization. The second stage encompasses the institutional framework and capacity building. In that respect the Act on the State Commission for the review of public procurement has been adopted by Parliament. The setting up of the Commission will be completed by the end of 2003.

Technical legislation

With reference to Article 73, SAA, a national strategy for harmonization of technical legislation with the legislation of the EU has been adopted. The strategy envisages the following legislation will be adopted by the end of 2003:

- Act on the Technical Requirements for Products;

- Accreditation Act;

- Standardization Act;

- Product Safety Act;

- Metrology Act.

Consumer protection

In order to fulfil the obligation stemming from Article 74, SAA, a Consumer Protection Act has been adopted. The Act systematically regulates the area of consumer protection for the first time. Another important Act for this area is the recently adopted Food Act. Its primary goal was harmonization with the newly adopted Regulation 178/2002/EC, as well as the implementation of a new organizational structure for official food control, regulation of competency in the area of food safety, and the role and financing of laboratories in the food control sector.

Company law/accountancy

Concerning the area of takeovers, the Croatian Parliament has adopted the Act on the Takeover of Joint Stock Companies 2002, as well as the Company Act, to a large extent harmonized with the EU *Acquis*. A Draft Proposal on the Accounting Act is due to be reviewed in accordance with standard Government procedure during the final quarter of 2003.

Financial services

In July 2002, a new legislative package was adopted to regulate the provision of financial services: the Banking Act, Savings and Loans Association Act, Securities Market Act and Act on the Takeover of Joint Stock Companies.

In 2003, 83 legislative Acts will be adopted. Most important, all five legal areas marked as priorities under Articles 70 to 74 of the SAA will be regulated, thereby fulfilling the obligations arising from the Articles. This, in the understanding of the Croatian representatives, represents the end of the first phase of legal approximation as set forth in Article 69, SAA. Figure 1.8.2 shows the current status of these Acts.

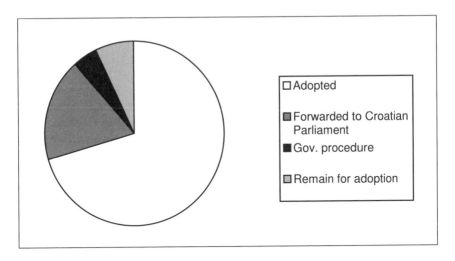

Figure 1.8.2 Status of legislation related to the SAA

National Programme for the Integration of the Republic of Croatia into the European Union

Taking into consideration the experience of candidate countries in the preparation of similar programmes, the Republic of Croatia has prepared its first National Programme for the Integration of the Republic of

Croatia into the EU – 2003,[4] which the Parliament adopted on 18 December 2002. The focus is on harmonization of legislation with the *Acquis* in the priority areas defined by the SAA. It provides a detailed plan for harmonization of legislation for 2003, thus complementing the Implementation Plan, which, in addition to legal measures, contains economic, institutional and other measures.

Given that the National Programme is the central steering mechanism of the Government of the Republic of Croatia in the move to European integration, its implementation will be the subject of future reports on the evaluation of the stabilization and association process for the Republic. Also, the National Programme is a document in which the Republic of Croatia addresses the assessments and recommendations of the European Commission and undertakes appropriate amendments.

The defining of priorities to determine the direction of the National Programme and its contents demanded that special attention be paid to the balance of needs and possibilities. The preparation of the National Programme, through working groups for the harmonization of legislation, included representatives of the legal profession, the judiciary, stakeholders, non-governmental organizations and private enterprises, which confirms the growing interest of society in the effects of the European integration process. Their participation is an important factor in gaining a general understanding of the reforms that need to be implemented. The Government will consider strengthening the existing mechanisms for a regular and structured dialogue with state administration bodies and the non-governmental sector.

Setting the priorities laid out in the National Programme was based on a number of sources, including the Operational Plan of the Implementation of the Programme of the Government of the Republic of Croatia 2002–2003, the SAA, the Agreement Implementation Plan, the progress evaluation of the Republic of Croatia in the Report of the European Commission, cooperation with the Delegation of the European Commission in the Republic of Croatia, etc. The National Programme thus reflects Croatia's readiness to implement the short- and medium-term priorities of the EU integration process, with an accent on 2003. The National Programme focuses on several issues:

- meeting the criteria stipulated by political policy;

- economic adjustments;

- harmonization of the legislation of the Republic of Croatia;

- strengthening administrative capacity for the implementation of the reforms;

---

[4] www.mei.hr.

- communication strategy for informing the Croatian public about the European integration of the Republic of Croatia.

Public administration reform

The Government of the Republic of Croatia initiated public administration reform by a Decision adopted on 7 November 2002. There are two exceptional, mainly complementary challenges: finalization of the transition to a market economy and transformation of the public administration into a service provider for citizens. Both should be considered in the light of EU standards and practices of individual member states.

A Task Force was established in the preparatory stage, located within the Ministry for European Integration, and completed the Programme Document for the beginning of implementing reform within six months. The document was submitted to the Government in June 2003. The reform of the state administration is necessary for the success of existing and future reforms in Croatia.

The main goal of the Task Force is the creation of a smaller and more efficient public administration system, capable, in addition to its everyday duties, of protecting citizens' interests and making rational use of existing resources. Furthermore, public funds need to be in complete accordance with European standards. For this purpose the Task Force has been using the experiences of other countries, chosen as 'reform models', and comparing them with the situation in Croatia.

The Croatian state administration must compensate for the lag in development. This means it must stabilize a clear, legal and democratically responsible administration. The other objective is to achieve the highest possible level of flexibility and openness towards future and world trends, especially in the context of integration into the EU.

The programme is in compliance and coordination with the CARDS 2001 Public Administration Reform project (see below) and has been established in cooperation with experts from the SIGMA programme and the OECD.

EU Technical assistance to Croatia

In order to support the participation of South-East European countries in the Stabilization and Association Process, the Council of the European Union adopted at the end of 2000 an assistance programme called CARDS – Community Assistance for Reconstruction, Development and Stabilization.[5] Croatia is among the countries that benefit from the national and regional components of the CARDS programme.

Since 2001, Croatian state bodies have been actively participating in the preparation and implementation of projects funded by the

---

[5] www.europa.eu.int/comm/europeaid/projects/cards/index_en.htm.

European Community. Under the national component of the programme, Croatia has received €179 million over the budget period 2001–2003. A further €68 million has been earmarked for Croatia in 2004 and more financial assistance is to follow in 2005 and 2006. In addition to national CARDS allocations, Croatia also benefits from the regional component of the programme, under which an additional €94 million has been allocated over the period 2001–2004 to support regional cooperation among the countries of South-East Europe.

The assistance provided to Croatia is in line with the priority areas outlined in the European Commission Strategy for Croatia for the period 2002–2006, and the first Multi-annual Indicative Programme for the period 2002–2004. It focuses on the following areas:

- democratic stabilization;

- return of refugees and internally displaced people;

- development of a civil society;

- economic and social development;

- promotion of trade in line with the provisions of the Stabilization and Association Agreement;

- creation of favourable conditions for foreign investments;

- promotion of social cohesion;

- justice and home affairs;

- modernization of justice;

- assistance with policing and the fight against organized crime;

- support for the integrated management of state borders;

- administrative capacity building;

- reform of public administration;

- national, regional and local development;

- reform of the public finance sector;

- the environment and natural resources.

In addition to the CARDS programme, Croatia is included in some other Community programmes such as: LIFE III (environmental protection), http://www.europa.eu.int/comm/environment/life/life/third_countries.htm; TEMPUS (higher education), http://www.europa.eu.int/comm/education/programmes/tempus/index_en.html; the sixth Framework Programme for Research and Development (scientific research and technological development), http://www.europa.eu.int/comm/research/ fp6/index_en.html; Youth (informal education of young people), http:// www.europa.eu.int/comm/youth/index_en.html; and Interreg (promotion of cross-border, transnational and interregional cooperation).

The Interreg III initiative covers the period 2000–2006 and is designed to strengthen economic and social cohesion throughout the EU, by fostering the balanced development of the continent through cross-border (strand A), transnational (strand B) and interregional (strand C) cooperation. Croatia is actively participating in following Interreg programmes:

- Adriatic Cross-border Programme between Eastern Adriatic Countries and Italy and Trilateral Operative Programme Hungary/Slovenia/ Croatia (still to be approved);

- Interreg III B CADSES (http://www.cadses.net);

- Interreg III C East Zone (http://www.interreg3c.net).

Croatia also benefits from a number of bilateral programmes and is recipient of loans from international financing institutions such as the European Investment Bank, the European Bank for Reconstruction and Development, the World Bank and others. Recognizing the importance of coordinating the overall foreign assistance in Croatia, the Government has established a permanent working group for this purpose and the Ministry for European Integration has set up an interactive database of foreign assistance in Croatia (http://www.mei.hr/default.asp?ru=173& akcija=).

If Croatia's application to become a candidate for EU membership proves successful, further assistance is expected from the European Community to support Croatia in the process. It is anticipated that future assistance may be modelled upon the pre-accession programmes open to the current acceding states and that support in the process of economic structural reforms would be provided, as well as assistance for the agricultural sector, protection of the environment and the upgrading transport infrastructure.

Part Two

Market Potential

Business & Leisure
Croatia

OBZORHOLIDAYS

CROATIA AIRLINES

2.1

Tourism in Croatia

Ministry of Tourism of the Republic of Croatia

Introduction

Croatia's travel and tourism industry started to develop in the early 1960s and for the next 25 years or so the country became an increasingly important player in the Mediterranean sun and beach market. By the 1980s, Croatia was an established holiday destination, representing serious competition for the Mediterranean leaders such as Spain, Italy, France and Greece. The primary reasons for its success were its natural geographical attractions – notably its beautiful coastline and unspoilt, natural environment – the warmth and friendliness of the local people, and the fact that it offered excellent value for money.

Tourist resources and attractions

Croatia has three distinctive geographical and climatic regions – the Pannonian and Peripannonian mainland, the mountains and the coastal region. The coast enjoys a typical Mediterranean climate with hot, dry summers and mild, humid winters, while the mountainous region can actually be quite cold in winter, with a lot of snow.

Croatia enjoys a unique geographical landscape, with more than 1,000 islands set in pristine waters of the highest quality and clarity. A number of these have been grouped together as national parks. The country boasts some of the most attractive coastline in the Mediterranean region, much of which is unspoilt, as well as lowlands and highlands culminating in the mountainous region of Lika and Gorski Kotar.

There are literally hundreds of cities, towns and villages – primarily along the Adriatic coast – that can provide tourists with basic accommodation and board, as well as a limited supply of sporting activities, entertainment, sightseeing and shopping. In addition to the old coastal towns of interest, such as Porec, Rovinj, Korcula, Trogir and Hvar,

DIA Yachting

Join the adventure

HEAD OFFICE (CENTRAL BOOKING)
Maksimirska 96
10000 ZAGREB
CROATIA
Tel: +385-1-2306000
Fax: +385-1-2307962
GSM: +385-98-708234
E-mail: renata.banozic@dia.tel.hr

CHARTER BASE OFFICE
Marina Kornati
23210 BIOGRAD n/m
CROATIA
Tel: +385-023-386509
Fax: +385-023-386510
GSM: +385-98-351635
E-mail: velimir.mestrovic@dia.tel.hr

Marina Kornati is a modern nautical center, that is situated at **Biograd na moru** in the middle of the Adriatic sea, just 18 nautical miles from the Kornati Archipelago. It is equipped in a modern way and it attracts boaters from the whole world with its overall facilities and possibilities of entertainment. Transfer from nearby airports (**Split** and **Zadar**) is possible.

The Kornati islands are the densest and most indented island group on the eastern Mediterranean. The Kornati island group consist of a labyrinth of 140 islands, islets and reefs making up a total area of 69 square kilometers and covering some 300 square kilometers. More than 50 restaurants with traditional dalmatian kitchen are available on Kornati islands. The island group was proclaimed a national park on 24th July 1980.

Owner and general manager of Yachtzentrum Greifswald, Michael Schmidt, a distinguished shipbuilder and sucessful yachtsman is one of the four main reasons why *Hanse* yachts are so splendid. The other reasons are superb design, quality and special wood processing.

Hanse started his great adventure in 1992 by exhibiting the model *Hanse 291* on the Hamburg Boat Show. Nearly ten years later, HANSE yachts are sailing by all world's seas and get more and more friends every day.

Here you can find out why we, at DIA Yachting, have decided to *join the adventure*.

Yachtzentrum Greifswald GmbH & Co KG
Salinenstraße 22
17489 Greifswald
Germany
Tel: +49-3834-5792-0
Fax: +49-3834-5792-30

CHARTER SEASON 2003

Price list 2003	Hanse 301	Hanse 311	Hanse 341	Hanse 371	Hanse 411	Elan 36	Beneteau 36.7	Elan 431	Baveria 44	Beneteau 50
Length in Meters	8,99	9,45	10,35	11,25	12,35	10,94	11	13,5	13,95	15,48
Berths/Cabins	4/2	4+1/2	6+1/3	6+1/3	8/4	6+2/3	6/3	8+1/4	8+1/4	8+2/4+1
Motor HP	10	19	19	30	40	35	29	50	55	75
Built Year	2002	2002	2002	2002	2002	2001	2003	2000	2002	2003
Till 19.04. From 04.10.	700	900	1.000	1.100	1.500	1.000	1.300	1.600	2.000	2.900
19.04.-24.05. 20.09.-04.10.	800	1.000	1.100	1.300	1.700	1.200	1.500	1.900	2.200	3.600
24.05.-28.06. 06.09.-20.09.	900	1.100	1.300	1.500	2.100	1.400	1.700	2.200	2.500	3.900
28.06.-19.07. 23.08.-06.09.	1.100	1.300	1.500	1.800	2.400	1.700	2.000	2.600	2.750	4.300
19.07.-23.08	1.300	1.500	1.700	2.100	2.700	2.000	2.200	3.000	3.150	5.200
Deposit	1.000	1.000	1.000	1.500	1.500	1.500	1.500	1.500	1.500	2.000

Included: Diesel-heating, furling genoa, main sail/drop-system, auto-pilot, GPS and chartplotter, electric windlass, wind direction/speed indicator, depth indicator, radio/CD player, VHF-radio, dinghy, warm water, stern shower, bedlinen, furling main sail (Elan 36, Elan 431, Bavaria 44), radar (Beneteau 50), bow thrusters (Bavaria 44, Beneteau 50).

Extras: skipper **80** per day + food, outboard motor **70** per week, permit **60** (obligatory), cleaning **60** (obligatory).

Discounts for more than one week reservations: 5% for 2 weeks, 10% for 3 weeks:

Check in: Saturday 18:00   **Check Out:** Saturday 08:00

Payment: 30% when signing the Contract   70% the latest 4 weeks before rental

www.diayachting.com

Croatia has a large number of little villages, which have preserved their historical character and traditions. And the hinterland of Croatia offers much more than just the capital city of Zagreb, boasting dozens of medieval fortresses, castles and mansions.

Despite the country's huge potential for tourism development, the number and type of attractions and activities – beyond pure sun and beach relaxation – are limited. There are very few facilities for golf, health and fitness, or special interest activities, for example. Developing these segments would undoubtedly help to extend the current tourist season – May to September – and to increase tourism expenditure.

The country's cultural and historical traditions have been maintained thanks, in part, to its strategic location at the crossroads of Europe. No fewer than 10 of Europe's key international land routes and railway links, including the historic Europe to Asia route, pass through Croatia. Numerous passenger and cargo ports are located along the coast, which is also home to nine international airports.

Location and transport

Croatia is situated in the very heart of Europe. This exceptional location provides easy access to all kinds of transport and travel from the key tourist markets.

Currently, 83 per cent of tourists come to Croatia by road. Despite the huge growth in sales of air package holidays to Croatia, air travel – scheduled and charter flights combined – accounts for less than 4 per cent of all arrivals. Croatia has nine international airports, four of which are located on the coast: Pula, Zadar, Split and Dubrovnik. Three are on the islands: Krk near Rijeka and the islands of Losinj and Brac, and two are in the central plain (Zagreb and Osijek).

The country also has six international seaports – Pula, Rijeka, Zadar, Split, Ploce and Dubrovnik – and dozens of small ports of local and regional importance. However, arriving in Croatia by sea, and the connections between the islands, are not well organized.

The Croatian Railways are not currently seen as attractive to the tourism industry. Due to very low cargo and passenger traffic, more time and much investment will be needed to modernize the railways and adapt the product to the needs of tourists.

Return to growth

During the 1990s, Croatia suffered the devastating impact of political instability and war, but from 2000 tourist traffic, especially international, recorded rapid grow (see Tables 2.1.1 and 2.1.2).

Table 2.1.1 Tourism trends

	1990	1999	2000	2001	2002	Index 2002/ 1990	Index 2002/ 1999
1. Arrivals in 000							
– domestic	3.477	1.307	1.282	1.316	1.376	39.6	105.28
– foreign	5.020	3.443	5.338	6.544	6.944	138.3	201.68
– **Total**	8.497	4.750	6.620	7.860	8.320	97.9	175.16
2. Overnight in 000							
– domestic	18.474	5.215	5.099	5.020	4.981	27.0	95.51
– foreign	34.049	21.349	33.307	38.384	39.711	116.6	186.01
– **Total**	52.523	26.564	38.406	43.404	44.692	85.1	168.24

Note: In 1990 domestic tourist figures are inclusive of all tourists coming from former Yugoslavia.
Source: Central Bureau of Statistics

Table 2.1.2 Tourist overnights in 000

Major markets	1990	1999	2000	2001	2002	Index 2002/ 1990	Index 2002/ 1999
Germany	12.264	4.515	7.598	9.686	10.789	88.0	239.0
Italy	5.365	2.578	4.360	4.724	4.883	91.0	189.4
Austria	2.975	2.377	3.159	3.601	3.543	119.1	149.1
Slovenia	5.415	4.237	4.968	5.119	4.993	92.2	117.8
Czech Republic	1.525	2.845	4.713	4.921	4.560	299.0	160.3
Hungary	517	813	1.403	1.554	1.733	335.2	213.2
Poland	232	679	1.805	2.514	2.186	942.4	321.9
Great Britain	4.522	270	410	542	661	14.6	244.8
Netherlands	2.465	592	895	1.059	1.204	48.9	203.4
France	766	88	180	224	418	54.6	475.0

Note: The 1990 domestic tourist figures are inclusive of all tourists coming from former Yugoslavia.
Source: Central Bureau of Statistics

Accommodation

Croatia currently has a total of 752,600 beds in different types of tourist accommodation (hotels, aparthotels, guesthouses, apartments, private rooms, etc) and camping places, of which 717,300 are located in the coastal area (see Figure 2.1.1).

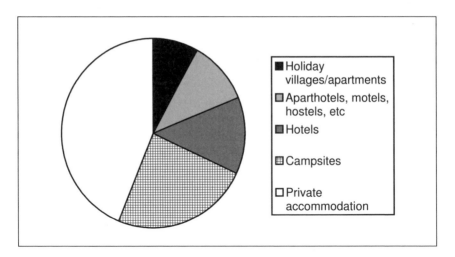

Figure 2.1.1 Accommodation types

The hotel sector

According to 2002 data from the Central Bureau of Statistics, there are 419 hotels in the country with a total of 96,607 beds, of which 49 per cent are three star and 12 per cent four and five star.

The hotel sector is the one that is suffering most from damaged and ageing bed stock. In fact, the expansion and renovation of Croatia's hotel supply is probably one of the greatest challenges facing the country's tourism industry – not to mention a critical competitive factor that could determine the growth of demand over the coming years.

One big disadvantage is that there are few well-known international hotel brands operating in the country. Sheraton, Starwood (Westin and Four Points), Sol Meliá, Club Méditerranée, Iberostar and Riu already have a presence in Croatia and a Hilton International property is scheduled to open in Dubrovnik before the end of 2003. In addition, a number of international hotel groups have expressed interest in establishing a presence in Zagreb, as well as in key resort locations, and local developers are looking to sign agreements with international operators for properties under construction.

Existing local hotel operators tend to be reminiscent of former, state-owned, locally managed enterprises. In some locations these companies have been more or less successfully privatized and operate to international standards. In most places, however, this is not the case, so the hotels leave a lot to be desired.

Tourism Satellite Account

Undertaken by WTTC, together with research partner Oxford Economic Forecasting, this report quantifies all aspects of travel and tourism demand, from personal consumption to business purchases, capital investment, government spending and exports.

In 2003, travel and tourism is expected to contribute 22.4 per cent of Croatia's GDP and it is expected to increase its share by more than 9 percentage points to 31.6 per cent in 2013. Travel and tourism in Croatia today account for 294,000 jobs, which is 27.4 per cent of total employment, and this is forecast to rise to 33.9 per cent by 2013. Current forecasts suggest that, if certain key factors are assured, Croatia will continue to record above-average growth levels over the next 10 years.

Privatization

The process of privatization of the state portfolio, in times of political and economic transition of the Republic of Croatia, represents one of the most significant preconditions for recovery and further development.

Determined to speed up the privatization process, the Government of the Republic of Croatia in its Programme of Work has set the privatization of the business sector, including the tourism sector, as one of its priority tasks.

Despite the difficulties during the past 10 years, tourism is one of the most resilient and recognizable Croatian products internationally. It has great potential for development and good market prospects, which the growing interest of investors has confirmed.

Privatization of the state portfolio is handled by the Croatian Privatization Fund, following two established models of privatization: a) the sale of stocks/shares by public auction on the stock exchange, for the companies in which the Government holds a small number of shares; and b) the sale of stocks/shares by public invitation of tender for other strategically important companies.

The Republic of Croatia holds over 25 per cent of shares of the capital stock in 35 hotel and other tourist companies. Many of those companies own, in addition to hotels, other facilities such as campsites, apartments, restaurants and shops. Out of those 35 companies, 12 are undergoing the process of privatization (some have invited tenders, the others are waiting for the final decision after completing the bidding process). Besides purchasing the stocks, potential investors can also buy the real estate from tourist companies.

Croatia expects that hotel chains and other quality investors, guaranteeing the introduction of international standards and quality, new technologies and know-how, market position and fresh capital, will take part in the privatization of the tourist sector. Croatian tourism is seeking partners able to successfully take part in its further development, making profits not only for themselves but also for their employees, the local community and the Croatian economy as a whole.

Long-term tourism planning

Long-term planning at a national level is a prerequisite for the successful development of travel and tourism in Croatia, since the industry can be fragile and adversely affected by short-term political considerations. The Croatian Strategic Development Commission for Tourism, McKinsey & Company and the German Investment & Development Company are in the process of developing a new Croatian Tourism Strategy, which will replace the existing one launched in 1993.

The prospects for growth in Croatia's travel and tourism sector are very good. Croatia has all the necessary natural resources on which to build the new tourism products required by the new, quality-conscious and increasingly sophisticated consumer. Though there will always be a need to provide low-cost tourism, diversification would ensure the sustainable growth of the industry for the benefit of all stakeholders.

As the international market becomes increasingly aware of the environmental friendliness of Croatia, as well as the unique attractions of destinations such as the national parks, this should encourage further tourism growth. It should also help Croatia to clarify its image generally.

A wealth of information to support the development of the Croatian Tourism Strategy 2010 can be found in the Strategic Marketing Plan – Croatian Tourism 2001–2005, commissioned by the Croatian National Tourist Board and prepared by THR International Tourism Consultancy and Horwath Consulting Zagreb. This plan proposes targets to reinvent and restructure Croatia's tourism products. It identifies eight regional clusters within the country and proposes that each cluster develop competitive and complementary tourism products and experiences. The focus is on enhancing the quality of tourism products and services, as well as developing a new brand identity for Croatia.

The strategic aim is the development of high-quality tourism based on the principles of sustainable development, including:

● maximum level of protection and rational use of land, especially on the coastline;

● preservation and protection of natural and other tourist resources and the environment;

● renovation, modernization and upgrading of existing hotels and other types of accommodation;

- development of new hotels and other accommodation capacities based on cautious plans;

- development of complementary and new competitive products (golf, fitness, etc);

- integration of all of Croatia into tourism through the development of selective types of tourist products.

2.2

Food and Beverages

Igor Mataic, Raiffeisenbank Austria d.d. Zagreb

This overview is divided into three parts:

1. The importance of the food and beverages industry in the Republic of Croatia.

2. The most important companies in the sector.

3. The latest trends.

The importance of the food and beverages industry in the Republic of Croatia

Food industry – production of food and beverages

Output of the food industry went up by 6.8 per cent in 2002. Production of food and beverages is the most important branch of the processing industry, with a 20.9 per cent contribution to the industry's overall results.

Food and beverage production contributes significantly to the gross added value of the production industry, but its share of the overall industrial results was lower in 2001 than a year earlier, dropping from 22.2 per cent in 2000 to 17.1 per cent in 2001 (see Table 2.2.1). Its industry share also contracted, as the participation in the overall income of Croatian entrepreneurs fell to 6.53 per cent in 2001, from 6.79 per cent in 2000.

The food and beverages industry employs the highest number of staff of all sectors in the processing industry; in 2001 it averaged 46,093, representing a small increase on the previous year's total of 44,852. The number of employees was the only item that registered a relative increase, thus worsening the cost–efficiency ratio compared to the rest of industry.

Table 2.2.1 Indicators of the size and importance of the food and beverages industry in the processing industry sector

	1999 (%)	2000 (%)	2001 (%)
Share in total income of entrepreneurs	6.77	6.79	6.53
Share in total income of the processing industry	21.10	21.10	20.90
Share in the total profit of the processing industry	18.70	22.20	17.10
Share in the total losses of the processing industry	14.50	25.00	14.20
Share in the total number of employed persons	4.11	4.15	4.16

Source: Central Bureau of Statistics (DZS), FINA

In 2001, the food and beverages production industry made significant improvements, registering a net profit of HRK458.33 million (see Table 2.2.2). Income in this sector is growing significantly faster than costs, resulting from investment in production-line modernization and cuts in operating costs, combined with rising income. Consolidated net margin amounted to 2 per cent, indicating that there is room for further rationalization.

Table 2.2.2 Basic financial results of the food and beverages industry

	At year-end in HRK000			Change (%)	
	1999	2000	2001	2000	2001
Total income	18,868,039	20,542,327	22,425,463	8.9	9.2
Total expenditures	19,218,067	20,690,786	21,731,497	7.7	5.0
Profit after tax	638,850	984,119	1,115,770	54.0	13.4
Loss after tax	1,125,274	1,342,255	657,439	19.3	−51.0
Net profit (+)/loss (−)	−486,424	−358,136	458,331	−26.4	228.0
Profit loss ratio	1.76	1.36	0.59	−22.6	−56.8

Source: DZS

During 2001, 886 business entities were active in the food and beverages industry, which is a rise of 3.5 per cent on 1999 when 856 entities were registered. The income of the 10 largest companies in the sector accounted for a 42 per cent share, while their share in overall profit totalled 58.2 per cent, reflecting their strength (see Table 2.2.3).

Table 2.2.3 Overview of the industry's largest entrepreneurs in 2001, listed by total income volume

Company name	Rank income in HRK000			Profit in HRK000		ROE %	
	2001	2001	% change	2001	% change	2001	2000
Vindija d.d., Varazdin	1	1,897,313	21.7	21,049	20.4	6.7	11.4
Podravka d.d., Koprivnica	2	1,583,375	4.6	36,275	24.3	1.9	1.5
Lurra d.d., Zagreb	3	1,514,057	10.5	101,622	25.9	16.1	13.2
Coca-Cola Beverages d.d.	4	883,856	1.7	84,169	27.7	13.6	9.2
Zagrebacka pivovara, Zagreb	5	771,365	19.3	214,494	43.6	39.5	31.8
Kras, Zagreb	6	736,755	–2.6	39,807	–48.4	5.7	11.4
Franck, Zagreb	7	593,391	4.8	59,860	–2.3	12.7	13.7
Ledo, Zagreb	8	547,628	–2.2	28,364	6.0	11.4	11.9
Zvijezda, Zagreb	9	523,221	–21.7	11,917	–76.9	3	13.3
Jamnica, Zagreb	10	463,679	12.1	52,314	111.2	23.2	14.6
Total food and beverages production		**22,425,463**		**1,115,770**		**8.6**	**8.0**
Total first 10		**9,514,638**		**649,870**			
Share of the first 10 in the branch		**42.4**		**58.2**			

Source: Privredni Vjesnik business magazine FINA

The most important companies in the sector

Agrokor

Agrokor is a food and beverage producer and retail concern, with a consolidated income of HRK6.67 billion (€0.9 billion) in 2002. Agrokor's core businesses are frozen food, beverages, oil, mayonnaise and retail. Ledo, Jamnica, Zvijezda and Konzum are the key companies in the Agrokor portfolio. Ledo produces ice-cream, pastry, fruit and vegetables, as well as fish. Despite strong foreign competition, Ledo's domestic market share is around 80 per cent. With a market share of 75 per cent, Ledo is also a market leader in the neighbouring Bosnia and Herzegovina. Jamnica is the biggest mineral water producer in this part of Europe with a tradition of over 170 years as the market leader in Croatia. In 2000 Jamnica acquired Kiseljak Sarajevo (Bosnia and Herzegovina). Sarajevski Kiseljak is the biggest and oldest mineral water producer in Bosnia and Herzegovina with a tradition of over 110 years and has a leading position in the domestic market. In 2003 Jamnica natural mineral water was awarded the EAUSCAR as the best natural sparkling mineral water. Zvijezda is the major producer of edible oils and the only producer of margarine, vegetable oil, mayonnaise and delicacy products made on a mayonnaise base. Zvijezda also produces ingredients for other food industries. In a few years Konzum grew from a local into a countrywide retail store chain through organic growth as well as acquisition.

Podravka

The organizational structure of Podravka is based on eight strategic business units: Vegeta, podravka dishes, desserts, fruit and vegetables, drinks, milling and bakery, Danica (meat industry) and Belupo (pharmaceutical industry). Belupo, in terms of market share, is the second largest pharmaceutical manufacturer in the Republic of Croatia. Podravka's most famous product is Vegeta, a universal food seasoning. Vegeta was launched in 1958 and is currently exported to more than 30 countries worldwide.

Vindija

Vindija's core activity is the production of milk and dairy products, juices, chicken meat, bakery products and other meat and meat products. During the past 40 years Vindija has been the only producer of blue cheese in the region. Vindija exports 12 per cent of its products, and the company has invested more than €50 million in production facilities.

Kras

Kras began operations in 1911, with the foundation of 'Union' – a chocolate and sweets factory. Over the years, 'Union' expanded the range of its activities and merged with 'Bizjak' – a biscuit factory. Kras emerged from the amalgamation of those two factories.

Kras is Croatia's leading confectionery manufacturer. Its main products are a wide range of chocolate, biscuit and sweets products. The current assortment of Kras chocolate products is known under the name of Dorina. During 60 years of production, Bajadera has become the best-known name of the Kras assortment and has gained the status of the ultimate Kras product worldwide. The main export markets are the countries of the former Yugoslavia and the CEE.

Lura

Lura is the leading Croatian producer of dairy products. It was founded in 1999 through the merger of Lura Group d.o.o. and three dairy producers – Dukat d.d. Zagreb, Sirela d.d. Bjelovar and Zadar Dairy d.d. Today Lura is one of the largest companies in Croatia and employs 1,700 workers. Due to its long-term development of business relations with farmers, Lura d.d. purchases milk from 25,000 dairy farmers throughout Croatia using 70 own and rented lorries and 2,000 lacto-freezes. The Lura d.d. product range includes more than 120 branded products.

Lura-Pica d.o.o. is a producer of non-alcoholic beverages and also has the exclusive right to bottle, sell and distribute soft drinks with Pepsi, Pepsi Max, Mirinda and 7Up brands. Lura d.d. Livno Dairy situated in Bosnia and Herzegovina is a company owned by Lura d.d., specializing in cheese production.

Zagrebacka Pivovara

Zagrebacka Pivovara was founded in 1892 and has been majority-owned by Interbrew Corporation since 1994. Its products consist of Ozujsko Pivo, the best selling lager beer in Croatia, dark Tomislav, Bozicno Pivo, and premium beer Stella Artois.

The latest trends

Modernization

Modernization of factories and increased effectiveness accompanied by reduced costs – companies have learnt that if they want to survive they must improve their productivity. The most vivid recent examples have been the construction of Podravka's new Vegeta factories in Croatia and Poland, as well as the construction of a soup factory. Kras consolidated production at one location, modernized the production line and built a state-of-the art warehouse for its finished products. Vindija invested in a new milk-processing plant and spent more than €50 million in the modernization of production facilities over the last few years. In the first six months of 2003, Agrokor invested more than €60 million in the new plants, technology and knowledge. In the last six years Lura invested over €100 million in production and technology, distribution and protection of the environment.

Establishing international standards

International standards of quality have in recent years been applied in the largest food companies in the Republic of Croatia. Vindija received an ISO 9001 certificate in 1996, the first food company in Croatia to do so. Koka (a member of the Vindija concern) received the certificate at the beginning of 2000 as the first meat-processing company in Croatia. Kras was issued the certificate in 1997, while Podravka's ISO 9001 certificate encompasses production of Vegeta, Podravka meals (soups, ready-made food and seasonings) as well as Lino baby food, Dolcela sweets and Kviki snacks. Lura was awarded the ISO 9001 certificate of quality for its entire production as well as the ISO 14001 certificate for its environment-friendly production system. Several companies within the Agrokor concern have received certificates for ISO 9001 and the HACCP (Hazard analysis critical control point) system .

Growth through acquisitions

Agrokor registered the most significant growth through acquisitions in more than one segment. The retail chain store Konzum registered a growth rate of 58 per cent in 2002 and 72 per cent in 2001. Such rapid growth was based on acquisitions of private companies in Croatia. The second segment where Agrokor registered above-average rates of growth is Ledo, the ice-cream maker. In 2002 it acquired Barpeh of Bosnia and Herzegovina, the local market leader with a share of over 75 per cent of the market. In early 2003, it acquired a frozen food and ice-cream factory, Frikom in Yugoslavia. All this enabled Ledo to become the strongest regional company in the frozen food segment.

In 2002, Podravka acquired Ital-Ice, a local food producer and thus entered into this fast-growing market segment. The company's first acquisition outside Croatia's borders was completed in the Czech Republic in 2002 with the acquisition of the Lagris factory. Lura acquired Sloboda from Osijek, starting its rise from a dairy into a food company.

In the last two years there have been horizontal mergers between food companies. Smaller local producers such as Ital-Ice, Sloboda Osijek and Irida from Daruvar have been acquired by local market leaders. Although attempts have been made to make the largest companies of the industry targets for multinational companies, to date all offers have been rejected. Lura negotiated a strategic partnership with the French company Danone and with the local tobacco producer, Tvornica Duhana Rovinj. Kras refused merger offers from Lura and Kraft Food and announced penetration into the regional markets through acquisition as well as cooperation with a confectionery producer, Koestlin.

The region of former Yugoslavia, especially Serbia and Montenegro, are markets where Croatian food companies are well known and where they plan their growth. In our opinion, the main reasons why domestic companies rejected the offers from well-known multinationals are that, firstly, domestic food companies are strong enough to be able to push for acquisitions in the regional markets on their own, and secondly, their brands (as a foundation for organic growth) are well known. After consolidating the entire market of former Yugoslavia, we believe that the leading domestic food companies will be more open to strategic alliances with big multinational companies for the purpose of further growth and development.

In addition to horizontal consolidation there have been some vertical moves. The first was the acquisition of the chain store Unikonzum by Agrokor back in 1994. Today, Konzum is the market leader and the main growth driver of the company, with an income of HRK4 billion and a 22 per cent share of the domestic food and beverages retail market. Vindija took over the chain store Zagrebcanka, with a network of 70 self-service shops. With the entrance of large foreign chain stores, such as Billa, Mercatone, Merkator, Kauflan and Metro, to the market, other domestic food companies started moving towards vertical consolidation. A consortium of domestic food companies has acquired Diona.

The only segment of the food industry that is almost entirely in the hands of foreign-owned multinational companies is the brewing industry. Out of Croatia's seven breweries, the four largest have foreign owners. The market leader is Zagrebacka Pivovara, the Zagreb-based brewery owned by Interbrew, which holds 48 per cent of the market. Early this year, the second largest local brewery, Karlovacka Pivovara, based in Karlovac, was acquired by Heineken. Karlovacka Pivovara's market share is 19 per cent. Panonska Pivovara is owned by Caltenberg, while Jadranska Pivovara was purchased by Slovenian producer Pivovarna Lasko. These four large breweries cover 80 per cent of the domestic market.

Creating well-known brands

The food industry in Croatia has concentrated on creating well-known brands. According to a survey by the company Accent, in 2002 the leading brands on the chocolate market were Milka, Kras and Dorina. Kras' strongest products are Dorina (chocolate) and Bajadera (a soft-centred chocolate); the company's products are market leaders. In the mineral water market the best known are Jamnica by Agrokor and Studena by Podravka. In the ice cream market the uncontested leader is Ledo (Agrokor) with over three-quarters of the market. In the mayonnaise and margarine market Zvijezda (Agrokor) and Margo hold around 80 per cent, while in the coffee market the company Franck with its brand Frank dominates, with a 59 per cent share and is followed by Minas and Nescafé. The relatively low participation of Nestlé in the market could soon change: it has signed a product distribution agreement with Podravka. Dukat (Lura) and Vindija (Vindija) are the two brands holding over 70 per cent of the dairy market.

Podravka is currently working on establishing brands such as Dolcela (confectionery) and Lino (baby food), Podravka soups and Podravka (meat products). Agrokor created the brand Konzum (retail segment) while Lura launched its Frutisima line (yoghurts). Vindija is pushing its Cekin (meat) line in the smoked and cured meat segment, where Gavrilovic and its Gavrilovic brand hold the leading position.

Growth of imports and exports

According to the preliminary results for 2002, Croatia's exports in this industry segment realized a rise of 23.29 per cent on a year earlier, while imports of food and beverages went up by 20.29 per cent (see Table 2.2.4). The rise in imports is due to the large foreign chain stores

Table 2.2.4 Trade in the food and beverages sector

US$ million	1999	2000	2001	2002*
Exports	276	223	249	307
Imports	393	363	414	498
Balance	−117	−140	−165	−191

* Preliminary data.
Source: Croatian Chamber of Economy (HGK)

Table 2.2.5 Average share of food and non-alcoholic beverages in the cost of living index

Year	%
2000	38.63
2001	36.81
2002	35.84
2003 (estimate)	35.25

entering the market, improved standards of living of Croatian consumers, and reduced customs duty on agricultural products.

It is evident from Table 2.2.5 that expenditure on food and drink is contracting, resulting in lower sensitivity to price movements. This generates increased demand for international brands and less dependence on and demand for cheaper products.

The structure of the retail trade also has a substantial influence on the rise in imports. Small privately owned shops dominate in Croatia and owners are traditionally more inclined to local brands. However, with the change in shopping habits and numerous new foreign chain stores opening, this advantage is expected to disappear soon.

Local vs multinational producers – trends

As can be seen from the data on leading brands in Croatia, domestic companies still hold the dominant position in almost all sub-segments. This is attributable to long-standing relationships with individual brands. The development of individual brands can be illustrated through the results of a survey showing that young consumers prefer Milka chocolate, while older consumers opt for Kras. Domestic producers will probably maintain their position in the mid-term thanks to the comparative advantage of being well known and knowing their markets. Longer term, only those that improve the competitiveness of their products will be able to increase their production volumes and be equipped to take on the largest players such as Nestlé, Unilever, Danone and Kraft. The best examples of this are Ledo's acquisition of Frikom, followed by Podravka's acquisition of Lagris. In cases like these, the benefits of synergy are achieved.

The second possibility is cooperation with international companies through distribution agreements, as we have seen in Podravka's example. Podravka signed an agreement with Nestlé on the distribution of its products throughout Croatia, Bosnia and Herzegovina, Serbia, Montenegro and the former Yugoslav Republic of Macedonia. It also signed an agreement with Unilever for distributing its products in Croatia.

2.3

Healthcare and Pharmaceuticals

Igor Mataic, Raiffeisenbank Austria d.d. Zagreb

Demographic data

According to the latest population census (2001), the Republic of Croatia has a population of 4,437,460. The proportion of inhabitants over 65 years of age reached 15.7 per cent, more than double the figure in the 1961 census (see Figure 2.3.1). The proportion of inhabitants under 14 years of age fell to 17.1 per cent.

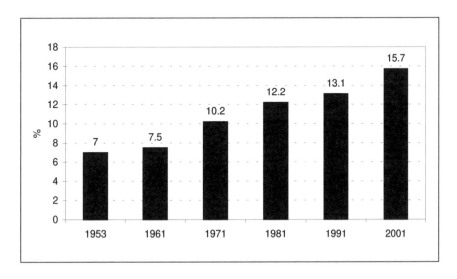

Source: Ministry of Health of the Republic of Croatia

Figure 2.3.1 Share of inhabitants under 65 in the population

Institute of Immunology

Imunološki zavod

FOUNDED IN 1893

TRADITION
OF
110 YEARS

Institute of Immunology, Inc., Zagreb has over a century old tradition in the production of immunobiological substances. The production started with the Small-Pox Vaccine in Zagreb at the institute founded by the Croatian Government in 1893. From this beginning production of an ever-increasing range of bacterial vaccines and animal sera followed.

The broadening of knowledge on the prevention and curing off infectious diseases imposed new requirements on the production of immunobiologicals substances. Consequently, the Serovaccinal Institute, today known as the Institute of Immunology, was established in 1956 to continue and extend the production of sera and vaccines. The Institute's goals today are the continuous improvement of existing products and the creation of new ones.

Institute of Immunology, Inc. is the only Croatian and one of the major regional manufacturers of immunobiologicals. It has a series of high quality products, production technologies, and expert personnel, on which it can rely for the future development and progress.

The basic activity of the Institute is the manufacture of viral and bacterial vaccines and blood products; scientific research; wholesale; and representation activities.

Institute, with its technology and products (generics), could compete in the market for viral vaccines and animal antisera on a global scale and for bacterial vaccines, as well as in plasma fractionation on the regional level.

The competency of the company on the global market of viral vaccines is best shown by the results of measles and MMR vaccines sold in over eighty countries.
Institute of Immunology, Inc. has its own master measles virus seed ("Edmonston-Zagreb") of highest quality. The measles virus strain Edmonston-Zagreb is the most immunogenic and least reactogenic strains in the world. A licence to produce the vaccine against measles with the Edmonston-Zagreb strain has been issued to institutions in the following countries: Belgium, France, India, Mexico and Switzerland.

wnership

Small shareholders
31%

Funds*
69%

* Croatian Privatisation Fund, Croatian Institute for Health Insurance, Croatian Institute for Pension Insurance

rganizational structure

he structure of the Institute has not substantially modified over the past decades, and is ontinuously based on the activities of particular manufacturing units. The activities are erformed through 11 departments headed by the Management Office that includes epartment of Internal Audit and Control and Department of Quality Assurance.

eneral Administrative and Technical Services Department covers the logistics common to all anufactures (legal affairs and general administration, accounting division, purchasing ivision, marketing and distribution, sales and ingredient/material store, technical affairs, oiler-room).

t the Department of Research and Development, a number of scientists are employed who re engaged in basic and applied research as well as in educational activities at the University f Zagreb.

ive long-term research projects supported by the Ministry of Science and Technology have een conducted at the Institute of Immunology.

ince the end of 2001, the Institute has been actively included in the Croatian Program of nnovative Technological Development through the work on six technological research-evelopment projects, with Institute affiliates as principal investigators.

anufacture was and is the main activity of the Institute, which makes it a profit-oriented rganization.

he manufacture is organized in six departments:
- Department of Viral Vaccines
- Department of Bacterial Products and Allergens
- Department of Transfusiology
- Department of Experimental Animals and Antisera
- Department of Plasma Processing
- Department of Manufacture Preparation and Finalization

uality Control Department performs supervision of all manufacture steps, from the control f ingredients and materials through the control of final products, for all Institute products, nd puts together registration documentation for the Institute products.

luman resources

s per December 31, 2002 Institute of nmunology, Inc. has 382 employees, 97 having university degree (18 hold a masters degree nd 19 a PhD degree). The activity of the stitute can be roughly divided into: roduction and services and research and evelopment (including teaching).

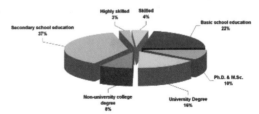

Highly skilled 3%
Skilled 4%
Secondary school education 37%
Basic school education 22%
Ph.D. & M.Sc. 10%
Non-university college degree 8%
University Degree 16%

Leading the way in the production

Viral Vaccines against: measles, mumps, rubella, and combined MMR

Bacterial Vaccines against: diphtheria, pertussis, tetanus, meningococcal meningitis

Croatia is self-sufficient in human plasma products: Human Immunoglobulins, Albumin, Specific human immunoglobulins against Hepatitis B, rabies, tetanus

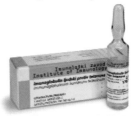

Animal antisera: Tetanus and diphtheria antitoxins, European Viper Venom Antiserum, Black widow antiserum

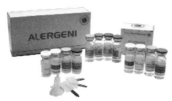

Other biologicals: Human leukocyte interferon, Allergens for diagnostics and hyposensibilization

Strategic guidelines for development of the Institute of Immunology

IN CROATIA

- ⊕ according to the decision issued by the Ministry of Health, Institute of Immunology manufactures, imports and distributes vaccines from the compulsory program of vaccination in the Republic of Croatia; and

- ⊕ according to the decision issued by the Ministry of Health, Institute of Immunology is in charge of plasma collection and processing to albumin and immunoglobulin for intravenous administration, and specific immunoglobulins to cover the needs of the Republic of Croatia.

ABROAD

- ⊕ Further development of the Institute of Immunology relies on the development and extension of the manufacture of vaccines for domestic and especially export requirements.

- ⊕ Intensive breakthrough on the international market through the development of new products and basic research is necessary.

- ⊕ Until 1998, Institute of Immunology sold its products on the world market via UNICEF and PAHO. The goal is to qualify measles vaccine production for selling through these agencies in 2004. At present, there is the need of product registration on the markets abroad, which is the primary task in this stage of development. Registration of the products is completed in Mexico, Slovenia, Russia, and is under way in India and Korea.

In order to realize these goals, recapitalization of the Institute of Immunology is required, whereby the following preconditions have been met:

- ➢ a decision has been issued by the respective Ministry and Croatian Privatization Fund, stating that the Government retains 25% +1 share to protect the strategic interest of the state, while the rest can be privatized through recapitalization;
- ➢ feasibility studies for the construction of the plant for the manufacture of viral vaccines and construction of the plant for human plasma processing have been elaborated; and the procedure of strategic partner selection is under way.

Contacts:

Director:
Professor Sabina Rabatić, Ph.D.
Rockefellerova 2
HR-10000 Zagreb
Croatia

e-mail: ured@imz.hr
url: www.imz.hr

Phone: +385 1 4684 500
Fax: +385 1 4684 303

Commercial Unit:
Dalibor Milković, B.B.A.
e-mail: kom@imz.hr
Phone: +385 1 4684 302
Fax: +385 1 4684 445

In 2001, the average life expectancy of both men and women in the Republic of Croatia was 74.65 years of age, that is 78.17 and 71.03 respectively (source: Ministry of Health of the Republic of Croatia). Compared to more developed countries (see Figure 2.3.2), Croatia is about four to five years behind (for example in Finland life expectancy is 78.17). It still lags two years behind Slovenia, where the average life expectancy is 76.49, but the situation is one and a half years better than the average in Central and Eastern Europe, of 73.29 in 2001.

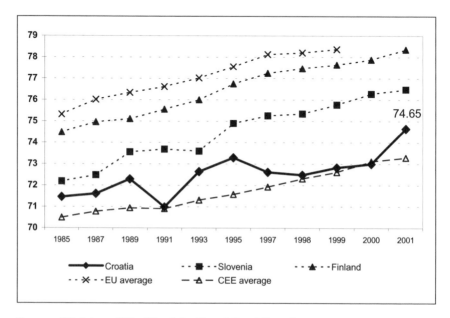

Source: Ministry of Health of the Republic of Croatia

Figure 2.3.2 Life expectancy in Croatia as compared to some other European countries

According to the available data on natural migration of the population, Croatia has a natural decline in the number of its inhabitants. In recent years, the number of deaths (49,552) has exceeded the number of newborns (40,993) by 8,559. The birth rate totalled 9.2/1,000, whereas the mortality rate was 11.2/1,000 (see Figure 2.3.3). Declining birth rates have been registered all over Europe and a comparison with the average throughout the European Union and Central and Eastern Europe shows that Croatia has a somewhat lower birth rate.

Age structure of the population

Similar to other European countries, Croatia has an ageing population and an increase in age-related illnesses is to be expected (see Figure

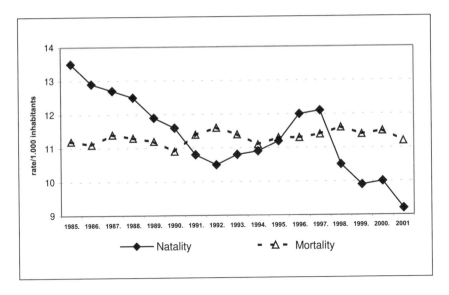

Source: Ministry of Health of the Republic of Croatia

Figure 2.3.3 Birth and mortality rates in Croatia in the period from 1985 to 2001

2.3.4). In addition, the baby-boom generation, which is more health-conscious, is entering the second half of its life, so combined with drugs for treatment of cardiovascular, musculoskeletal and other age-related diseases we can expect an increase in the sales of 'lifestyle' preparations (regulating weight, help in giving up smoking, etc).

Pharmaceutical pricing and reimbursement

Prices of drugs

Cuts in medical costs are to be achieved with new pricing methods in line with the changes and amendments to the Act on drugs and medical products implemented in 2000 (*Official Gazette* 53/01) and the Rulebook on determining wholesale drug prices (*Official Gazette* 84/01), which regulates prices of drugs under the principle of comparable or bench-mark prices.

Furthermore, changes and amendments to the Rulebook on methods of determining wholesale prices (*Official Gazette* 124/97, 53/01 and 129/02) introduced for the first time generic pricing of drugs, which reduced prices by 5 to 10 per cent, cutting overall healthcare costs.

Croatian Institute of Transfusion Medicine

During the last ten years, transfusion medicine has faced major challenges consequential to newly discovered blood-transmissible diseases (AIDS, hepatitis C, Creutzfeld-Jacob), better recognition of side effects (infectious diseases, bacterial contamination of blood products, immunosuppression, GVHD, etc.), new technologies of blood product manufacture (leukocyte-poor preparations, recombinant coagulation factors), new tests (anti HIV, anti HCV, anti HTLV), requirements for prevention of infectious disease transmission (legal acts, regulations, recommendations regulating blood collection, preparation of drugs derived from human blood, and transfusion therapy), and rising costs of health service, which also has an impact on transfusion medicine posing limitations on the procurement of new and more expensive reagents, materials and instruments. These processes, characteristic of industrialized countries, have not skipped Croatia either.

Croatia is a new state, founded in 1991. In spite of the war in Croatia (1991 - 1995) the high standards of Croatian Blood Transfusion Service was maintained and improved. Restructuring of work, centralization of some activities, and increasing of collected number of units per blood bank/transfusion center and increase of efficacy of the preparation of blood products are indispensable for transfusion service reorganization. The geographical layout of Croatia does not allow similar implementation and reorganization with the same degree increasing in size and merging of transfusion units and restructuring that is applied in many other European countries (large centers where blood collection and production of blood products are performed from hundreds thousands of donors). Therefore, the organization of transfusion service from any other European countries cannot be simply extrapolated to Croatia. The Croatian transfusion centers inevitably will be smaller. Transfusion medicine in Croatia has responded to these challenges by its organizational adjustment to the new conditions, adoption of new technologies, and more economical management of this complex service.

Pictures on the left from the top are showing Croatian Institute of Transfusion Medicine and facilities.

Today, we are facing the reorganization of Blood Transfusion Service. There are 21 Blood Transfusion Centers (BTC) and 1 national Blood Transfusion Center (Croatian Institute of Transfusion Medicine, CITM) that collect and test donors blood. Additional 13 hospital Blood Transfusion Services (BTS) perform only hospital service of pretransfusion testing of donor and patient's blood. As compared to most other European countries, Croatia has a lower proportion of blood donors per 1,000 inhabitants. However, the >36 blood donors /1,000 inhabitants meets the needs of cell concentrates, but not plasma requirements for the manufacture of plasma derivatives. Therefore, there is a small fractionation center at the Zagreb Institute of Immunology, working since 1968. Some 25 000 L plasma are being fractionated per year, and albumins, IVGG and specific IMGG are obtained from it. In spite of inadequate seasonal amounts of blood products (cell concentrates and fresh frozen plasma), there are no major shortages of these products in Croatia. Only Croatian Red Cross up to 1996 did recruitment of donors and since than by CRC and CITM. Blood donors are volunteers and are not reimbursed for their donation. The following laboratory tests are routinely performed on each unit of the blood/plasma collected from blood donors: determination of ABO and Rh of the donor's blood group; testing for the irregular antibodies in the donor's blood; testing for infectious disease markers (HBV, HCV, AIDS, syphilis) in the donor's blood.

Croatian Blood Transfusion Service, adapted to the new conditions, is characterized by progressive computerization, automation, robotics, quality assurance, traceability of blood-derived products, reorganization, restructuring of work, enlargement of transfusion units issuing of a National plan for meeting the needs of blood-derived drugs, and work organization consistent with Good Manufacturing Practice (GMP), ISO standards and Standards for Transfusion Service based on Council of Europe recommendations and directives on the preparation, use and quality assurance of blood components.

You can visit us at http://www.hztm.hr

Pictures from the top are showing couple of posters that invites blood donors.

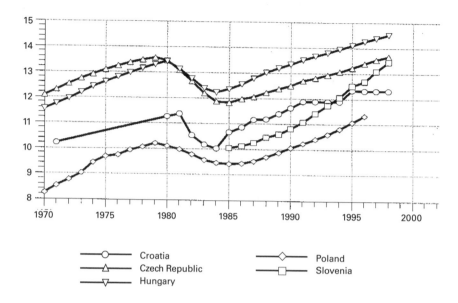

Source: Ministry of Health of the Republic of Croatia

Figure 2.3.4 Movement of the proportion of population over 65 years of age in some CEE countries

Pursuant to this Rulebook, individuals engaged in the production or transport of drugs were obliged to determine wholesale drug prices in line with five other countries: Slovenia, Italy, France, Spain and the Czech Republic. After calculating comparable prices in line with the methodology prescribed under the Rulebook, prices were adjusted as follows: those which were below 70 per cent could be increased, those between 70 and 95 per cent remained the same, while those above 95 per cent had to be reduced.

After completing the procedure the Croatian Institute for Health Insurance (HZZO) published these new prices as part of the Institute's drug list (*Official Gazette* 20/01). Out of 1,373 different drugs, prices increased for 82 (5.92 per cent), remained unchanged for 720 (52.44 per cent) and were reduced for 571 (41.59 per cent). The procedure of price adjustment is scheduled to be repeated after six months, which will lead to additional cuts in the prices of individual drugs.

Customs duty on drugs, governed by the Regulations on customs duty, was in 2002 cut from 9.6 to 4.3 per cent for countries outside the European Union or to 2.6 per cent for member countries of the European Union (*Official Gazette* 113/01).

Reimbursement

Pharmacists collect part payment from the patient and seek reimbursement of the remainder of their entitlement from the HZZO. The total payment to pharmacists is the drug cost plus a service fee that is determined by a points system. The service fee is negotiated with the HZZO. There are no constraints on the charges that apply for other products (including private prescriptions) sold by pharmacies. For private prescriptions and drugs without a prescription, a mark-up of about 35 per cent applies.

To collect their payment from the HZZO, pharmacists need to complete claim forms, which are lodged weekly. The payments to pharmacists from the HZZO usually take around 180 days to process. As pharmacists are unable to sustain the cash flow associated with carrying this debt, wholesalers are often asked to bear the burden of this delay in payment.

The governing body of the HZZO has established a special fund for: drugs for the treatment of chronic diseases such as AIDS, haemophilia, Gaucher's disease, multiple sclerosis and leukaemia; Paklitaksel and Cisplatin for the treatment of ovarian cancer; and drugs needed for heart, kidney, liver, lung, bone marrow and corneal transplant procedures. Twenty-five per cent of the expenses accrued in the treatment of these conditions are paid by hospitals themselves and 75 per cent is covered by a special fund. These arrangements have been in force since 1 May 2002.

Healthcare Reform Project, July 2000

A major new health reform project was approved by the Croatian parliament in July 2000. Overseen by the Ministry of Health, and supported by various international organizations, the project has the following major objectives: to prolong life expectancy, to improve health-related quality of life, and to reduce inequalities in health and access to healthcare.

These objectives are to be achieved through the following areas of reform:

- restriction of health expenditure growth and establishment of financial stability;

- improved healthcare planning and management;

- reorganization of the system of health service financing and payment;

- improvement in the efficiency and quality of health services;

- strengthening preventive and primary care.

The reform process will maintain the principle of universal access to healthcare, funded principally through the National Insurance scheme. People will be able to take out supplementary private health insurance to cover areas not included under the NI scheme. Healthcare services will be provided through a mixture of public and private facilities, subject to government capacity planning. This will aim to provide equal access to services and avoid unnecessary duplication of services.

A number of measures have been made a priority, and have already been undertaken or begun:

- increased funding for the Croatian Institute for Health Insurance (HZZO);

- revision of the NI-funded drug formulary list;

- starting the World Bank-supported project 'New Direction of Health Policy' (see below);

- reorganization of the blood transfusion system.

Following these, a number of reform projects will be undertaken in a wide variety of areas:

- institutional reform;

- promotion of healthcare structural organization (World Bank-assisted);

- reorganization of the healthcare financing system;

- definition of a basic package of services;

- improvement of the healthcare reimbursement system;

- provider capacity planning;

- state hospital reform;

- introduction of clinical guidelines;

- improvement of preventive healthcare services;

- national drug policy project;

- health information system project;

- strengthening of international cooperation;

- increasing awareness of human rights and ethics in the healthcare system;

- research and development;

- policy of professional development in medicine and health system reform.

Distribution channels

Wholesalers must hold a licence, issued by the Ministry of Health, in order to distribute and sell both domestically produced and imported medicines. There are 115 registered drug distributors in Croatia. The largest, Medika, Oktal Farma and Farmacija make up 82 per cent, while the eight largest make up as much as 90 per cent of the market. Other smaller distributors specialize in particular areas such as orthopaedic aids, diagnostic equipment, veterinary medicine, dental medicine or only one or two products. Around six distributors cover the whole range of products on the pharmaceutical market. By law all distributors must purchase products from a local producer directly, and trading among themselves is forbidden.

The pharmaceutical market

The Croatian market for pharmaceuticals is estimated at US$415 million in 2003, equal to US$92 per capita. After a period of accelerated growth (up to 15 per cent annually) a growth rate of around 6 per cent is expected in the next five years. The market is dominated by two local producers (Pliva and Belupo), which together hold around 43 per cent of the market (see Table 2.3.1). Krka and Lek are Slovenia-based companies that cover around 13 per cent of the market. Their long presence in the market is the reason for their success. All major pharmaceutical companies are present in the market; MSD holds the largest share at 4.5 per cent of the market.

Table 2.3.1 Top five pharmaceutical companies

	Rank	Sale HRK 2002	Market Share %
MARKET		**3,132,107,091**	
Pliva	1	891,108,623	28.45
Belupo	2	468,214,548	14.95
Krka	3	209,458,764	6.69
Lek	4	182,677,251	5.83
Merch Sharp & Dohme	5	140,688,744	4.49

Source: MIS

Around 30 million prescriptions are written each year, equal to seven per insured person. The market is dominated by brand generics. The leading therapeutic group in terms of prescription sales is the C (cardiovascular) ATC group, with sales of nearly US$100 million in 2002.

Other leading therapeutic areas include J (anti-infectives) and A (gastrointestinal and endocrinological drugs), with sales of around US$50 million, and US$45 million respectively.

Market structure

The majority of pharmaceutical companies sell their products exclusively through distributors, apart from Belupo which sells 50 per cent of its products directly. The pharmacy segment of the industry is larger, although distribution through hospitals is also on the rise in terms of value due to the use of more expensive items such as citostatic drugs.

The OTC (over-the-counter) market

The size of the OTC market is around HRK48 million a year, with around 78 per cent made up by Rx (prescription) drugs, and 22 per cent by OTC. The OTC market growth rate is around 14 per cent.

OTC trends

Pharmaceutical companies have realized the advantages of OTC drugs: first, there is the importance of word of mouth recommendations among consumers, not just prescriptions from a doctor. Secondly, they are paid immediately. The distribution and sale of OTC drugs through consumer channels is gaining in importance, and consequently all OTC companies are intensifying their marketing activities. 'Lifestyle' preparations are also becoming increasingly important:

- vitamins and minerals;
- giving up smoking;
- hair loss;
- 'emergency' contraceptives.

Rx trends

The market is on the rise in terms of value rather than volume. There is an evident switch to more expensive, modern drugs. The highest growth rates are achieved in products connected with the ageing of the population (drugs for the treatment of cardiovascular, musculoskeletal and nervous diseases) and the CNS group.

The main domestic producers

Belupo
Belupo is the second biggest producer of drugs in the Republic of Croatia, and is wholly owned by Podravka d.d. It develops and produces human

pharmaceuticals, herbal medicinal products and dental preparations. Other Belupo products include disinfectants for skin, surfaces and instruments, as well as cosmetic and hygienic products. Belupo has three product lines:

1. Prescription drugs for:

   - the digestive system;

   - the cardio-vascular system;

   - the skin;

   - the genito-urinary system;

   - treating infections;

   - the musculoskeletal system;

   - the nervous system.

2. Over-the-counter drugs:

   - herbal products;

   - dietary products.

3. Cosmetic products.

Belupo has cooperation agreements with a number of business partners – Merck Sharp & Dohme, Solvay Pharmaceuticals, Hoffmann-La Roche, GlaxoSmithKline and Janssen Pharmaceutics. Belupo's principal export markets are Slovenia, Bosnia, Macedonia, the Czech Republic, Slovakia, Russia and other countries of the former Soviet Union. The company operates a network of representative offices in Moscow, Bratislava, Prague, Skopje and Sarajevo, as well as its Slovenian subsidiary in Ljubljana. Belupo is not listed on the stock exchange, but it is expected that the public offering of Belupo shares and the listing of Belupo d.d. in Quotation I of the Zagreb Stock Exchange will take place during 2003.

Pliva
Pliva is the largest pharmaceutical company in Croatia and the largest in Central and Eastern Europe (see Table 2.3.2). Pliva became a joint stock company in 1993 and was listed on the London Stock Exchange in 1996. The company manufactures and supplies a wide range of prescription and OTC pharmaceutical products. The company has concentrated on its core business and sold its foodstuff and cosmetic businesses in 2001 and 2002.

The main event in 2002 was the acquisition of the American pharmaceutical company Sidmak. With that acquisition, Pliva gained entry into the world's largest pharmaceutical market. In 2002, Sidmak launched

Table 2.3.2 Pliva vs peer group companies (in US$ million, 2002)

	Country	Mkt Cap	Freefloat	Revenues	Net profit
Gedeon Richter	Hungary	1,216	875	431	122.4
Pliva	Croatia	1,208	812	892	175.7
Krka	Slovenia	672	531	407	50.8
EGIS	Hungary	253	124	240	28.9
Polfa Kutno	Poland	78	20	52	5.7
Jelfa	Poland	71	49	61	6.3
Slovakofarma	Slovakia	62	24	125	6.1
Terapia	Romania	40	13	32	7.2
Sicomed	Romania	23	5	39	4.8

Source: Bram Buring, Raiffeisen Centrobank

a range of new generic and speciality products: Ethosux-imide, Fluoxe-tine, Tramadol, Vitamin D and VoSpire ER (albuterol sulphate).

Pliva has expanded in Western Europe, primarily by acquisitions. AWD is Pliva's largest acquisition in Western Europe, acquired in 2001. The company is focused on the development, manufacture and distribution of generic products in Germany and the CEE. AWD's leading products in Germany are Katadolon (flupiritine), Quadropril (spirapril), Cordanum (talinolol) and Corinfar (nifedipine). The other Pliva companies in Western Europe are Pliva Pharma Ltd and 2K Pharmaceuticals. Pliva Pharma is a UK-based company, while 2K Pharmaceutical is a Danish company with a subsidiary in Scandinavia.

Pliva's first acquisition was made in 1997 when it bought Polfa Krakow, one of the biggest Polish companies. Lachema, from the Czech republic, was the second acquisition in the CEE markets. Through these acquisitions Pliva has transformed from a regional to a global pharmaceutical company.

In 2002, Pliva posted a net profit of HRK1,263 billion on revenues of HRK6,143 billion, a rise of 22 per cent in local terms and of 30 per cent in US dollar terms. Prescription drugs (Rx) and bulk azithromycin were the main growth drivers. Rx sales rose 49 per cent (plus 58 per cent in US dollar terms) year-on-year after the consolidation of Sidmak and AWD. Royalty revenues fell by 8 per cent in 2002 to HRK1,104 billion (flat in US dollar terms). New markets and new drugs were responsible for top-line growth in prescription drugs in 2002. Sales in Western Europe and the USA added HRK975 million to the top line, or 85 per cent of the 2002 increase in absolute terms. All of this is essentially from AWD (Germany) and Sidmak (US). Five of Pliva's top 10 drugs are now from the AWD or Sidmak portfolios and appear to be the main sales drivers. Bulk azithromycin sale to Pfizer was the other main performer in 2002. In percentage terms azithromycin sales in 2002 rose 28 per cent in HRK and 36 per cent in US dollar terms.

Research and development

Among a range of generics in different stages of development, Pliva obtained first marketing authorization (MA) approval for carvedilol in Croatia and for citalopram and simvastatin in Germany. Furthermore, Pliva obtained additional MA approvals for five molecules (carbamazepine, clomipramin and isoniazid in two CEE countries and fluconasol and torasemid in one Western European country). Thirteen molecules were submitted for registration in three CEE countries and four molecules in three Western European countries, representing 48 products. Overall, there are currently 361 MA approvals pending in six CEE countries, 149 in six Western European countries and 10 ANDAs (Abbreviated New Drug Application) in the USA. Three new chemical entities (NCEs) are currently advancing through clinical studies, and an additional one has been selected as a new candidate for clinical trials (see Table 2.3.3). Several NCEs are advancing through different stages of discovery/pre-clinical trials.

Table 2.3.3 Status of the most advanced NCE projects

NCE project	Indication	Status
PLD-116	Peptide drug for treatment of inflammatory bowel disease (IBD)	Undergoing Phase II
PLD-117	Thrombocytopenia (TPO) agonist	Phase I completed
PLD-118	Novel oral antifungal	First Phase II completed
PLD-147	Novel oral cytostatic agent	Phase I to start in H2 2003

Source: Pliva

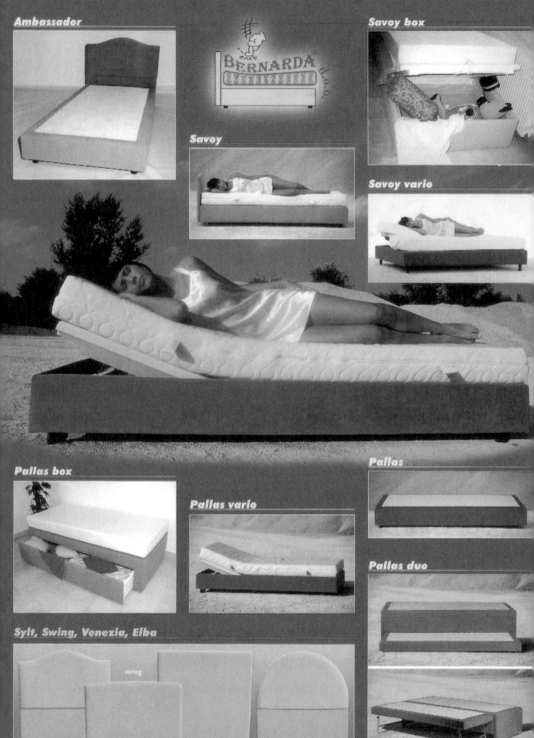

Ambassador

Savoy box

Savoy

Savoy vario

BERNARDA d.o.o.

Pallas box

Pallas vario

Pallas

Pallas duo

Sylt, Swing, Venezia, Elba

swing

sylt

venezia

elba

...utura Medico

DEKORATIVNA TKANINA
PAMUK / VUNA 500 g/m²
KAŠMIR 400 g/m²
OŽEPIČASTA JEZGRA 5-zona Ø 1,6 - 1,8 mm
SPUŽVA RG 28 (10x5 cm)
LATEX 30 mm

...enera

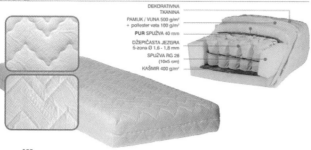

DEKORATIVNA TKANINA
PAMUK / VUNA 500 g/m² + polïester vata 100 g/m²
PUR SPUŽVA 40 mm
DŽEPIČASTA JEZGRA 5-zona Ø 1,6 - 1,8 mm
SPUŽVA RG 28 (10x5 cm)
KAŠMIR 400 g/m²

...rtosilk

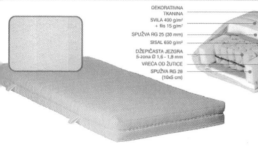

DEKORATIVNA TKANINA
SVILA 400 g/m² + flis 15 g/m²
SPUŽVA RG 25 (30 mm)
SISAL 650 g/m²
DŽEPIČASTA JEZGRA 5-zona Ø 1,6 - 1,8 mm
VREĆA OD ŽUTICE
SPUŽVA RG 28 (10x5 cm)

Madraci / Karakteristike	Elegant Specijal	Elegant	Kompakta (BS)	Stabila (BS)	Perfekta	Perfekta V	Rubin	Superlux	Siesta	Prima	Safir	Stela	Palma	Luxima TFK	Futura Medico	Venera	Ortosilk
...eto - Zima	X	X	O	O	O	O	O	✓	✓	O	✓	✓	O	✓	✓	✓	X
...tibakterijski	O	O	O	O	O	O	O	O	O	O	O	O	O	O	O	O	O
...agorivo	O	O	O	O	O	O	O	O	O	O	O	O	O	O	O	O	O
...žina (kg)	do 80	do 80	do 80	80 do 110	više od 110	80 do 110	80 do 110	više od 50	više od 50	do 80	do 80	do 80	80 do 110	više od 50	više od 50	više od 50	više od 50
...edicinski	X	X	X	X	X	X	X	✓	✓	X	X	X	X	✓	✓	✓	✓

✓ da   X ne   O opcija

BERNARDA d.o.o.

Čakovečka 136 A, Puščine, 40305 Nedelišće
Centrala: 040 **895 300** Fax: 040 **895 333**
http://www.bernarda.hr/
e-mail: bernarda@ck.hinet.hr

...a proizvodnju namještaja, trgovinu i posredovanje u trgovini

Kutna garnitura "Boris"

Kutna garnitura "Boris" je namijenjena manjim stambenim prostorima gdje se dnevna soba uvečer pretvara u spavaču. Kutna garnitura (slika 1) može se vrlo jednostavno modificirati u bračni krevet koji nudi visoku kvalitetu spavanja (slike 2, 3, 4).

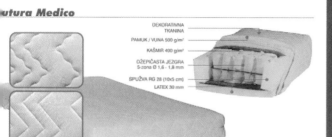

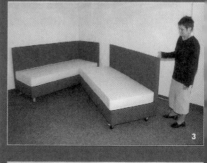

Garnitura se može izraditi u svim dimenzijama i sastoji se od kreveta SAVOY, triju stranica VENEZIA i madraca po izboru.

2.4

Croatian Textile, Knitting and Garment Industry

Mirjana Gambiroza-Jukic, Croatian Chamber of Commerce Industrial Sector, Zagreb

Introduction

The textile, knitting and garment industry of Croatia is characterized by lower business activities (fewer companies surviving in the market, a smaller number of employees and gross income somewhere above HRK4 billion, while the foreign trade balance is negative for the first time since 1991). The main reason for the situation is the fact that the industry is undergoing technological and organizational restructuring. The efforts of the employees and management in this branch of industry are aimed at higher productivity and reduced production costs, as well as selecting profitable programmes.

The manufacturing of textiles and clothing in Croatia has traditionally been open to international cooperation and trade, as it has developed under the principles of quality production processes and competitiveness in both price and costs. The technological and expert potential of the employees within the textile and clothing industry has won the industry a leading position on the European market thanks to its ability to quickly adapt the manufacturing process to new fashion trends. For this reason the Croatian textile industry has long been a recognized partner to European and international customers.

The main characteristics of the textile and clothing industry are:

- representation of various processes in manufacturing of textiles and clothing;

- large dispersion of factories in almost all Croatian counties;

- labour-intensiveness;

Chairman of the Varteks Board

Mr. Miljenko Vidacek BSEcon

1. Could you explain Vartek's main line of business?
Varteks d.d. Varazdin owner of the Varteks brands is one of the best know producers of woolen fabrics and has manufactured under the woolmark license for over 30 years. We are known for high quality ready-made garments sold under our own developing trademarks: Di Caprio, Edora, Varteks International and Focus. We also have the licence agreement to Levi Strauss company.

Annual production shows our size: Yarn: approx. 400 tones

Fabric: approx. 1.700,000 mtrs

Clothing: 1.400.000 uts (Levi's excluded)

We produce both fabrics and clothing for the domestic and Western European market. Even GB known as the cradle of textile production with its demand of high quality woollen products does not produce as much.

To keep the business market orientated, we constantly develop our range to include:

- wool fabrics and blends with silk, linen, viscose, lycra and polyester
- men's clothing: suits, jackets, trousers, overcoats, raincoats
- ladies' wear: costumes, jackets, skirts, trousers, overcoats, raincoats, blouses
- sportswear: jackets, trousers for both sexes
- jeanswear

2. How large is the whole enterprise? How many production plants do you have, where are they and how many employees do you have?
The Head Office was established in 1918. It has one operation for fabric production (400 workers) and 3 ready-to-wear garments production, a printing factory, transportation facilities and offices. Also there are 4 ready-to-wear garments productions located outside of Varazdin but within the same county. The core business is fabrics and rtw garments. All together, there are 4,258 people employed including the retail operations all over Croatia (80 shops, 9 department stores). Internationally we have 19 outlets in Bosnia and Herzegovina, 2 in Macedonia, 9 in Slovenia, 5 in Montenegro and 29 in Serbia. It is interesting to know that the premises in Serbia were taken away at the beginning of the war in 1990 though we now have control of them today. Though the financial damage of this loss cost us approx 11 million Euros; indirect loss is valued to be approx. 70 million Euros.

3. Please give a brief historical account of the company development. If it was founded as a government enterprise and then privatised, you may like to comment on how it was managed when owned by the government compared to how it became privatised and run by private entrepreneurs.

The largest Croatian textile manufacturing company was founded in late 1918 bearing the name Tekstilna tvornica Varazdin (Textile Industries Varazdin) as a share holding company. The main constituent assembly was held on October 23 that year on the site of the former cotton and linen manufacturing plant. The founding of the company was the crowning event in the long tradition of textile manufacturing in the region according to the oldest written records, present in Varazdin as early as the 15th century. The dominating area of production throughout history has been that of goods made of cotton, silk and linen. Business commenced on November 29 1922 with the manufacture of woollen yarns and fabrics. The largest shareholder was from Brno resulting in much of the second-hand machinery and equipment being imported from Czech factories. Good business acumen coupled with the initial capital meant the business had quadrupled in 13 years and in 1926 this spurred the owners to start the manufacture of ready-to-wear garments so by 1929 the retail network was beginning to develop. Up to 1948, the company bore the name Tekstilna industrija d.d. Varazdin or Tivar for short, which changed to Varteks (Varazdinska tekstilna industrija) under which it grew into the country's largest textile manufacturing and exporting company. The 1960s were marked by intensive development in manufacturing and retail capacities. Several new plants were built to accommodate the manufacture of woollen fabrics and ready-to-wear garments. In addition, power stations, a computer centre plus a number of new retail stores were built. In this period, Varteks entered a competitive world market where it has remained to figure for more than 40 years.

Today, the company is a completely integrated operation, focusing on yarn and fabric manufacturing, ready-to-wear garments and marketing through its own network of department and retail stores, as well as its own international companies.

The 85-year development of Varteks is a living example of a long lasting tradition of textile manufacturing in this region that has trained numerous skilled craftsmen whose work has influenced top-quality products that fulfill the needs of millions of domestic and foreign buyers.

4. Market share and your competitors: What is your market share for your product and who are your main competitors? Do you operate only in Croatia or in much of the former Yugoslavia and beyond? What are your company's strengths and weakness vis a vis foreign competition? Would

Croatia's membership of the EU be of benefit for your company?
Our company's strengths are the Licence Agreement with the International Wool
Secretariat and from 2001 Varteks is the owner of ISO 9001 quality Certificate.
Ex Yugoslavian "situation" has been covered in point **2.**, and the other in point **3.**
Regarding the European market, we have our representative offices to "cover" the
concerned territories:

- Varteks Trade d.o.o., Ljubljana, Slovenia
- Malved d.o.o., Maribor, Slovenia
- Varteks Mont V.R., Podgorica, Montenegro
- Varteks Trgovina d.o.o., Siroki Brijeg, Bosnia and Herzegovina
- Varteks d.o.o. E.L., Skopje, Macedonia
- Varteks Plus d.o.o., Belgrade, Serbia
- Varteks Textiles, London, GB
- Burgtrade, Eisenstadt, Austria
- Vartimpeks Italia, Firenze, Italy

**5. Basic financial and legal status: What is your annual turnover? What is
the legal status of your company (i.e. private closed joint stock company,
etc?) What do you understand by the term corporate governance and how
is it applied at your company (if at all)? Do you employ international
accounting standards?**
Varteks is a share holding company. Shares are divided as follows (dd. 30.09.2002):

Small shareholders	34,6%
Privatization Investment Funds	32,6%
Financial institutions (of other kinds)	3,5%
Cro Privatization Fund	7,6%
Vault shares	21,7%

6. What is your strategic vision for Varteks d.d. in the future.

The management has devised firm guidelines for future
growth and development. Investment in modern
technology and the company's own sales facilities, full
computerisation of the entire operation, continual
training and care for every employee will optimize
success.

We aim to improve the style of fashion in this country
through well thought – out and designed collections
presented in aesthetically attractive retail stores that
will sway even the most demanding buyer. Detailed
market research on the needs and desires of buyers are a prerequisite for
determining the sales of Varteks products in a highly demanding foreign market.
From a traditional garment industry that has been manufacturing and retailing

clothes intended for a large segment of consumers, Varteks is growing into a top fashion design company that can successfully sell its products under its own name (Di Caprio, Edora, Focus, Varteks International) in both the domestic and international arena. Varteks enters the 21st century firmly rooted in tradition and expertise that is striving to become a strong successful market leader.

7. Do you feel that the government of Croatia has created an adequate business environment in which your company can operate? Are the laws of business clear? What, if any, are the main problems for your firm while doing business in Croatia?

With its 4200 employees, Varteks' employs 14% of the county's workforce. Regarding our county export, it "occupies" 19% in total while 62% in textiles and garments export.

Varteks employs 11% of textile workers in Croatia that produce over 70% of total wool fabrics and exports more that 9 per cent of total textiles.

If we track the percentage several years back, it becomes obvious that they are

increasing in our (Varteks) favour. This reflects our good planning but unfortunately it also shows the (macroeconomic) frame inside of which we operate: during a certain period of time, we were "foreign currency bringers" but in 2001 we were (on state level, of course) importing more (612.000.000 US$) than exporting (575.000.000 US$). Two years earlier, export valued 600.000.000 US$ and import 360.000.000 US$.

Therefore it is more than obvious that all doors were opened to each and every competitor to enter Croatia. One of the reasons is the healthy rate of exchange to the importing companies.

8. What are the main benefits for operating an enterprise of your type in the Republic of Croatia in general and in Varazdin in particular?

Running the textile industry is not a matter of being privileged but it is ultimately about taking care of the existence of the workforce in an area where it is possible to combine tradition in textile production with the standards of high quality merchandise.

- pronounced export orientation;

- manufacturing organized through small, medium and large companies;

- openness to international cooperation;

- readiness to quickly adopt fashion demands;

- respect for deadlines for delivery of goods;

- high quality of work and in many cases design of finished textile products and ready-to-wear clothing.

Today, the primary production of textiles covers the following activities:

- preparation and spinning of textile fibres;

- manufacture of fabrics;

- dressing of textiles;

- manufacture of finished textile products (except fashion clothing) and other textile products;

- manufacture of knitted and embroidered fabrics and products.

The clothing industry consists of the manufacture of leather clothing, other clothing and fashion wear, and dressing and dyeing of furs and fur products.

Within the Croatian textile and clothing industry there are 33,246 employees. This represents 3.21 per cent of the total number of employees in the Republic of Croatia or 13.99 per cent of the total number of employees within the manufacturing and mining industries.

Exports of Croatian textile and clothing industry accounts for 12.10 per cent of total exports. During 2001 the export surplus amounted to US$37.3 million for this branch of the economy, one-eighth of the total for 1999. Exports are mainly covered through sub-contracting work, which occupies 80 to 95 per cent of production capacities. Full exports, ie exports of goods of Croatian origin, are realized through the manufacture of clothing, especially men's suits for the UK, Italian, Slovenian and Bosnia and Herzegovinian markets, and women's clothing for the Slovenian, Czech Republic and Bosnia and Herzegovinian markets. Knitted goods are exported to Germany, Austria and Slovenia, and yarns and fabrics are exported mainly to the Italian, German and Bosnia and Herzegovinian markets.

The textile industry holds a 4.5 per cent share of the total manufacturing revenue of Croatia, with primary textile production representing 34.18 per cent of that amount and the manufacturing of fashion apparel and dressing and dying of furs representing the remainder.

Restructuring

Today the Croatian textile and clothing industry finds itself in a restructuring phase, which is being carried out in two ways. These are: finding a majority owner through the sale of shares on the stock market and through the voucher privatization scheme; and through increasing labour productivity and lowering costs by selecting profitable programmes. In the majority of cases factory managers are being successful. Most of the time this means accepting new technology, which is the key method in modernizing manufacturing processes, which in turn improves the quality of products and services.

The primary textile industry sector is acquiring new weaving machines, which will improve the quality of fabrics and allow a smaller production run of fabrics manufactured to the particular design requirements of customers. In the clothing industry sector, depending on the financial strength of each factory, automated tailoring machines are purchased as well as new ironing equipment so that new fabrics (a mixture of various fibres) can be fashioned to suit market trends.

In general, investment in the textile and clothing industry is primarily in technology equipment (70 to 90 per cent), while the construction of new facilities accounts for up to 31 per cent. The clothing industry makes significantly higher investments because it employs more people, and investment per employee is much lower than in the primary industry.

Top 10 companies

There are a total of 688 textile companies registered in Croatia. The top 219 companies account for 91 per cent of total revenue in the whole industry, and they employ 88.5 per cent of the workforce. Most (286) of the remaining 469 companies employ up to five workers each.

The top 10 companies earn 45.82 per cent of the sector revenue, or 15.66 per cent of the total industry (see Table 2.4.1). Similarly, the top 10 fashion clothing industry companies earn 34.48 per cent of total textile and clothing industry revenue, which is 52.38 per cent of fashion wear and fur industry revenue (see Table 2.4.2).

Fairs and exhibitions

The textile and clothing industry traditionally participates in the Zagreb Fair's 'Intertextile' annual event. Also, Croatian textile and clothing manufacturers take part in specialized fairs and exhibitions throughout Europe. Members of the primary textile industries group, TKZ Zagreb, Kelteks Karlovac, Cateks Cakovec and Pamucna Industrija Duga Resa exhibited successfully at Heimtextil in Frankfurt in January 2003. Four companies will attend the Heimtextil in Frankfurt scheduled for April

Table 2.4.1 The top 10 textile and apparel manufacturers according to total revenue in 2001

Company	Production programme
DN-17 Production of textiles	
Cateks d.d., Cakovec	artificial leather mixed fabrics – linens, bed and table fabrics, kitchen cloth
Pazinka d.d., Pazin	cotton fabrics, bed fabrics
TKZ d.d., Zagreb	cotton damask, bed and table fabrics and fabrics used for special purposes: military assortment
Pamucna ind. Duga Resa	cotton damask, bed and table fabrics and fabrics for military cloth, ladies' and men's underwear and nightwear
Lola Ribar d.d., Karlovac	sterile surgical gauze sterile gauze compresses various types of bandages hygienic and cosmetic cotton wool elastic woven and elastic knitted bandages
Regeneracija d.d., Zabok	felt (of wool or fine animal hair or of other textile materials) wadding PES geotextiles and technical textiles other clothing accessories
Jadran d.d., Zagreb	fine ankle socks, knee socks, stockings with Lycra, patterned pantyhose with cotton gussets, men's socks and children's socks
MTC, Tv. carapa d.d., Cakovec	thread for embroidery
Unitas d.d., Zagreb	sewing thread and thread for embroidery
Dalmatinka d.d., Sinj	
DB-18 Production of apparel	
Varteks d.d., Varazdin	ladies' wear (jackets, skirts and trouser suits) overcoats, mackintoshes men's clothes, suits, trench coats, trousers woollen fabrics and mixed fabrics
Benetton Croatia, d.o.o., Osijek	ladies' and men's knitwear and cloth
Kamensko d.d., Zagreb	ladies' and men's apparel
Heruc – Izrada odjece d.d., Zagreb	ladies' and men's apparel

Table 2.4.1 (cont'd)

MTC d.d., Cakovec	haberdashery knitted fabrics
Galeb d.d., Omis	ladies' and men's underwear
Betex d.o.o., Belica	protective garment and shoes
Kotka d.d., Krapina	men's cloth
MTC, tv. rublja d.d., Cakovec	briefs, boxer shorts, pyjamas, nightgowns, housecoats, swimwear
VIS Konfekcija d.d., Varazdin	ladies' garments

2003: Regeneracija Zabok, Cateks Cakovec, Kontex Karlovac and TKZ Zagreb.

Professional association within the CCE

The Association of Textile and Clothing Industry Manufacturers is organized through the Industry and Technology Department of the Croatian Chamber of Economy (CCE).

Useful industry contacts

Croatian Chamber of Economy
Industry and Technology Department
Managing Director: Miljenko Babic, BSc Mech
Contact Person: Dr Mirjana Jukic-Gambiroza, PhD
Draskoviceva 45, 4th Floor
HR-10 000 Zagreb, Croatia
PO Box 630
Tel: +385 (0)1 46 06 755
Fax: +385 (0)1 46 06 737
Email: industrija@hgk.hr

Croatian Chamber of Economy
Headquarters
Rooseveltov trg 2
HR-10 000 Zagreb, Croatia
PO Box 630
Tel: +385 (0)1 45 61 555
Fax: +385 (0)1 48 28 380
Email: hgk@hgk.hr
Web site: www.hgk.hr, www.biznet.hr

Table 2.4.2 Textile production

Production Main indicators for the total volume of industrial production of textiles, fashion apparel and dressing and dyeing of furs

Production of selected industrial products by sections and divisions of NCEA

17. Manufacture of textiles

		1995	1996	1997	1998	1999	2000	2001	2002
Hemp fibre	t	361	127	0	0	0	0	0	0
Cotton yarn	t	8,867	5,276	5,415	5,088	3,946	4,238	4,919	4,126
Wool yarn	t	3,333	2,490	676	468	411	375	257	220
Hemp yarn	t	99	68	0	0	0	0	0	0
Rope, cord and straps	t	272	316	364	406	398	370	384	324
Sewing thread	t	1,343	1,088	1,117	1,056	857	743	616	622
Cotton fabric and blankets	m² (1,000)	22,200	18,941	15,797	16,749	13,179	13,873	14,059	13,914
Wool fabrics and blankets	m² (1,000)	6,678	4,809	6,915	6,550	4,018	4,155	3,583	3,645
Knitted fabrics except jerseys	t	3,373	3,053	2,981	3,064	2,595	2,513	2,749	4,829
Socks	'000 pairs	20,262	21,876	21,851	21,191	18,818	18,172	21,371	22,032
Haberdashery	t	462	326	67	94	66	75	71	57
Household linen	'000 m²	9,161	7,758	7,677	8,088	6,928	7,229	6,506	6,272

18. Manufacture of apparel; dressing and dyeing of fur

		1995	1996	1997	1998	1999	2000	2001	2002
Manufacture of knitted underwear	t	2,493	2,753	1,216	1,520	1,467	1,239	1,191	1,226
Manufacture of knitted clothing	t	997	689	580	510	581	559	684	1,187
Manufacture of linens	m² (1,000)	7,017	6,722	7,802	7,123	5,940	5,945	6,038	5,784
Ready-to-wear clothing	m² (1,000)	32,353	28,597	26,643	26,640	24,740	24,397	24,468	19,508
Leather clothing	m² (1,000)	176	246	306	286	203	187	0	214
Ready-to-wear plastic clothing	m² (1,000)	98	60	0	0	0	0	0	0

Source: CBS, processed by Croatian Chamber of Economy

Table 2.4.2 (cont'd)

Foreign trade and employment statistics

	1995	1996	1997	1998	1999	2000	2001	2002
Total revenues, in HRK	–	4,584,924	5,011,049	4,275,974	4,284,578	4,038,979	4,689,360	–
Imports (1,000 US$)	463,421	472,608	472,063	442,889	369,556	522,257	612,343	
615,883								
Exports (1,000 US$)	785,103	732,126	717,214	642,568	608,060	548,811	575,043	
592,953								
Total no. of employees	55,700	50,400	45,300	44,500	40,600	39,200	37,600	33,246

Source: CBS, processed by Croatian Chamber of Economy

Indices of industrial production and employment by divisions of NCEA
1995 = 100

Sub-section	Production (index)							Employment (index)
	1996	1997	1998	1999	2000	2001	2002	
DB 17 Manufacture of textiles	82	92.9	96	84.8	86.2	94.3	96	
DB 18 Manufacture of fashion apparel; dressing and dyeing of fur	91	90.1	89	81	79.5	80.3	69.38	
DB total	90.5	81.3	79.9	72.9	66.7	59.69		
Manufacturing industry		101.3	105.2	108.6	105.5	108.6	115.6	115

Source: CBS, processed by Croatian Chamber of Economy

Table 2.4.2 (cont'd)

Total investment by branch

Activity	Total Investment by year (in 1000 HRK)					
	1996	1997	1998	1999	2000	2001
Textile and apparel industry (DB)	121,324	83,354	124,446	152,120	142,600	91,724
Primary textile industry (DB17)	21,672	27,138	16,522	53,823	27,943	215,875
Apparel industry (DB18)	99,652	56,216	107,924	98,297	114,657	307,599

Source: CBS, processed by Croatian Chamber of Economy

Total revenue in 2001 according to size of business entity

Division of business entities according to the Law on Accountancy (NN 90/92)	Total revenue of the textile and clothing industry in HRK	Share of total industry revenue as percentage
Small	910,209,011	19,41
Medium	978,114,628	20,86
Large	2,801,036,655	59,73

Source: CBS, processed by Croatian Chamber of Economy

Table 2.4.2 (cont'd)

Number of employees in the textile businesses that submitted a financial statement for 2001

Number of employees	Total number of textile industry companies (688) Number of people in the top 219 companies according to total revenue (HRK2 million or more)	Number of people in the remaining 469 companies according to total revenue
0		60
1–5		286
5–20		103
20–50		18
75		2
Less than 50	107	
50–100	41	
100–500	52	
500–1,000	15	
1,000 or more	4	

Table 2.4.2 (cont'd)

The top 10 textile and apparel manufacturers according to total revenue in 2001

Production of textiles company	Production of apparel company
1. Cateks d.d., Cakovec	1. Varteks d.d., Varazdin
2. Pazinka d.d., Pazin	2. Benetton Croatia d.o.o., Osijek
3. TKZ d.d., Zagreb	3. Kamensko d.d., Zagreb
4. Pamucna industrija Duga Resa	4. Heruc – Izrada odjece d.d., Zagreb
5. Lola Ribar d.d., Karlovac	5. MTC d.d., Cakovec
6. Regeneracija d.d., Zabok	6. Galeb d.d., Omiš
7. Jadran d.d., Zagreb	7. Betex d.o.o., Belica
8. MTC Tvornica carapa d.d., Cakovec	8. Kotka d.d., Krapina
9. Unitas d.d., Zagreb	9. MTC Tvornica rublja d.d., Cakovec
10. Dalmatinka d.d., Sinj	10. VIS konfekcija d.d., Varazdin

Source: Payment Transfer Agency, Zagreb

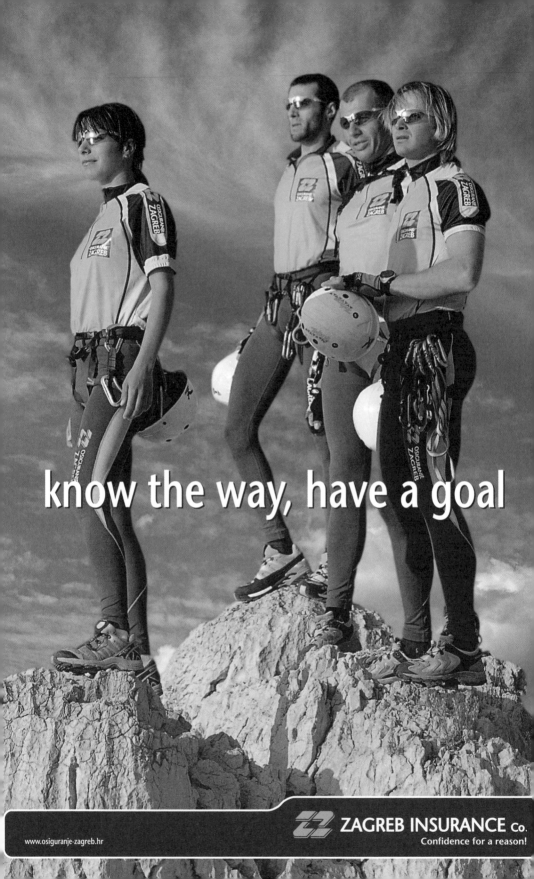

know the way, have a goal

ZAGREB INSURANCE Co.
Confidence for a reason!

www.osiguranje-zagreb.hr

Osiguranje Zagreb Team

know the way, have a goal

It takes strength and wisdom to live a good life. The best and the widest insurance program in Croatia offers you an opportunity to get your privilege, to live your life free from care. Be relaxed, feel safe. **Your way and your goal.**

2.5

The Croatian Insurance Industry

Ms Petra Tarle, LLB, President of the Management Board, Zagreb Insurance Company Ltd

Introduction

The insurance market in Croatia is considered to be relatively undeveloped. However, economic indicators in this segment herald significant growth. In 2002, growth in life insurance premiums was over 20 per cent. Five insurance companies together hold over 70 per cent of the life insurance market. The growth in life insurance was contributed to by tax benefits on life insurance introduced in mid-2001. Non-life insurance had far smaller growth in 2002 – only 6.6 per cent. Moreover, in early 2003 some non-life insurance products were additionally taxed, and it is necessary to wait and see what impact the new taxes will have on this segment of insurance in Croatia.

Despite the relatively small market of a total of 4.5 million inhabitants, in Croatia there are 23 insurance companies and one reinsurance company. The greatest share of the insurance market overall continues to belong to Croatia Insurance, the only insurance company that is primarily in Government ownership. In Croatia, in addition to insurance companies, there are insurance agencies, individual agents and brokers for insurance and reinsurance.

A permit for a company to function as an insurance company is issued by the Insurance Companies Supervisory Authority, which also supervises insurance company operations.

The Croatian Insurance Bureau plays an important role. It is in charge of green cards, conducts the Guarantee Fund for the Processing and Settlement of Claims for Damage Caused by Unknown and Uninsured Motor Vehicles, and represents Croatian insurance in the European Insurance Committee, as an associate member.

The Croatian Nuclear Pool insures Croatian interests in the Krsko Nuclear Power Plant located in Slovenia, in the immediate vicinity of the Slovenian border with Croatia.

Insurance companies

The legal framework that regulates the establishment, operations and termination of insurance companies is stipulated by the Insurance Act (*Narodne novine* (Official Gazette of the Republic of Croatia), Nos 46/97, edited text, 116/99 and 11/2002).

According to the amendments to the Insurance Act since 1999, it is no longer permitted to establish insurance companies that are engaged in both life and non-life insurance (composite insurance companies). Insurance companies established after these amendments are permitted to be engaged in life insurance, or non-life insurance, or reinsurance. However, insurance companies that were already engaged in both types of insurance when this amendment came into force are permitted to continue. Those insurance companies which also performed reinsurance were required to decide within one year whether they would be engaged in the insurance or reinsurance business.

In addition to insurance companies founded in Croatia, insurance business can also be performed by branches of foreign insurance companies if they are registered in Croatia.

The stock capital of an insurance company ranges from 6 to 15 and even 18 million Kunas, depending on the groups of insurance that the insurance company handles. An individual is permitted to possess only 15 per cent of voting shares, while ownership of a percentage over 15 per cent requires the approval of the Insurance Companies Supervisory Authority.

Insurance agencies and brokers for insurance and reinsurance

At the time of writing, there are over 150 insurance agencies in Croatia, which is still the most widespread manner of selling insurance services. There are also a significant number of individual agents in the market.

The Insurance Companies Supervisory Authority issues approval for an insurance agency to operate when the following conditions are met:

● it has stock capital paid in cash in the amount of at least HRK100,000;

● it has a minimum of one employee who is an authorized insurance agent;

- it does not comprise a connected company with insurers or reinsurers or brokers in compliance with the Commercial Company Act; and

- it has made a preliminary contract or contract on the representation of an insurer or reinsurer.

In addition to agencies, insurance brokers have also appeared on the market recently, largely due to the Agency and Brokerage Firm in Insurance Act (*Narodne novine* No. 27/99), according to which a clear differentiation has been made for the first time between an insurance agency and an insurance brokerage firm. At the moment, there are eight brokerage firms founded in Croatia, of which the global brokerage firms such as Aon, Marsh, Mai and Eosrisq have opened subsidiaries, servicing mainly global companies. Among the foreign reinsurance brokers, the Heath Lambert Group has established a branch office in Croatia.

The Insurance Companies Supervisory Authority issues approval for a brokerage firm to operate so long as the following conditions are met:

- it has stock capital paid in cash of at least HRK200,000;

- it has two or more employees who are authorized brokers, of whom at least one must be a member of the company's board;

- it does not comprise a connected company with insurers or reinsurers or brokers or agents in compliance with the Commercial Company Act; and

- it has made a preliminary contract or contract regarding liability for damages that occur through the performance of activities on the amount of insurance for a minimum of HRK1 million.

Pension reform

Pension reform began in 2002 according to the 'three-pillar' system and has, in the opinion of many, exceeded all expectations. Taking into account the trend away from government-administered retirement pensions, the second pillar represents compulsory pension funds, while the third pillar represents voluntary pension funds. The Government is attempting to promote the further development of the third pillar through subsidies and tax benefits.

Future development of insurance in Croatia

The general opinion is that the life insurance market is continuing to grow and there is a markedly strong potential in this segment for growth. There are also expectations for the development of insurance-bank products such unit-linked policies, and a stronger connection between banks and insurance companies.

Croatia's moves towards joining the European Union imply continued legal coordination with EU directives. In insurance regulations, changes will have to be made in the legal framework regarding investment by insurance companies. The regulations currently do not permit an insurer to invest in foreign securities, and limit investment of life insurance premium reserves, of which a minimum of 50 per cent must be invested in Croatian Government bonds, without the option of investing in stocks or investment funds. Insurers are also not permitted to use financial derivatives, nor they can manage interest and currency risks.

Finally, in the coming years there will be a significant growth in the role of insurance brokers, which will signify new trends in the insurance industry, and a better overall quality of risk management by domestic companies.

The Zagreb Insurance Company

The Zagreb Insurance Company was established in 1991 as the first private insurance company in the Republic of Croatia. The company is headed by Petra Tarle, LLB. With the enthusiasm and devoted work of the employees, it has become one of the leading insurance companies in Croatia.

The company headquarters are in Zagreb, and the company operates throughout Croatia via a developed network of branch offices and agencies, and successfully covers the entire Croatian market. The branch offices are in Zagreb, Split, Rijeka, Pula, Zadar, Karlovac, Cakovec, Osijek, Dubrovnik and Vukovar.

In 2002, an average of 147 employees were employed by the Zagreb Insurance Company. Among the employees, most of whom have many years of experience in the insurance industry, 44 per cent were highly educated professionals. In the company, four certified actuaries are employed who are also full members of the Croatian Actuarial Association.

All the business processes are supported by a quality information system, which has been developed using modern information technologies with online access to a relation database. Online technologies provide in-time and complete information to all the decision-making structures.

The Zagreb Insurance Company currently has over 500,000 insured clients and contracts all types of insurance:

- life;

- accident;

- health;

- motor hull;

- marine and inland marine hull;

- cargo;

- property;

- motor third-party liability;

- ship owners' liability;

- other liability; and

- travel insurance.

In the portfolio of the Zagreb Insurance Company, life and non-life types of insurance are equally represented. The shares of life and non-life insurance within the total portfolios of the European Union, Republic of Croatia and the Zagreb Insurance Company are shown in Figure 2.5.1.

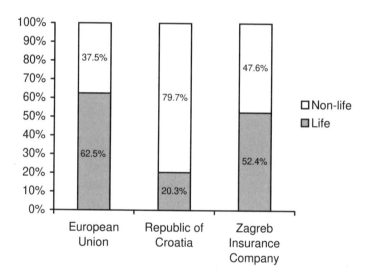

Figure 2.5.1 The shares of life and non-life insurance within total portfolios

The basic approach of the Zagreb Insurance Company in settling claims is the rapid, equitable and uniform payment of damages, which is summarized by the Company slogan: 'Confidence for a reason!'

The portfolio of the Zagreb Insurance Company is protected by reinsurance contracts with leading world reinsurers Munich Re, Scor Deutschland and Lloyd's.

The Zagreb Insurance Company is the first insurance company in Croatia that owns a company for the managing of investment funds – TT Invest, which manages three investment funds.

The performance of the Zagreb Insurance Company in 2002

The total assets of the Zagreb Insurance Company in 2002 were nearly HRK700 million, which is 31 per cent higher than in 2001. The premium revenues in 2002 recorded a growth of 6.6 per cent to HRK305.5 million.

In 2002, the Zagreb Insurance Company recorded an increase of 28.5 per cent in gross income, which amounts to HRK14.2 million. The income was 14.1 per cent higher than during 2001, while investments grew by 37.4 per cent.

According to the level of premium revenues in 2002, the Zagreb Insurance Company occupies fifth place among 24 Croatian insurance companies – with a market share of 5.5 per cent. In terms of the volume of life insurance business, it is in third place, and in terms of non-life insurance business it is in sixth place.

Insurance products in the portfolio of the Zagreb Insurance Company

Life insurance
The strategic product of the Zagreb Insurance Company is life insurance. In the life insurance portfolio of the Zagreb Insurance Company there are three basic products:

1. endowment insurance;

2. term insurance; and

3. pure endowment insurance for children.

In 2002, the share of life insurance in the portfolio of the Zagreb Insurance Company was 52.4 per cent. The insured persons' share in the life insurance profit was HRK16 million. A nearly 7 per cent increase in the number of newly contracted life insurance policies in 2002 indicates that life insurance is becoming accepted as a prerequisite for financial security, quality savings and creating additional assets for retirement.

In 2001 – with the beginning of pension reform and the introduction of individual capitalized savings – an opening was created for more significant life insurance growth in the Republic of Croatia. Since the share of life insurance in the total portfolio in the Republic of Croatia is only 20.3 per cent, the trend in the growth in the number of life insurance policies is positive and life insurance will continue to remain a strategic product of the Zagreb Insurance Company.

Starting in 2003, supplementary insurance for critical illness in addition to life insurance is offered. This new product insures payment in the event of a critical illness or condition, so that the insured person is paid an additional amount, while his or her life insurance continues.

Non-life insurance

Within the total portfolio of the Zagreb Insurance Company, in 2002 non-life insurance had a 47.6 per cent share (see Figure 2.5.1).

The structure of non-life insurance portfolio of the Zagreb Insurance Company is shown in Figure 2.5.1.

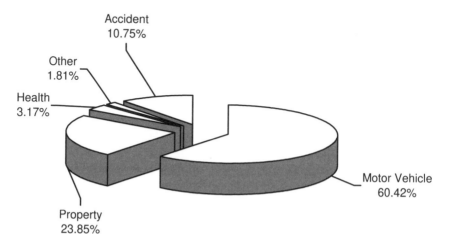

Figure 2.5.2 The structure of non-life insurance in the Zagreb Insurance Company

The level of development and profitability of non-life insurance in the Zagreb Insurance Company is based on adjustment to the demands and specific needs of the market. For example, the Zagreb Insurance Company is the only company on the insurance market of the Republic of Croatia to offer contractors all-risk insurance and some types of professional liability insurance.

The Zagreb Insurance Company devotes particular attention to the development of new products. In 1994, it was the first insurance company to offer compulsory occupational accident and occupational disease insurance, and in 2001, when such insurance was terminated, it was one of the first to offer a new type of insurance for compensation of wages.

In 2003, the range of products was expanded with the introduction of several new types of insurance, such as crop insurance, animal insurance and liability insurance; the most significant product that the Zagreb Insurance Company introduced to the market in October 2003 was private health insurance.

Plans

Taking into account the anticipated growth of the insurance market, the strength of the competition and the entry of foreign insurers into the Croatian market, the Zagreb Insurance Company anticipates growth of its market share.

In 2003, the Zagreb Insurance Company plans continued development of the sales network, a 12–15 per cent growth in premiums and achieving second place on the Croatian life insurance market during the next two years. By 2010, the Zagreb Insurance Company will attempt to obtain a 10 per cent share of the Croatian insurance market with an annual increase in its share of approximately 0.75 per cent.

In establishing company policy, the Board is guided by the following goals and values:

- confidence for a reason;

- insurance in which the insured person is the centre of interest;

- insurance that operates only according to market criteria throughout the territory of the Republic of Croatia;

- insurance that offers security, commercial excellence and the best coverage.

CROATIAN OIL AND GAS INDUSTRY

Oil industry has quite a long tradition in these parts. The beginning was in the 1870s when oil was mined from trenches and pits at several locations. The first exploration well was drilled in 1886 near the village of Peklenice in the Medjimurje region.

The first significant productive hydrocarbon accumulations that were discovered through exploration drilling were the Bujavica gas field (1917) and Gojilo oil field (1941) in the Sava Depression.

The Rijeka refinery was established in 1883 and the Sisak refinery in 1927.

INA was founded in 1964 when the operations of Naftaplin (oil and gas exploration and production) were merged with those of the refineries of Rijeka and Sisak. By the end of that decade INA had expanded to include the Zagreb Refinery, Marketing (retail network), the OKI and DINA petrochemical operations and the Kutina fertiliser plant.

In 1993 INA became a joint-stock company Industrija nafte d.d. with the Republic of Croatia as the only shareholder.

INA Industrija nafte d.d.
INA is a vertically integrated oil and gas company. It is the largest Croatian company but also a significant regional energy player.

Core businesses

1. Exploration and production of oil and gas
The upstream division of INA, previously called Naftaplin, is engaged in the

exploration, development, production and acquisition of oil and natural gas in Croatia and internationally. INA commenced upstream operations in 1952 with exploration in Croatia. Since then the division has been active in twenty countries and is currently active in Angola, Croatia, Egypt and Syria.

The majority of production comes from onshore Croatia, where INA owns 100% of all 50 of the producing oil and gas fields. Production offshore Croatia began in 1999 from the Ivana gas field, in which INA and Italian ENI have a joint interest based on a commercial contract between the two companies. The development of other satellite discoveries in the area south of Ivana is expected to start in 2003. Total gas reserves in the Adriatic offshore are estimated at 20 billion cm.

In 2001 INA produced a total of 2m mt of crude oil and 1.8bn cm of natural gas.

In Syria INA has two significant gas/condensate discoveries under appraisal.

2. Refining and Wholesale

INA d.d. owns and operates refineries and lubricant plants in Croatia, and supporting crude oil and product distribution networks. Crude oil is delivered to refineries by pipeline and products are distributed by ship, road and rail through a number of product depots. Product sales are made on a wholesale basis and also through a retail network.

The two fuels refineries are located in Rijeka (Urinj) and Sisak. The Rijeka refinery is a medium sized refinery located on the Adriatic coast with access to a deep-sea port and JANAF pipeline system. The refinery typically runs 3-3.5 million tonnes per year of crude oil, producing a range of petroleum products for the domestic and export markets. The Refinery has seven crude oil storage tanks with a total storage capacity of 356,000 m³.

The Sisak Refinery is located 50 km from Zagreb, the main consumption area in Croatia. It is also well located to serve other local markets in Croatia and northwestern parts of Bosnia & Herzegovina, north-eastern part of Slovenia and western and northern Serbia.

The refinery processes local crude oils (produced by INA) plus Russian crude oil imported via connections to Druzba 1 and Druzba 2 pipelines. It is also possible to supply crude oil from the Mediterranean through the JANAF pipeline.

The refinery typically runs 2.0-2.2 million tonnes per year of crude oil, producing a range of petroleum products for the domestic and near export markets.

Lubricant plants

The Mlaka lubricants plant is located within the Mlaka district in the town of Rijeka. It is also known as "Maziva Rijeka". It is currently operated as a profit centre within INA d.d. although there are plans to run the plant as a wholly owned subsidiary.

Operations started at the site in 1883 with one of the first refinery operations in Europe. The refinery has been substantially rebuilt with major investments being made throughout the last century. Today, the plant is focused on the production of base oils, lubricants and bitumen and is the key supplier of these products in Croatia.

The Zagreb lubricant plant is now a fully owned subsidiary company of INA d.d., known as Maziva Zagreb d.o.o.

The plant is located in the industrial zone of Zagreb and close to the markets with the strongest demand, namely the Zagreb area and its industry. It's main activities are production and trade of lubricants, tailor made lubricants and greases for industry, additives and related products.

Wholesale and distribution
Wholesale and distribution operations are managed within the Wholesale department within the combined Refining and Wholesale division of INA. The main aim of this part of the division is to manage efficiently the link between refinery production and INA's retail network and wholesale customers.

3. Marketing operations
The principal business activity of this segment is retail of fuels and other goods through a network of petrol stations and a certain amount of direct bulk sales of fuels. INA's retail network covers the whole of Croatia with 397 operating petrol stations plus 31 other specialised sales sites that include warehouses, marine terminals and retail shops.

In 2001 the Marketing segment sold on the Croatian market 2.2 million tonnes of oil products. The average throughput in 2001 was app. 2,650 tonnes per site.

The petrol station network gives INA the leading position in the Croatian fuels retail sector. The sector is opened to competition with a number of other companies owning and operating sites (mostly in turn still supplied by INA's refienries).

INA's retail operations in neighbouring countries are managed through subsidiary companies in these countries. The operations include 43 petrol stations in Bosnia and Herzegovina and 6 petrol stations in Slovenia.

INA also claims ownership of certain assets in Serbia comprising 194 petrol stations, seven terminals and other facilities. It has undertaken a legal action in order to regain title to the Beopetrol assets (the company that currently runs INA's petrol stations).

Prices of oil products are deregulated. They are based on CIF Med prices of derivatives and the exchange rate US$ and HRK, including some other parameters included in the formulae.

The company has several corporate functions that provide support to the core businesses and carry out activities in their specific areas: Finance and Controlling, Internal Audit and Control, Legal Department, HR and Payroll, Strategic Planning, PR and Promotional Activities and IT Sector.

Management
INA's management structure follows the German model and comprises the General Assembly, Supervisory Board and a Management Board.

The Management Board manages the day to day business of the company. It has direct control of commercial decisions and is empowered to enact the company's business. The Management Board is ultimately responsible to the Supervisory Board. INA's Management Board comprises 6 members and is headed by the chairman.

The Management Board chaired by Dr Tomislav Dragicevic was appointed in January 2000. Since then INA has carried out a comprehensive restructuring programme and significantly improved its operational and financial performance.

During the restructuring process INA reorganised itself as a vertically integrated oil and gas company with clearly defined key business segments. All other activities are being spun off as independent companies that still operate under the umbrella of INA Group. However, this new independence gives INA's individual operations much greater flexibility and market adaptability.

Key Subsidiaries

CROSCO Integrated Drilling & Well Services Ltd. is a wholly owned subsidiary of INA. Principal activities of Crosco comprise services in connection with the extraction of crude oil and natural gas, drilling, workover and well completion, well testing, coil tubing and nitrogen cementing, stimulation and well logging. The company has a fleet of 48 modern drilling, workover and geoservices rigs, as well as three offshore platforms (one semisubmersible and two jackups). CROSCO has over forty years of international service experience and has conducted operations in

23 countries throughout Europe, Africa and Asia.

Crosco has a contract for provision of drilling and other services to INA at agreed upon prices. These prices are set to reflect current market conditions. But also, Crosco provides services to a number of other operators in the target markets.

PROPLIN Ltd. Proplin comprises the wholesale and retail LPG business of INA. Effective January 2002, Proplin operates as a separate legal entity within the INA Group.

The distribution of LPG in bottles to households and tanks to industry started more than thirty years ago. Over the years, the business has grown as the number of customers have increased and the LPG consumption has diversified (bottles, small bulks, automotive gas, city gas, industrial consumers, etc.)

Proplin operations consist of eight distribution centres in Croatia, geographically well positioned to serve the customers all across the country. It has an estimated market share in Croatia of 98% in wholesale and 35% in retail.

STSI – Integrirani tehnicki servisi d.o.o. In December 2001 INA spun off into a wholly-owned subsidiary the assets used in performance of preventive and corrective maintenance services. Prior to establishment of STSI the maintenance services were performed as an operating division within INA.

STSI's mission is to ensure safe, efficient and quality maintenance services for properties and technical systems of INA's companies at prices that reflect those on the open market. STSI will focus on the development of the maintenance business to become a leader in the domestic and surrounding areas. In addition to maintenance services, STSI also provide organisation of specialised transport services, machining and manufacturing of spare parts, overhaul repairs of processing equipment and other equipment to INA and other customers.

INA's overseas trade companies act as distributors of INA Group products and as purchasers of raw materials. These companies also assist INA in trading of crude oil and obtaining foreign sources of financing for INA. Material trading subsidiaries are InterINA Limited London and InterINA (Guernsey) Limited.

INA has a 16.63% shareholding in JANAF oil pipeline system. JANAF has signed certain agreements for the implementation of Druzba Adria project that involves the export of Russian crude oil to the world market via the existing pipelines of the Druzba and JANAF systems, which extend from Russia, via Belarus, Ukraine, Slovakia, Hungary and Croatia to the Omisalj tanker port and terminal. Realization of this project can be made possible by modifying the Omisalj - Sisak sections so as to allow for the reversal of flow of crude oil.

 **Today, INA is a modern, well-organized company. The restructuring measures undertaken during the last three years have rendered results. The restructuring included streamlining of core operations, cost reduction and the closure of some facilities that were not commercially viable. As the result, efficiency and profitability of the company improved.**

In 2001 INA d.d. the parent company generated profit US$ 86 million, while the profit of INA Group was US$ 43 million. In 2002 INA parent company posted a profit of US$ 109 million and INA Group of US$ 125 million.

Privatisation of INA

In the context of consolidation of oil industry in the world and liberalisation of energy market in the European Union, the Croatian Government decided to privatise Ina. In March 2002 a special law on privatisation of INA was passed according to which 25% plus 1 share will be sold to a strategic partner. The public announcement for the expression of interest was published in May 2002 and it aroused considerable interest by the European and Russian companies. The three shortlisted candidates – OMV, Austria, MOL, Hungary and Rosnjft, Russia submitted their offers and carried out due diligence process.

MOL offered the highest price of US$505 million for acquisition of the 25% plus one share in INA. The signing of the transaction agreements took place on 17 July 2003. The Completion Date is scheduled for the end of October 2003.

This strategic partnership is expected to strengthen the position of both companies in the region and contribute to higher integrity of upstream and downstream operations with positive impact on efficiency.

It is likely that next year Croatia will put on offer a further 15% of shares in its oil and gas company INA Industrije nafte, following the successful sale of a quarter of the company's stock to Hungary's MOL.

2.6

The Regulatory Regime in the Croatian Energy Sector

Biserka Cimesa, INA

The Republic of Croatia has ratified the Agreement on Energy Charter Treaty, which aims at creating the legal framework for encouraging long-term cooperation in the field of energy.

In order to adjust the existing legislation and institutional framework to bring it into line with the legislation in force in the European Union, the basic terms of reference of the EU Directives on electricity market liberalization (96/92EC) and on gas market liberalization (98/30/EC) have been integrated in the set of laws regulating the energy system.

Essentially, the energy sector in Croatia is governed under three 'tiers' of law, each dealing with a different level of detail:

1. The Energy Law, which sets out the framework for Croatian energy policy (comprising oil, gas, heat and electricity) and the requirements and administration of the licences for participants in the respective markets.

2. The Energy Services Act, or the Croatian translation, Law on Regulation of Energy Activities, which outlines the powers, duties and constitution of the energy regulatory agency.

3. The Oil Law, Gas Law and Electricity Law, which have a more limited function, but set out such items as service standards and safety requirements.

These energy laws set out the objectives of regulation of the energy sector in Croatia:

- to promote competition in energy services;

- to ensure the financial and technical viability of licensed energy subjects;

- to protect customers;

- to promote environmental protection, efficient and economical use of natural resources, protection at work and social welfare.

The Energy Services Act also established the Energy Regulatory Agency, which is funded by fees charged to licence holders. This reflects the international view of the importance of a regulator funded independently from the government.

The duties of the Energy Regulatory Agency, as set out in the law, would be recognizable in most liberalized jurisdictions. These duties include supervision of market players, approval of energy plans as required under any relevant energy legislation, dispute resolution on the scope of business of a licensed party, collection of data on the operation of the energy market, issue of regulations and the imposition of fines.

The Energy Law is the main Act that sets out the requirement that certain activities in the energy market are prohibited unless licensed, and also lays out the framework for the issue, operation and termination of the necessary licences. Again, this reflects an EU-liberalized model. The Energy Law also outlines the energy policies and strategies (in high-level form) that the Government of Croatia intends to follow to and implement within Croatia.

Because the Energy Law and the Energy Services Act set out the majority of the necessary regulatory and supervisory regulations, the specific Acts for each particular energy source (eg gas, electricity or oil) are more limited, essentially setting out certain service obligations, for example the requirement of certain oil licence-holders to maintain a limited stockpile or to allow negotiated third-party access.

Liberalization of the energy sector in the majority of EU states has been implemented in two stages: first, restructuring the energy organizations, and then privatizing them. Croatia is following the same model. The two large players in the energy sector, INA Industrija nafte d.d., a vertically integrated oil company, and Hrvatska Elektroprivreda, the electricity company, have undergone considerable restructuring. INA has divested itself of non-core activities and is now focused on exploration and production of oil and gas, refining and marketing of oil products. In 2002 Parliament approved the law on privatization of INA according to which the Government will sell 25 per cent plus one share to a strategic partner in the first phase.

Natural gas transmission activities were spun off from INA in 2001. According to the Energy Law, gas transmission has a public service obligation. Before privatization of INA started, the Government decided to exempt the natural gas transportation business from privatization and acquired from INA the transmission company Plinacro d.o.o., which is now 100 per cent owned by the Government.

Also, in line with the new energy legislation, INA introduced separate accounting for different activities within the vertically integrated parent company. The LPG business was separated into a new subsidiary, Proplin d.o.o. INA is also active in natural gas distribution through Croplin d.o.o., an associated company that has entered into a joint venture with a German partner, MVV.

In September 2002 a new tariff system was introduced for natural gas. It includes a pricing system for the supply of gas to tariff or captive consumers, being industrial consumers connected directly to the natural gas grid and local distribution companies. The tariff system allows periodical adjustment of the natural gas price depending on input costs. The Energy Regulatory Council monitors the implementation of the tariff system.

The second tariff system regulates pricing of transportation services for natural gas suppliers and eligible customers. According to the Gas Law, eligible customers are those whose annual consumption exceeds 100 MCM or those who have co-generation. The eligible customers are entitled to select their gas supplier and even to construct their own direct pipeline if they cannot have access to the existing transmission system due to technical or other reasons. The third tariff system for distribution of natural gas is in preparation.

Given the present conditions in the gas market and configuration of the natural gas system, it is unlikely that other gas suppliers would enter the market in the near future. However, in the process of adjusting Croatia's legislation to EU standards, the Croatian Government has set a regulatory framework that enables liberalization of the energy market. During the last three years the reform of the energy sector has gathered momentum and further activities are on the agenda.

It is expected that privatization of INA and the entry of a strategic partner will contribute to further opening and expansion of the market. Hrvatska Elektroprivreda, the electricity company, has also been restructured. As of 1 July 2002 it was transformed into the HEP Group. The parent company is HEP plc, which is the holding company of the subsidiaries engaged in power generation, supply, transmission and distribution, as well as those engaged in gas and heat supply. There is also a system operator and electricity market operator.

The law on privatization of HEP has also been approved; however, the present Government postponed the sale, which will be effected by a new Government after the elections due to take place by the end of 2003.

Privatization of INA

In the context of global consolidation of the oil industry and liberalization of the energy market in the European Union, the Croatian Government decided to privatize INA. In March 2002 a special law was passed according to which 25 per cent plus 1 share are to be sold to a strategic partner. The public announcement for the expression of interest was published in May 2002 and it aroused considerable interest in European and Russian companies. The three short-listed candidates – OMV, Austria; MOL, Hungary; and Rosnjeft, Russia – submitted their binding offers. The bids were opened on 10 July 2003. MOL offered the highest price of US$505 million and met other conditions set by the Croatian Government. The signing of the transaction agreements took place on 17 July 2003, by which MOL acquires 25 per cent plus 1 share in INA.

The law on privatization of INA envisages a further sale of 15 per cent of shares through public offering on Croatian stock exchanges. Also, 7 per cent of INA's shares will be offered to employees and former employees and 7 per cent of shares will be transferred without compensation to war veterans.

The Government will keep 25 per cent plus one share until accession to the EU. The remaining 21 per cent will be distributed as compensation to former owners and sale or exchange in accordance with market conditions based on a government decision and Parliament's assent.

2.7

Telecommunications:
The Regulatory Framework

Raiffeisenbank Austria d.d. Zagreb

Introduction

The telecommunications sector is fundamental to any economy attempting to remain competitive in today's increasingly globalized world. Therefore a properly established regulatory framework is extremely important not only to companies or individuals that obtained or intend to obtain concessions but also to the economy as a whole, because more competitive telecommunication markets reduce costs, ie enhance the competitiveness of other sectors. Telecommunications as an extremely dynamic industry requires a dynamic regulatory framework. The latest decision by the regulatory authorities repealed the order on service charges that Internet Service Providers (ISPs) had to pay for using the telecommunications network of another provider, which amounted to 2 per cent of their annual gross income.

Since the regulatory authorities are continually improving the legal framework, this overview should not be considered as definitive; it provides insight into the current state of affairs.

Governing agencies

The Ministry of Maritime Affairs, Traffic and Communications is responsible for administrative and other tasks pertaining to domestic and international maritime, road, rail, air and postal transport and telecommunications. It performs the administrative supervision of the Croatian Telecommunication Institute and of the Telecommunication Council; it participates in making the subordinate regulations governing telecommunication activities under the jurisdiction of the Ministry; it suggests the telecommunication development strategy, and corresponding measures as well as pursuing policies in telecommunication activities.

On 1 January 2000 the CIT, Croatian Institute of Telecommunications, was created to take over the regulatory functions of the Ministry of Maritime Affairs, Transport and Communications. A new law on telecommunications is in preparation in order to meet European Union guidelines.

The Telecommunication Council (TC) is an independent telecommunication regulator in the Republic of Croatia. The TC is autonomous in performing its activity as specified by law, and is responsible to the Croatian National Parliament and the Government of the Republic of Croatia. On 1 January 2002, the Council started working on its statute in accordance with the Telecommunications Act. Since April 2002 it has been engaged in operative work.

Within the activities designated by the Telecommunications Act, the TC, as a public authority, performs the following activities: a) issuing decisions about granting concessions and issuing decrees on withdrawing concessions for activities in the field of telecommunications, with the exception of radio and television activities; and b) issuing decisions and decrees regulating the relationship between service providers in the telecommunications market.

The Council and the Institute are financed from the charges for the use of broadcasting frequencies, from the charges for the use of addresses and numbers, and from the 0.2 per cent of gross income generated by companies which were granted concessions for providing telecommunications or cable TV services (ISPs were exempt from this charge in April 2003).

Telecommunications Institute of Croatia

The Institute cooperates directly with the TC in such a way as to prepare the proposals of the Acts issued by the Council, conclude agreements on concessions granted by the TC and perform other professional and inspection jobs. The purpose of the TC is to ensure equal opportunities for all participants in the telecommunication market, promoting competition, enabling new service providers access to the market, preventing monopoly and other types of abuse, and implementing open network provision (ONP) as well as creating the same market conditions as those in the EU. It is also responsible for the resolution of disputes among undertakings (service providers) and, through the Telecommunications User Council, for resolving disputes among service providers and end-users. The regulatory institutions are shown in Figure 2.7.1.

The work of the TC is based on the legislation and regulation of the Republic of Croatia and on international agreements. The major statutory and subordinate regulations covering telecommunications in the Republic of Croatia are:

● Telecommunications Act (*NN* (*Official Gazette*), Nos 76/99, 128/99, 68/01,109/01);

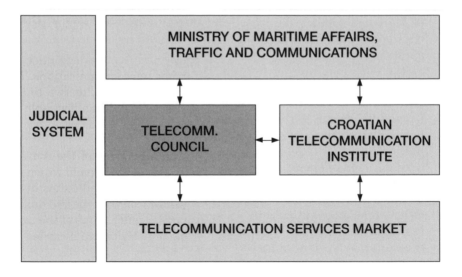

Source: CIT

Figure 2.7.1 Chart of the regulatory institutions

- General regulations for telecommunication service providers (*NN*, No 84/95);

- Regulations regarding concessions granted for performing public telecommunications activities (*NN*, No 88/01);

- Regulations of compensation for attending to telecommunication services and other telecommunication activities and payment (*NN*, No 88/01);

- Regulations regarding compensation for radio frequency applications and the way of their payment (*NN*, No 88/01);

- Regulations regarding technical conditions of construction and implementation of the telecommunication infrastructure (*NN*, No 88/01).

The Telecommunications Act regulates telecommunications, radio, TV and cable TV, and governs the relationship between telecommunication services providers and users, as well as the construction, maintenance and usage of telecommunication facilities, equipment and broadcasting services, and ensures that a defined set of minimum universal telecommunication services of a specific quality is available to all users in the Republic of Croatia, regardless of their geographical location, at an affordable price.

Concession holders of telecommunication services in the Republic of Croatia

The right to provide telecommunication services is obtained under the Regulations on granting concessions in public telecommunications. The concession scope may encompass the county, a region, or two to five counties, local areas, municipalities, or towns. In addition, for cable TV services the concession spectrum may include a city area or district, a municipality or part of a municipality.

A concession is granted in line with the provisions of the Act and depending on the type of service, level and size of the area in which the activity is performed. Concessions are given for a limited period of not longer than 30 years. The period is set depending on the type and quality of the service as well as its scope. In principle, concessions of the same type and significance and the same scope of activity are awarded for the same duration.

Licences are issued for providing the following services:

● public telephone network at a fixed location;

● mobile communication services – NMT-450i standard; E-GSM and DCS-1800 standard; GSM900 standard; UMTS standard; E-GSM, GSM900 or DCS-1800 with UMTS;

● broadcasting services – TETRA, VSAT, S-PCS, TFTS i sl;

● radio;

● TV;

● cable TV.

A request for obtaining a concession is submitted in writing to the TC. The request must contain the name and address of the company submitting the request, as well as copy of its registration, type and the scope of the service for which the concession is requested, evidence on available sources of finance, construction documents containing the estimated duration of construction, starting date and detailed description of all necessary equipment and facilities. A request for a concession for voice telephony in the fixed network at state level must include a commitment to invest at least €50 million in Kuna equivalent in the infrastructure of telecommunication facilities, network or system over four years from the date the concession was granted.

A company holding a concession for providing telecommunication services through the use of the radio spectrum allocated to the second generation mobile network (GSM, E-GSM, DCS-1800) must, within two years of obtaining the concession, ensure the following coverage: a) GSM and E-GSM – at least 75 per cent of the population or 60 per cent of the territory of the Republic of Croatia; b) DCS-1800 – at least 40 per cent of the population or 50 per cent of the territory.

The amount of the fee due during the first and subsequent years of providing market telecommunication services via the radio spectrum allocated to the second generation mobile network system (GSM, E-GSM, DCS-1800) is regulated by the Rule book on fees and charges for providing telecommunication services and other telecommunications activities.

The concession for providing telecommunication services in the UMTS network includes the right to provide new Internet access and data transmission services utilizing voice, data, video, multimedia, etc in a scope and manner that does not coincide with a concession for providing TV and radio services.

The UMTS services provided must meet minimum quality and availability requirements, meaning that they must be available to: a) at least 35 per cent of Croatia's population, within two years from the date the concession was obtained; and b) at least 50 per cent of the country's population, within three years.

The amount of the fee due during the first and subsequent years of providing the UMTS is regulated by the Rulebook on fees and charges for providing such services.

It was impossible to obtain a concession for a fixed network prior to 1 January 2002, and a company subsequently obtaining a licence cannot start providing telecommunication services until 1 October 2003.

Currently, **Fixed Network** Croatian Telecommunications Inc has a concession for providing public voice services and market telecommunication services in the fixed network, with a contract concluded on 22 September 1999 for a period of 30 years.

As regards the mobile network, VIPnet Ltd and Croatian Telecommunications Inc have concessions for providing public telecommunication services in the GSM mobile network (VIPnet concluded the contract on 30 October 1998 for a period of 10 years and Croatian Telecommunications Inc entered the contract on 22 September 1999 for a period of 10 years). As at June 2002, 15 concessions had been granted for providing cable television services.

Operators with significant market power

The law defines telecom services providers and users with significant market power (SMP). An operator has SMP if there is no or only scarce competition on the market. An operator has SMP measured by its income compared to the market size or control it has over the customer base, as well as access to financial sources or experience in providing products and services.

Every operator with SMP is obliged to issue a comprehensive price list of all its products and services. An operator with SMP must provide other market participants with services and conditions equal to those provided for its own purposes or to related companies. An operator with SMP can limit access to a network and linking only for reasons in line with the EEC guidelines and pursuant to other EU regulations.

With the Decree of the Telecommunication Council issued on 6 September 2002, and in accordance with the suggestion of the Croatian Telecommunication Institute, the following have been proclaimed service providers with SMP:

- Croatian Telecommunications Inc – the public voice telephony market in the Republic of Croatia;

- Croatian Telecommunications Inc – the fixed-line services market in the Republic of Croatia;

- Croatian Telecommunications Inc and VIPnet Ltd – the mobile network telecommunication services market in the Republic of Croatia;

- Croatian Telecommunications Inc – the Internet services market in the Republic of Croatia.

Market liberalization

The liberalization of the telecommunications market will be conducted in three phases. As part of the first phase Croatia signed the Protocol on the Republic of Croatia's joining the Marrakech Act on the foundation of the World Trade Organization (*NN*, No 13/2000; International Acts) which entered into force on 11 November 2000. In the second stage the exclusive rights of Croatian Telecommunications Inc expired and on 31 December 2002 the market opened to new service providers for the fixed network. In the third stage access to the local loop will be opened, starting in early 2005. HT, Hrvatske telekomunikacije d.d. (HT d.d.) had exclusive rights until 31 December 2002 to:

- operate the public fixed-phone network;

- provide voice telephony services in the fixed network; and

- provide international telecom services.

The Government of the Republic of Croatia entered an agreement with HT d.d. regulating its exclusive country-level right to operate the public telecommunication network until 31 November 2002, which governs the rights and obligations towards other market participants and the provision of basic universal services, as well as network enlargement, service quality and consumer protection. It also regulates the prices based on HT's published price list within the framework of consumer protection. The law on the Privatization of Hrvatske telekomunikacije d.d. (*Official Journal* 68/2001) specifies a transitional period until 31 December 2004, which starts after the termination of the exclusive rights of HT (on 31 December 2003).

During this one-year transitional period HT will not be obliged to give other operators and service providers unbundled access to its local loop, or to provide number portability and carrier pre-selection services. The Government of the Republic of Croatia and HT d.d. will sign an Annex to the agreement covering the rights and obligations during the transition period. Until the expiry of the transition period several Rulebooks will be drawn up to govern the access to the local loop, the obligation to provide telephone number transfer service and to enable the choice of operator.

Telecommunication equipment

Telecommunication facilities and equipment, installations and terminals intended for use in the Republic of Croatia must be projected, produced, constructed and maintained in line with Croatian regulations and technical conditions, as well as ETSI (European Telecommunications Standards Institute) standards and the rules, decisions and recommendations of the International Telecommunications Union (ITU) and the Conference of European Postal and Telecommunication Authorities.

A company that obtained a concession for providing universal basic telecommunication services, and that got the concession for TV and radio services, has the right, if technically possible, to use others' telecommunications infrastructure for a payment defined by a contract.

On 30 November 2000 the Republic of Croatia became the 140th member of the World Trade Organization. All the commitments that were undertaken are included within the Act of Acknowledgement of the Protocol by which the Republic of Croatia joined the Marrakech Act on the foundation of the World Trade Organization, published in the *Official Gazette* (*NN* 13/00; International Acts), Act of Acknowledgement of the Temporary Agreement regarding commercial and other related issues between the Republic of Croatia and the European Union (*NN* 15/01; International Acts).

Sources

Croatian Institute of Telecommunications, http://www.vzt.hr.
Ministry of Maritime Affairs, Transport and Communications, http://www.mppv.hr.
Narodne novine, http://www.nn.hr.

2.8

The Telecommunications Market in Croatia

Raiffeisenbank Austria d.d. Zagreb

Introduction

In early 2003, the first year of deregulation of the telecommunication market officially started. Until 31 December 2002 Croatian Telecom had the exclusive right to manage fixed public telecommunications, provide voice telecommunication services in the fixed-telephone network, and international telecommunication services throughout Croatia. Fee cancellation to ISPs for providing telecommunication services, as well as the final drawing-up of regulations that would integrate telecommunications and informatics, should also contribute to telecommunication and Internet market development in Croatia.

Telecommunications have realized around 3 per cent of the total income of all entrepreneurs in 2001 and account for around 4 per cent of the total profit realized by all entrepreneurs in Croatia. A 6 per cent increase in call duration per fixed network was realized in 2002 and the mobile communications saw an increase of 38 per cent in total call duration (there was a year-on-year growth of 37 per cent in expenditure of mobile minutes in 2001 too).

Macroeconomic indicators predict further increases in telecommunications. GDP and GDP per capita in 2002 have marked a significant increase (in 2001 GNI per capita adjusted for purchasing power parity was estimated at US$8,440) and the expected GDP increase rate for 2003 is 3.4 to 4 per cent. However, the limiting factor is the negative demographic trend that threatens the already low numbers of potential customers (see Table 2.8.1).

Fixed-line penetration varies from 38 to 41 per cent (if penetration is measured by the number of channels). Penetration of 65 per cent was the European average as recently as 2001, so there is still some opportunity for growth. The penetration of mobile telephony amounts to 53 per cent. Slovenia reached 61 per cent mobile penetration in 2000

Table 2.8.1 Macroeconomic trends in the Croatian economy, 1999–2002

	1999	2000	2001	2002
Population (mid-year estimate, thousands)	4,554	4,381	4,437	4,437
Population growth, %	−1.5	−1.5	−1.9	–
GDP, US$ billion	19.9	18.4	19.5	22.1
GDP growth, %	−0.4	2.9	3.8	5.2
GDP per capita, US$	4,424	4,095	4,403	5,056
CPI, % yoy	4.2	6.2	4.9	2.2
HRK/US$, avg	7.11	8.28	8.34	8.06
HRK/Euro, avg	7.58	7.64	7.47	7.41

Source: Republic of Croatia Central Bureau of Statistics; Croatian Chamber of Economy; World Bank

and Croatia can expect an increase in the number of mobile users in the coming years due to the improvement in living standards and competition. As the number of computer owners is on the increase in Croatia (up from 25 per cent to 30 per cent in 2002), Internet penetration, currently estimated at 18 per cent of the population, will follow the trend.

Major telecommunication companies in Croatia

Potential investors in the fixed telephony have to invest €50 million in a period of four years according to the Law and have to pay an annual concession fee for the fixed telephony of HRK 40 million. Up to the present date, no concession applications have been submitted. The concession fee is too high according to some experts. So far, only VIPnet has announced that it will apply for the fixed telephone network concession. VIPnet plans to enter the fixed telephony market in the first place as a service provider, and not as a fixed-network operator. Furthermore, there are indications of an ambitious project that would result in a new national telecom concern. A consortium of large Croatian companies, Koncar, HZ, HEP and Ericsson Nikola Tesla, see an opportunity in creating the new organization, that, starting from 2004, could take an estimated HRK 500 million of profit from HT. Public companies, HZ and HEP, have well-developed infrastructure in Croatia that cannot be used by any other company without concession. Optical cable could be laid down through HZ's rail tracks and HEP's transmission lines, expanding the existing capacity of the telecommunication network, and small telecom centres could be built at abandoned railway stations,. All parties have good reasons for merging together and embarking on this project; because of the advantages at their disposal there is no need for additional investments. The next step would be founding a joint company that would become the telecom owner. The financial justification for creating a new Croatian telecom business is the fact that HT alone realizes around HRK1 billion of net profit annually.

Croatian Telecom (HT d.d.) is the only full-spectrum telecommunication service provider in Croatia. As it is still the only provider of fixed-line telephony services (100 per cent market share), it is the major telecommunication player in Croatia (see Table 2.8.2). There are two GSM service providers, HT mobilne komunikacije d.o.o. (53 per cent market share) and VIP-net d.o.o. (47 per cent market share). HTmobile, a fully owned subsidiary of Croatian Telecom, for a long time was the only GSM operator, but in July 1999 the VIP-net was launched. Competition on the market is likely to increase, as authorities have announced the upcoming sale of the two new GSM concessions and liberalization of the fixed network.

Table 2.8.2 HT statistical indices

Operational Statistics	EOY				CAGR
	1999	2000	2001	2002	1999–2002
I Fixed line network					
Total no of channels (POTS + ISDN)	1,641,570	1,721,139	1,781,000	1,825,157	3.6%
No of POTS	1,641,570	1,681,910	1,678,279	1,626,423	
No of ISDN channels	0	39,229	102,721	198,734	127.7%
II Mobile network (GSM & NMT)					
Mobile phone subscribers (GSM & NMT)	258,654	580,467	875,013	1,241,842	72.4%
No of HTcronet post-paid subscribers	156,903	186,092	199,451	207,774	10.0%
No of HTmobitel subscribers (NMT NW)	94,674	73,000	42,297	26,971	
No. of Simpa pre-paid subscribers 1533.5%	7,077	321,375	675,562	1,007,097	
III Internet (HiNet)					
Dial-up users	74,955	148,041	238,586	370,013	71.3%
Leased line Internet users	148	206	262	377	36.8%

Source: HT Annual Reports

The principal activities of HT-Hrvatske telekomunikacije d.d. and its subsidiary HT mobilne komunikacije d.o.o. (together the HT Group) comprise the provision of telecommunication services, and the design and construction of communications networks in the Republic of Croatia. The Group's operations are performed through its three lines of business organized in two business units (fixed network and online) and one separate legal entity, HT mobilne komunikacije d.o.o. In addition to the basic fixed-line telephony, including local, long-distance and international calls, HT operates analogue (NMT) and GSM mobile telephone networks called Mobitel and Cronet, respectively, and the Internet (HTnet; HThinet). During 2002, HT d.d. experienced a further growth in the mobile pre-paid market and in fixed-line telephony partly as a result of an increased range of services and an increase in the number of subscribers, and partly as a result of tariff rebalancing performed in August 2001. The tariff rebalancing led to an increase in the local-call price, while the price of domestic long-distance calls has fallen. Revenues from telecommunication services for 2002 were HRK7,544 million, of which HRK5,052 refer to fixed-line telephony, HRK2,078 million to mobile telephony, and HRK414 million to data, Internet and other services. In 2002 revenue from HT's fixed telephone network increased by 7.31 per cent to HRK5,052 million from HRK4,717 million in 2001. The net profit for the financial year amounted to HRK1,664 million. HT's operating profit in 2001 was significantly impacted by revaluation, as HRK1,142 million of the written-off assets was reported as compared to the results in 2001; see Table 2.8.3.

Table 2.8.3 HT financial indices

	EOY HRK millions				CAGR
Earnings position	1999	2000	2001	2002	1999–2002
Revenue – by business	4,758	5,830	6,788	7,544	16.70%
Revenue from fixed telephony	3,529	4,346	4,717	5,052	12.93%
Revenue from mobile telephony	846	1,115	1,673	2,078	35.35%
Revenue from Internet and data services	224	272	353	349	16.69%
Other revenue	159	97	45	65	−16.05%

Source: HT Annual Reports

VIPnet d.o.o. is a consortium of Mobicom (Austria), Western Wireless (USA) and local Croatian partners. VIPnet's activities were helped by a €22.4 million loan provided by EBRD in 1999. Through energetic marketing, VIPnet has managed to increase its customer base rapidly. HTmobile had 340,000 and VIPnet 150,000 mobile users after only one year of VIPnet's operations. In late 2000, VIPnet, primarily a mobile telephone operator, entered the ISP market.

The Croatian Internet sector has expanded rapidly during the last two years. There are an estimated 550,000 users (600,000 to 700,000 if users in companies are counted), which represents roughly 18 per cent of the population. It is expected that Internet penetration will grow to 22 per cent by the end of 2003, what is much closer to EU levels. There has also been an increase in the amount of e-commerce conducted. HT offers a subsidized tariff amounting to 5lp/min (1 HRK = 100 lipas, lp) for Internet use via any of the ISPs in Croatia.

HThinet, a subsidiary of HT, controls more than 74 per cent of the dial-up market based on usage, and the rest is carved up between seven smaller Internet service providers (there are eight ISPs in Croatia).

Iskon and Globalnet are the second- and third-largest private service providers. Both of them received a boost in 2000 when foreign investors bought controlling stakes in them.

IskonInternet is the biggest private ISP in Croatia. During 2000 it was strengthened by significant investments from the USA and Germany (Adriatic Net Investors invested US$5 million; Dresdener Kleinwort Benson Private Equity invested US$6 million). European and American know-how has contributed to Iskon's development of Internet services, which are the most extensive in all the transition countries. It has 150 employees today, and regional offices and points of Internet-connection (POPs) in Zagreb, Rijeka, Split, Osijek, Dubrovnik, Pula, Porec, Varazdin and Cakovec. IskonInternet co-founders are Etours (e-commerce), Eona (the first domestic safe Internet service provider, CASP) and Sanoma Magazines Zagreb.

Globalnet Grupa d.d. was the first private Internet service provider in Croatia, receiving a concession in July 1999 for unlimited line numbers for providing of services via the public telephone network. The majority owners of Globalnet are Croatia Capital Partnership (CCP) investment fund and EBRD, which, during 2000 and 2001, increased the capital of Globalnet Group d.d. with US$4.2 million. M-San Group, one of the biggest distributors of IT equipment in Croatia, is part of the ownership structure. During 2000 Globalnet provided complete 'know-how' as well as programme back-up for the founding of two ISPs in Bosnia and Herzegovina. The first Globalnet Group POP outside Zagreb was opened in February 2000 in Rijeka, and provided the citizens of Primorsko-goranska county with access to the Internet at local tariffs.

There are also several companies that offer Voice Over Internet Protocol (VOIP). According to the existing Rules on fees for telecommunication services, the provider of the VOIP service will in the first year pay a fee of HRK500,000, and afterwards 2 per cent of income to the authorities. Transintercom d.o.o. is the VOIP provider with the largest share of the market.

Privatization of HT-Hrvatske telekomunikacije d.d.

HT d.d. is a joint stock company in majority ownership of Deutsche Telecom AG (DTAG). It was incorporated on 28 December 1998 under the laws of the Republic of Croatia pursuant to the terms of the Law on the Separation of Croatian Posts and Telecommunications into Croatian Posts and Croatian Telecommunications (*NN*, No 101/98), which involved the post and telecommunications business of the former HPT-Hrvatska posta i telekomunikacije being separated and transferred into two new joint stock companies, HT-Hrvatske telekomunikacije d.d. (HT d.d.) and HT-Hrvatska posta d.d. (HP d.d.), which commenced their operations on 1 January 1999.

Pursuant to the terms of the Law on Privatization of Hrvatske telekomunikacije d.d. (*NN*, Nos 65/99 and 68/01), on 5 October 1999 the Republic of Croatia sold a 35 per cent stake in HT d.d. to DTAG and on 25 October 2001 DTAG purchased a further 16 per cent stake, becoming the majority shareholder with a 51 per cent stake. DTAG is now represented on the Supervisory Board by five members, the Republic of Croatia with three, and one member is appointed by the Workers Council of HT d.d.

The Law on Privatization of HT prescribed the privatization of 70 per cent of the shares of the company. Ownership of remaining 30 per cent would remain in the hands of the Croatian government, and only the Croatian National Parliament (Sabor) can make decisions on its distribution.

Croatia currently has 49 per cent of HT shares that should, according to the Law, be privatized as follows:

1. transfer of 7 per cent to Croatian soldiers and members of their families without payment;

2. sales of 7 per cent to the employees and former employees of HT and Hrvatske poste d.d. and former employees in Javno poduzece postanskog i telekomunikacijskog prometa HPT-Hrvatska posta i telekomunikacije, under special conditions that will be prescribed by the Croatian government;

3. in the public offering in accordance with the Law on the issuing and selling of treasury stocks; at least 20 per cent of HT shares will be offered:

   – the sales through public offering to the Croatian citizens according to the Law on the issuing and selling of treasury stocks (*NN*, Nos 107/95 and 142/98), with priority rights, privileges and conditions prescribed by the Croatian government for listing of HT shares on the stock exchange,

- the sales through public offering to domestic legal persons and foreign investors in accordance with the Law on the issuing and selling of treasury stocks (*NN*, Nos 107/95 and 142/98), with no privileges;

4. the sales of remaining shares in accordance with the market situation to a strategic investor or on the capital market according to the decision of the Croatian government.

These share percentages were determined according to the share capital of HT on the date of passing of the Law on Privatization of HT (June 1999), when the share capital of HT amounted to HRK8,189 million and included 81,888,535 ordinary shares valued at HRK100 each. Recent and future developments for HT are shown in Table 2.8.4.

Table 2.8.4 Wireline – timeline of market development

1990	Croatian Posts and Telecommunications (HPT d.d.) founded
December 1998	Croatian Posts and Telecommunications split into two separate companies: Hrvatski Telekomunikacije (HT) and Hrvatski Poste
September 1999	Deutsche Telekom acquires a 35% stake in HT
1 January 2000	Creation of Croatian Institute of Telecommunications – CIT
September 2000	HT undergoes name and logo change in a bid to boost its image, becoming Hrvatski Telekom
October 2001	Deutsche Telekom pays €500 million for an additional 16% stake in HT
Q1 2002	HT reorganizes its businesses, adopting a three-pillar structure
1 January 2003	Fixed-line market officially opened up to competition
1 January 2005	HT required to offer LLU

Source: Croatian Institute of Telecommunications – *CIT, Telekom* (Croatian Telecoms magazine)

HT shares and ownership rights will remain in the ownership of the Republic of Croatia until the sale. Dividend realized from shares in the ownership of the Republic of Croatia are the revenue of the national budget. As long as the Republic of Croatia has at least one share of HT with voting rights, Hrvatske telekomunikacije d.d., ie its branches, can

Table 2.8.5 HT financial indices

	1999	EOY HRK millions 2000	2001	2002	CAGR 1999–2002
Revenue	4,758	5,830	6,788	7,544	16.70%
Own costs capitalized	314	299	167	49	−39.86%
Other income	112	91	89	111	1.26%
Total operating income	5,184	6,220	7,044	7,704	14.20%
Material costs	−1,314	−1,773	−2,075	−2,170	18.85%
Staff costs	−1,033	−1,241	−1,224	−1,278	7.73%
Depreciation, amortization and write-down of fixed assets*	−1,335	−1,533	−1,208	−1,307	0.61%
Write-down of fixed assets from appraisal	–	–	−1,142	–	–
Write-down of current assets	−242	−65	−125	−98	−0.81%
Other costs	−372	−450	−646	−679	23.21%
Total operating costs	−4,296	−5,062	−6,420	−5,532	10.28%
Operating profit	888	1,158	624	2,172	77.46%
Net profit for the year	717	920	310	1,864	154.43%
Assets and liabilities					
Fixed assets	8,365	8,108	10,586	10,618	9.26%
Current assets	936	1,851	3,337	4,618	72.14%
Prepayments and accrued income	19	20	22	21	3.57%
Issued capital and reserves	7,925	8,486	11,365	13,198	19.04%
Subscribed share capital	8,189	8,189	8,189	8,189	0.00%
Short-term liabilities	913	911	1,337	1,143	10.68%
Accruals and deferred income	96	147	214	190	29.16%
Total assets and liabilities	9,320	9,979	13,945	15,257	18.74%
Financing					
Net cash inflow from operating activities	2,127	2,924	2,734	2,828	11.47%
Net cash outflow from investing activities	−1,401	−1,845	−2,535	−1,799	13.35%
Net cash outflow from financing activities	−752	−473	5	−502	–
Ratios					
Assets turnover*	55.7%	62.7%	51.30%	50.49%	−2.39%
Current ratio	1.0	2.03	2.50	4.04	62.59%
Financial leverage ratio (total liabilities/subscribed capital)	17.0%	18.2%	32.0%	25.1%	20.49%
ROE*	9.0%	10.8%	2.7%	14.1%	120.99%
ROA*	7.7%	9.2%	2.2%	12.2%	131.38%

*Data for 2001 are significantly affected by the asset appraisal.
Source: HT's Annual Reports

undertake the following actions only with the consent of the Croatian government:

- reach a decision on termination of the company;
- give up the concession, licence or authorization for performing its main activity, or cancel the agreement on concession;
- modify the company;
- reach a decision on relocation of HT's headquarters outside Croatia.

HT d.d. holds, besides INA, the Croatian oil company and, with HEP, Hrvatska elektroprivreda, the most important natural monopoly that is in the process of privatization. The Croatian capital market impatiently awaits further privatization of HT d.d, among which the banks and pension funds will be the most important investors. Considering the size of HT shares, they will be listed on domestic and foreign stock exchanges. What differentiates HT from other telecom companies is its low debt level: the percentage of total liabilities amounted to 12.6 per cent in 2002. HT's financial position is shown in Table 2.8.5.

2.9

Mobile Telecommunications

Ivana Robic, Raiffeisenbank Austria d.d. Zagreb

Introduction

Early in May 2003 the Telecommunications Council published an invitation for the expression of interest in a 3G mobile communications network concession. Thus a public tender for three 2G mobile network concessions was launched (DCS 1800 MHz) as well as a tender for four concessions for 3G mobile networks (UMTS). Two concessions of the third generation are reserved for HTmobile and VIPnet, which are currently using the GSM 900 network (which has a smaller scope than DCS 1800). According to the Rules the price for a combined concession (DCS and UMTS) would amount to HRK172 million payable in a lump sum at the time the concession is granted, plus HRK12 million annually. For DCS the lump sum to be paid is HRK105 million, plus HRK5 million annually, and a UMTS concessionaire would pay HRK130 million in a lump sum and HRK12 million each year.

As both VIPnet and HTmobile have confirmed their interest in a UMTS concession, they will upgrade the existing transmitters with additional equipment and gradually add new locations. The new operator will have to establish a completely new network, at the pace that is required under the concession terms regarding a particular territory coverage level. According to regulators' estimates, the establishment of a new GS network will cost, in addition to the concession price, around €250 million. Following the introduction of the UMTS, ie WCDMA (Wideband Code Division Multiple Access) technology in mobile communications, Croatian customers will have the convenience of voice communication and data transfer at a considerably higher speed, real-time information and access to live pictures such as video streaming and video telephony. Customers will be able to check in only a few seconds traffic reports, weather forecasts or sports results. The total cost of the introduction of UMTS technology for VIPnet and Cronet in Croatia should be as high as the investment in GSM technology.

Regulation

Currently three bodies regulate the mobile market in Croatia: the Ministry of Maritime Affairs, Transport and Communications, the Telecommunications Council and the Croatian Telecommunications Institute. To resolve some questions arising from the Telecommunications Act of 1999, the regulator has drafted a new Act. In addition to continued adjustment to meet EU guidelines and norms, the proposed Act provides for the organization of a user council and a more transparent distribution of the duties and responsibilities of certain bodies.

Other than the initial and annual concession fees, GSM operators also pay an annual frequency fee of HRK100,000 per duplex channel. GSM operators are also obliged to pay an annual fee of HRK150 per mobile radio station (ie subscriber). Operators have the right to recharge this fee to their subscribers.

Subscriber base and usage

Subscribers
The latest data from operators (March 2003) show that there were 2,417,000 GSM users in Croatia, which gives mobile penetration of 54.5 per cent (according to the 2001 Census Croatia has 4,437,000 inhabitants). Mobile penetration is round 55 per cent if we count the NMT users. At the end of 2002 GSM users were equally shared between VIPnet and HTmobile (a 50 per cent market share each). Of the total number of mobile users (27,000 NMT users counted), HTmobile held 53 per cent of the market at the end of 2002. HTmobile had 53 per cent of the post-paid market and VIPnet a little over 50 per cent of the pre-paid market. As for post-paid users, while VIPnet entered this market three years after HT d.d., it has managed to improve the weak share of business users it had in the beginning by presenting a VPN service (the first to do so in the market).

Research by GfK Market Research Center has confirmed that the possession of mobile phones increases in proportion to household income growth, so further growth will depend in part on rising living standards.

Minutes spent
According to data from the State Statistics Bureau, 1,498 million mobile minutes were used in 2002, up 38 per cent year-on-year, with a 37 per cent annual growth recorded the year before.

SMS usage

On average a mobile user in Croatia sends 70 SMSs per month, ie 2.5 SMSs per day, which is rather high in comparison to other EU countries (only Irish users have similar SMS usage; Spanish users send 50; Germans around 40; and the French around 15 SMSs per month. European citizens send 25 SMSs on average).

M-commerce

The operators offer various micro-payment options (in the amount of €5–10 per month, through their account, without agents or registrations) and they have started to develop a macro-payments offer. Macro-payments (HRK500–5,000 monthly per user) are made through agents (banks, credit card companies), as required by law.

Mobile payment of parking by SMS (micro-payment) is widely used; Croatia is ranked as the leading country in the use of mobile payments. Around €50,000 was invested in the m-parking project, and SMS parking is nowadays used more widely than the parking machines. In January 2003, INA, the national oil company, launched a pilot project for payment by SMS messages at petrol stations, thus enabling mobile payment for all INA's 140,000 card holders. The research on this sample has shown that the necessary technology is in place, and INA is seeking a strategic partner to develop this system for all users (involving banks and card companies). This way Croatia became, besides South Korea, the only country where clients can pay for fuel at the filling station by mobile phone.

Local services

In order to make the stay of foreign tourists in Croatia more convenient, both Croatian mobile communication operators – HTmobile and VIPnet – offer general and tourist information, which helps the tourist to get around cities and find interesting sights. According to the draft Act, data on location that refer to users or subscribers to mobile networks can only be processed where the users or subscribers' consent has been obtained. Users and subscribers must always have the option to withdraw their consent for location data processing.

GPRS

According to the information available in early 2003 VIPnet had around 26,000 GPRS users. Assuming that HTmobile has the same number of GPRS users, we have a very small base of only 2 per cent of total mobile users that use the 2.5 generation of mobile communications, or only 1 per cent GPRS penetration.

HT Mobilne Komunikacije d.o.o.

In 1991 HT d.d. began to offer analogue mobile telephony services, ie the NMT network. In 1996 it launched GSM for post-paid users. During 2002 HT d.d. made a decision to transfer the mobile telecommunication business to a wholly owned subsidiary, HT mobilne komunikacije d.o.o. (HTmobile). The total interest of HT d.d. in this wholly owned subsidiary amounts to HRK1,478 million. HT mobile commenced its commercial activities on 1 January 2003, until when GSM and NMT services had been provided by HT d.d. Legislation passed in the second half of 2001 provides for the right of HTmobile to be awarded the UMTS concession under prescribed conditions and for a fixed concession fee. HTmobile has a GSM Concession Agreement, which lasts for 10 years, and the NMT Concession Agreement, which lasts for 30 years starting from 16 September 1999. In addition to the initial concession fee paid of HRK100 million, HTmobile currently pays an annual concession fee of HRK4 million for the NMT concession, and HRK5 million for the GSM concession.

Until separation, HTmobile was part of HT and it was possible only to compare the income of these two operators and the number of users. With the creation of a separate company, HTmobile is certainly going to improve efficiency, and investors will be in a better position to compare these two companies in terms of efficiency and profitability.

HT d.d. revenue from mobile networks increased by 44 per cent from HRK1,162 in 2000 to HRK1,673 million in 2001. This growth in revenue was achieved by having a stronger customer base. Revenue growth was also supported by improvements in the quality level and territory coverage of the GSM network (capacity extension and upgrading of technical platforms).

VIPnet d.o.o. was founded in 1998. On 7 September 1998 VIPnet won a 10-year concession for the construction and operation of the second GSM network in Croatia. The concession was granted and the contract was signed on 30 October 1998. VIPnet's network, established in the record time of eight months, went 'on air' in July 1999. VIPnet d.o.o. is the first private GSM operator in Croatia. The shareholders are Austrian Mobilkom Austria AG (80 per cent), Western Wireless International and Croatian investors. Foreign investors own the majority share of the consortium (99 per cent), while domestic investors control the remaining 1 per cent. VIPnet is considered to be one of the most successful start-up companies in the industry. The 1 million customer mark was passed in the third quarter of 2002; growth rates among the most important key figures are impressive.

VIPnet's development reflects the economic upturn in Croatia that began in 2000. After the launch of the first full-coverage GPRS network in Croatia in May 2001, VIPnet made m-commerce a priority. The most popular service is VIP.parking, which allows users to pay their parking fees by mobile phone.

When entering the market VIPnet estimated that it would move into profit by 2004. However, as early as 2000 it had HRK25 million of profits, or 2.1 per cent of its total income. Market data and information on VIPnet's performance are shown in Figures 2.9.1 to 2.9.5.

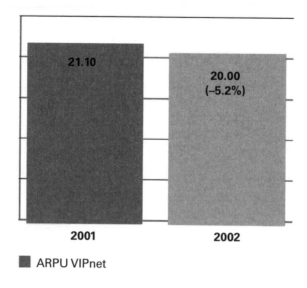

Status: EOY 2002; Source: Mobilkom Austria

Figure 2.9.1 Average revenue per user (ARPU) VIPnet

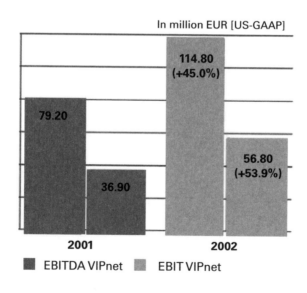

Status: EOY 2002; Source: Mobilkom Austria

Figure 2.9.2 EBITDA & EBIT VIPnet

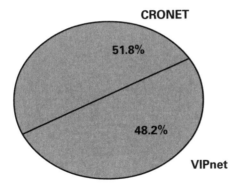

Status: EOY 2002; *Source*: Mobilkom Austria

Figure 2.9.3 Market share VIPnet vs HT

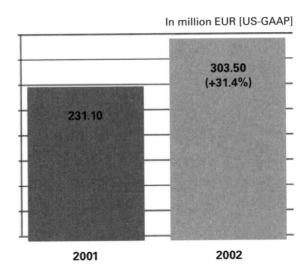

Status: EOY 2002; *Source:* Mobilkom Austria

Figure 2.9.4 Revenues VIPnet

GSM penetration in 1999 was only 7 per cent. Between 1999 and 2002 it grew to 52 per cent. The subscriber growth was highest at the end of 2000, when the customer base of both operators grew by more than 200 per cent. VIPnet took almost half of the market in only one year of operations.

Although HTmobile's customer base is higher than VIPnet's, VIPnet's total revenues from operations were higher in all years. This doesn't

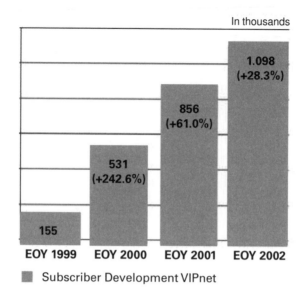

Subscriber Development VIPnet

Status: EOY 2002; *Source:* Mobilkom Austria

Figure 2.9.5 Subscriber development VIPnet

mean that VIPnet's customers have higher ARPU than HTmobiles'. HT d.d., when reporting revenues from mobile operations, consolidates the interconnection revenues and costs within the group, so HTmobile's interconnection revenues from fixed network were not included in the HT 'revenues from mobile business'.

The cumulative average mobile revenue growth from 1999 to 2002 was 63 per cent, which is heavily influenced by VIPnet's revenue growth of 400 per cent in 2002. The CAGR revenue growth for both operators from 2000 to 2002 was around 37 per cent. The Croatian mobile market volume in 2002 amounted to HRK4.3 billion (around €580 million).

What can a third GSM operator expect? The Croatian GSM market is mature in terms of service and penetration. By the time the third concessionaire gets ready for the commercial operation, the penetration will have reached at least 60 per cent. VIPnet has invested round HRK1.5 billion in network construction, of which 28 per cent is for the purchase of equipment from Siemens and Ericsson Nikola Tesla. The new operator will have to invest several hundred million euros to set up the network and cover operating losses in the initial years. The third operator will probably reduce prices in order to acquire a 20 per cent market share, which is estimated to be the minimum for survival. The price of calls and other services in Croatia are on or below the European level, which is an additional burden for a potential third mobile operator.

The third operator will therefore have to focus on the market segment that has not been covered by the existing two operators. The experience from Western Europe shows that a third operator mostly targets younger pre-paid users.

Sources

http://www.vipnet.hr/
http://www.htmobile.hr/

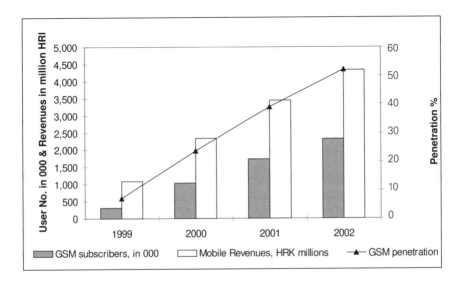

Source: Croatian Institute of Telecommunications – CIT, Annual Reports of Croatian Telecom and Mobilcom Austria, Central Bureau of Statistics (Republic of Croatia)

Figure 2.9.6 Mobile revenues, users and penetration

The Advertising and Marketing Industry in Croatia

Lowe Digitel d.o.o.

Introduction

The transition from a 'socialist' to a market economy in Croatia has led to the development of commercial media, advertising and marketing, all of which have grown in quality and volume, with a much higher rate of growth rate than the GDP.

Marketing and advertising had been important in Croatia much earlier (mid-1960s) than in most of the other transitional countries. The major reasons for this were: emigration, primarily economic, which brought Western standards directly to the Croatian families without state interference; highly developed industry; national political structures that perceived marketing as a vehicle for autonomous development; and tourism, which was mainly an individual/family business, market-oriented and hard to control. These circumstances provided the conditions for the development of agencies and commercial media, long before the capitalist economy was introduced. As a result, marketing and market communication have a significant tradition and their subsequent progress had solid foundations. This is particularly noticeable in the functional integration of local and global communications.

Development can be summarized in one sentence: a high level of integration of the local and global marketing industry has been achieved in Croatia, resulting in a quality service for local and multinational companies and their brands. Whether the task is to launch a new brand or to support an international brand, integrated communication can be performed professionally and efficiently, according to global industrial standards yet compatible with the local market.

Media overview

The advertising market in Croatia has faced some big changes in the past couple of years.

The state-owned media monopoly ended a few years ago. The growth trend in the past five years has been extremely high and was gradually slowing down in 2003 due to the stabilization effect.

Not only the media, but also advertisers, advertising agencies and research agencies have gone through an evolutionary period. In 1999 there were only two subsidiary/representative offices of international agencies, whereas in 2003 there were 15 international agencies (media and creative) as well as dozens of locally owned agencies. A similar situation is found in PR, although the number of agencies in this field is much smaller. Interestingly, the biggest advertising and PR agencies are locally owned but affiliated to international networks.

Media research is available for all media, using recognized methods such as diary, CATI and telemetric/electronic measurement of TV viewing, and also single-source research on brand usage, exposure and perception of media and lifestyles.

Characteristics of media channels in Croatia

TV

The first year of real changes in the TV market was 2001; other media underwent the privatization process years ago. HTV, the national TV service with three channels was a monopoly until the end of 2000, when a licence for commercial TV was issued to Nova TV. HTV is still the market leader with more than 65 per cent audience share. Nova TV holds approximately 25 per cent audience share, while the rest is distributed among several local/regional TV stations. By the end of 2003 there will be another commercial TV station as a result of the reduction of HTV broadcasting from three to two programmes, whereupon the third HTV channel will be privatized.

Print

The ownership of print media is highly concentrated and private, and overall quality is continuously improving. There are three big international players: Waz, Styria and Sanoma. Political and female magazines dominate the market. There are Croatian editions of international magazines – *Cosmopolitan, Playboy, Story, Elle* and *Lisa*. Regarding readership, although there is no spill over from neighbouring countries, most Croatian magazines are also read in Bosnia and Herzegovina, Serbia and Slovenia.

Radio
Overall, with six national networks and more than 130 private local and regional radio stations, the radio market is highly developed with diverse offerings. National stations include the state-owned radio station, Hrvatski radio, which broadcasts three national programmes, and three private radio stations – Otvoreni radio, Narodni radio and Hrvatski katolicki radio.

Outdoor
There are four international (Europlakat Proreklam, Metropolis Media, Outdoor, Akcent) and one local network operating throughout Croatia with more than 8,200 billboards and 2,300 city lights.

The Internet
Approximately 28 per cent of households have Internet access in Croatia. Use of the Internet as an advertising media is a question of prestige at the moment (less than 1 per cent share), although this is slowly changing. The main Internet advertisers include software and hardware manufacturers, financial institutions, car manufacturers, ISPs and telecommunications companies.

Cinema
With a share below 0.5 per cent, cinema is not important in terms of advertising. However, with the arrival of the first multiplex, the interest of audiences and thus advertisers has increased. New multiplexes will be opened in the near future.

The advertising market in numbers

Estimates from the Mediana-Fides Agency are shown in Tables 2.10.1 to 2.10.4.

The legal framework (media and advertising)

The Croatian Parliament has recently passed two bills relevant to this subject: the Consumer Protection Law and the Law on Electronic Media, both of which are in line with the recommendations of the European Union. A third law is also under way: the Law on Media. These laws will provide a solid base for the development of the Croatian marketing industry as a whole, in line with EU standards.

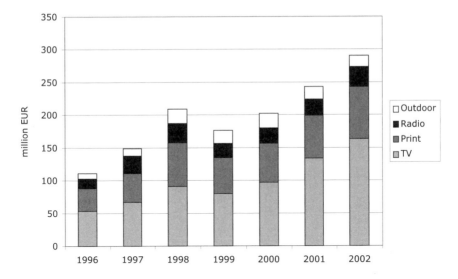

Figure 2.10.1 Advertising expenditure

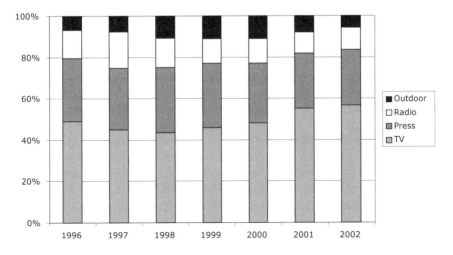

Figure 2.10.2 Share by medium

Conclusion

In this domain, business in Croatia is completely compatible with the marketing industry worldwide. All those considering coming to Croatia, or who have already decided to come, can count on marketing support in the media, agencies, legislators and the regulatory body. Croatia has ensured a high-quality welcome to all those who wish to do business with or within Croatia.

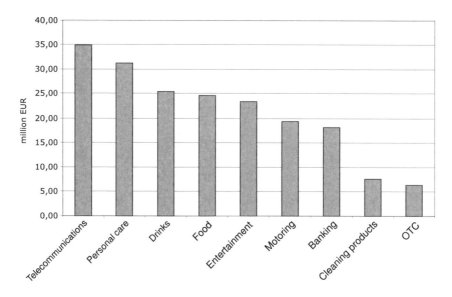

Figure 2.10.3 Top 10 advertising categories

2001	Gross Sum	2002	Gross Sum
Advertiser	EUR	Advertiser	EUR
Hrvatski telekom	19,449,064	Hrvatski telekom	19,592,094
VIP Net	12,662,539	VIP Net	14,336,772
P&G	6,919,215	Beiersdorf	12,221,384
Beiersdorf	5,792,509	P&G	7,923,309
Reckitt Benckiser	4,628,969	Henkel	5,363,495
Henkel	4,269,725	Hrvatska lutrija	4,987,595
Zagrebačka pivovara	4,044,591	Karlovačka pivovara	4,450,995
Coca-Cola	3,889,962	Coca-Cola	4,368,633
Unilever	3,788,690	Unilever	4,355,886
Privredna banka Zagreb	3,512,001	Zagrebačka pivovara	4,282,494

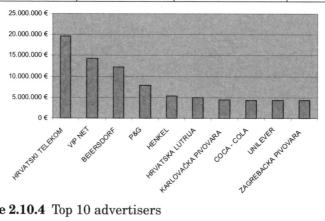

Figure 2.10.4 Top 10 advertisers

2.11

The Power Sector

HEP

In terms of electricity generating capacity and electricity demand, the Croatian power system is among the smaller European systems. The system has a history of electricity transit, and is crucial for the electricity supply of neighbouring countries. Croatia has played this important transit role as a UCTE member state since 1975.

Former 400 kV and 220 kV interconnections between Croatia and Slovenia, Bosnia and Herzegovina and Serbia are partly out of operation due to war damage. Reconstruction work is underway and all the facilities will be fully operational within the next two years. The construction of the 400 kV transmission line towards Hungary was completed in 1999, which significantly improved the east–west transit of electricity.

The existing generating capacities in Croatia can meet current electricity demand under average hydrology conditions (a significant number of hydro power plants provide generating capacities). However, electricity generation in obsolete liquid-fuel-fired thermal power plants, which is very expensive, is, for economic reasons, being replaced by cheaper imported energy, so that Croatia's average electricity imports account for 25 per cent of the total annual demand.

Key data (2001)

Electricity generation capacity	4,809 MW
Electricity generation	11.26 TWh
Electricity consumption	14.45 TWh

Generation mix: 50 per cent conventional thermal, 7 per cent nuclear and 43 per cent hydro.

The activities related to electricity in Croatia are almost exclusively performed by a state-owned vertically integrated company for electricity generation, transmission and distribution – Hrvatska Elektroprivreda (HEP). HEP is the only authorized electricity trade entity, and is responsible for electricity supply to 2 million customers in Croatia.

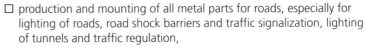

△ DALEKOVOD

joint-stock company for engineering, production and construction
ZAGREB - CROATIA

Since its foundation in 1949., DALEKOVOD d.d. has developed into a modern organisation with over 1.600 employees, that offers services of

- □ design,
- □ production and
- □ erection

of the following fields of service and engineering that DALEKOVOD is specialized in:

- □ design and production of suspension and jointing equipment for all types of transmission lines and substations from 0,4 up to 500 kV,
- □ design, production and erection of steel lattice and lighting towers and other metal structures,
- □ design, production and erection of electric power facilities, especially transmission lines from 0,4 up to 500 kV,
- □ design and erection substations of all types and voltage levels up to 500 kV,
- □ mounting and laying of aerial, underground and submarine cables up to 110 kV,
- □ erection of telecommunication facilities, all types of networks and antennas,
- □ production and mounting of all metal parts for roads, especially for lighting of roads, road shock barriers and traffic signalization, lighting of tunnels and traffic regulation,
- □ electrification of railways and tram lines in the cities.

Dalekovod d.d. is entirely a privately owned company. 85% of the company shares are owned by small shareholders (mostly former and present employees of Dalekovod). Two Employee Stock Ownership Plans (ESOP 2000 and ESOP 2001) have been carried out so far at Dalekovod and 60% of the company employees have taken part in it.

In order to ensure independent auditory control of the company, PriceWaterhouseCoopers has been engaged by the Supervisory Board and the Management Board of the Company. The shares of Dalekovod have been listed at the Zagreb Stock Exchange since March, 2001. under the stock exchange symbol **DLKV-R-A.**

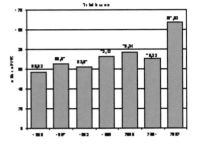

Dalekovod is a company engaged in design, production, and assembling of electric power, traffic and telecommunication facilities, as well as consultancy services on the domestic and international market. It is a fully customer-oriented company which insists on quality of its products and services based on specific know-how and qualifications of it's labor force, as well as the ability of prompt adjustment to the impacts of the environment by developing competitive capacities.

Our mission is to provide a complete service to the infrastructure industry (electric-power, road and railway traffic, telecommunications) based on the principles of professional excellence and top quality. Our base are our people who possess specific knowledge and skills, highly appreciated by our customers. We are a learning organization with the ability to adapt quickly to turbulent environmental influences. The operation of our company is characterized by a stakeholder approach, reflected particularly in the fact that the company is majority owned by its current and former employees. We shall always be a responsible member of the society making sure that our sustainable development be harmonized with the interests of the wider community and requirements of environmental protection.

Our highly educated personnel can solve each challenge related to the design, production and construction technology from company's line of business. By developing fundamental competencies and skills which are important to this industry, we are trying to add new values to our products and services.

It should be noted that along with our already traditional business efficiency, implementation of the ISO 9001:1994 system, certificated by the Lloyd's Register Quality Assurance in 1995, has contributed significantly to the improvement of our business operations. In order to ensure constant quality monitoring, Dalekovod is carrying out adjustment of ISO 9001:1994 to ISO 9001:2000. The clean and healthy environment is ensured by the application of the International ISO 14001 standard, whereby we give our full contribution to the environmental protection.

By fostering principles of our profession and by applying acknowledged world quality and environmental protection standards, Dalekovod is trying to continously improve our customer's satisfaction. Dalekovod today is a reliable, renowned and acknowledged partner throughout the world in our wide ranging area of product and services.

The results of our business policy and our cooperation with domestic and international partners are high-quality equipment and services, which along with acceptable prices, are highly appreciated and accepted by our customers worldwide.

Besides above mentioned standards, Dalekovod was also awarded: EN 729-2, BSI OHSAS 18000, ISO/IEC 17025.

Beeing a fully customer oriented company demands strong research and development. Strategy to continuously develop new prodacts or to improve existing products in order to improve our customer's satisfaction has forced DALEKOVOD d.d. to prepare and carry out two large investments in year 2003.

The first one is a hot dip galvanizing plant in Dugo Selo, located some 20 km from Zagreb. This plant will be the biggest hot dip galvanizing plant in the region and commission date is set to August 2003. The capacity of this

plant is 31.000 tons of steel per year. It has two production shops.The first one is for polygonal poles and high masts, guard rails & accessories, transmission towers and other products up to 12,50 m in length. Dimension of the zinc kettle is 13,00 x 1,80 x 2,80 (h) m. The second shop is for nuts & bolts, suspension and jointing equipment, hollowware, anchor bolts and other small materials. It is equipped with automatic suspended spinning equipment. This galvanizing plant will satisfy following quality and environment standards: EN ISO 1461, ASTM-A 123, ISO 9001 and 14001.

The galvanizing plant DALEKOVOD-CIN?AONICA d.o.o. is founded as limited liability company in 100% ownership of DALEKOVOD d.d.

The second investment is the new laboratory for vibrations, which is expected to be the best equipped in the south-east Europe. The present DALEKOVOD's laboratory is mostly oriented toward testing of new or improved DALEKOVOD's products and quality control. After the new vibrations lab is commissioned, DALEKOVOD's laboratories will be able to offer their services on the market as well.

Dalekovod has specially equipped teams of experts for the terrain work at its disposal. They can execute works under all climatic conditions and on all terrains by using special machines and tools of Dalekovod. Besides the application of special derricks for lifting up loads during the erection process, the experts of Dalekovod take pride in having wide experience and knowledge in the use of special work helicopters for erection.

Our expert teams are specially prepared and trained in order to measure up to the requirements of construction of particular projects. The references of Dalekovod concerning erection of 0.4-500 kV electric power transmission projects, 0.4-500 kV substations, laying of underground and submarine power and telecommunication cables, lighting of roads, sports grounds and industrial facilities, railroad contact networks, installation of aerial and TV towers and mobile telephone towers (GSM), guard-rails on motorways, traffic signpost portals, indicate enough that Dalekovod is a safe and reliable business partner.

Our design department utilizes up to date software (Catia V) for 3D modelling and generating software for machining of tool components which are fabricated on the CNC processing machines. Thus, DALEKOVOD's design department is able to swiftly respond to the new customers or even markets demands. Accumulated experience, references, extensive data - base and specialized know - how, are today coupled with the most sophisticated CAD/CAE technology.

Products from our production program have been manufactured in our own production workshops by means of technologies for forging, casting, mechanical processing, welding, sand blasting, hot dip galvanizing, mounting and other. DALEKOVOD d.d. in own production has special tool workshop for production of all tools, devices and facilities which are necessary for quoted technologies.

Our half a century of experience in development, design and production of suspension and jointing equipment, testing results and experience from building and service of transmission lines are a guarantee of the quality, reliability and functionality of our products. DALEKOVOD d.d. today is one of the leading companies in production of suspension and jointing equipment worldwide. Today, about 80% of products is assigned for international market.

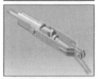

Our contacts:

DALEKOVOD d.d.	DALEKOVOD-CINCAONICA
	d.o.o. Galvanazing plant
Ul. grada Vukovara 37	Trno??ica b.b.
10000 ZAGREB	10370 Dugo Selo
CROATIA	CROATIA

General manager
phone: ++385 (01) 6171 287   phone: (++385) (01) 2753 602
Contracting
phone: ++385 (01) 2411 214   telefax: (++385) (01) 2753 652
International sales
phone: ++385 (01) 6227 202   e-mail: galvanize@dalekovod.hr
telefax: ++385 (01) 6170 450

e-mail: dalekovod@dalekovod.hr
web: www.dalekovod.com

In Croatia, HEP owns 21 hydro power plants and eight thermal power plants and is co-owner of a thermal power plant (Plomin 2 TPP) with RWEE. HEP also owns 50 per cent of a nuclear power plant (Krsko NPP) located in Slovenia and 650 MW in thermal power plants located in Bosnia and Herzegovina and Serbia. Due to unsettled ownership conditions following the independence of certain republics of the former Yugoslavia, the facilities in Slovenia, Bosnia and Herzegovina and Serbia totalling 1,004 MW are currently not generating electricity for Croatian needs.

In addition to HEP's output, electricity in Croatia is also generated in small industrial plants and privately owned renewable electricity sources. However, such generation accounts for only approximately 1 per cent of total electricity generation.

Electricity sector reform strategy

The Government and the Parliament of the Republic of Croatia have embraced the concept of energy sector reform consistent with European energy regulations. The basic principles of the reform were outlined in a document adopted in July 2000.

In July 2001, the Energy Law was passed along with the Law on Regulation of Energy Activities and a number of specific laws governing individual energy activities, eg the Law on Electricity Market regulates electricity-related activities; In March 2002, privatization Acts were passed for the national energy companies INA (oil industry) and HEP (electricity). In November 2001, the Croatian Energy Regulatory Council was established (the Regulator). Following the passage of secondary legislation in the course of 2002, all formal and legal conditions for the establishment of an electricity market and HEP's restructuring and privatization will be met.

The Law on Electricity Market stipulates that the activities related to the operation of the Croatian electric power system should be divested from HEP and performed by a separate company, Croatian Independent System and Market Operator (CISMO), to be entirely owned by the state. CISMO was established and started its operations in 2002.

The Law on Electricity Market sets out the obligation to restructure HEP into a group of associated, legally independent companies performing particular core electricity activities (generation, transmission, distribution and supply). HEP Group is governed by a parent company HEP Parent, which is the founder of the companies carrying out individual activities. It has been envisaged that HEP Group will be engaged in other energy and infrastructure activities (gas, district heating, water, telecommunications) in separate companies. HEP Group and CISMO have a public service obligation related to electricity supply to tariff customers and are obliged to provide electricity transmission and distribution services. In competitive activities, appropriate companies of the HEP Group will compete with other electricity undertakings under fair market conditions. The restructuring of HEP in line with these principles was carried out in 2002.

The privatization of HEP will be implemented through the sale of corporate shares in the HEP Group. In the first phase, until Croatia's accession to the European Union, up to 49 per cent of HEP will be privatized, and the remaining 51 per cent will remain in state ownership. The scope and method of HEP's privatization after Croatia's accession to the European Union will be determined in a separate law. The privatization of up to 49 per cent of HEP will be carried out upon completion of the restructuring phase.

Individual companies within the HEP Group, as well as all new electricity undertakings in the Croatian electricity market, will have to apply to the Regulator for a licence for carrying out energy activities, submitting proof of their technical, expert and financial qualifications for carrying out particular activities. Electricity consumers with an annual electricity consumption over 40 GWh are eligible customers and are allowed to choose their electricity supplier.

The electricity price in Croatia is on average below the economic price due to the former policy of the state to set 'social' prices. With the establishment of market conditions, the price of electricity for tariff customers in Croatia will rise; a formula will be devised to adjust the price of electricity should there be a change in operating costs over which HEP has no influence (hydrology, fuel prices, or currency exchange rates). The new tariff system for electricity has been passed. The prices of individual infrastructure services (transmission, distribution, system operation, system services, etc) will be the same for the companies belonging to HEP Group as for all other system users.

Implementation of the Electricity Directive by Croatia

The Energy Law, Law on Regulation of Energy Activities and Law on Electricity Market were adopted on 27 July 2001 (*NN*, No 68/2001) with an implementation date of 1 January 2002. These laws regulate all issues relevant to carrying out electricity activities, and for the functioning of the electricity market in the Republic of Croatia.

Market opening

The law establishes that all electricity consumers with annual electricity consumption exceeding 40 GWh can become eligible customers, provided

TEP d.d.

TEP was established August, 3rd 1949. We are based in Zagreb with production plants in Zagreb, Krapina and Desinic. TEP is an ISO 9001 certified company – satisfying the highest standards in manufacturing and assembly. Our products are found in small and large projects all over the world.

Main technologies:

Processing of metal materials by milling, turning and cutting on CNC machines

- Metal sheet processing on CNC machines
- Injection moulding and press moulding
- Surface treatment and surface protection
- Assembling
- Laboratory testing

Today TEP maintains three basic production programmes:

- Lighting fittings and devices
- Installation material
- Distribution devices

Lighting
- Street lamps
- Park and garden lamps
- Tunnel lamps and lights
- Sports stadium floodlights
- Assembly lamps
- Decorative
- Custom design
- Industrial lights and lamps

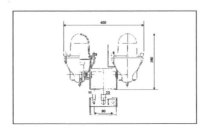

Distribution Devices
- Low voltage distribution boards
- Distribution cabinets
- Cable accessories for power and telecommunication cables
- Installation systems
- Industrial electronics

Installation
- Mounting installation systems
- Mounting program
- Surface mounting installation systems
- Plugs and sockets for industry

Medarska 69, 10090 Zagreb, Croatia
Tel: 00-385-13782-202
Fax: 00-385-13782-247

email: tep-rasvjeta@tep.hr
www.tep.hr

that they apply to the Regulator for such a status. This legal provision provides for a 10 per cent opening of the electricity market in Croatia.

Access to the network

A regulated third-party access (TPA) is applied to all legal entities that have been issued a licence for carrying out energy activities or have been approved as eligible customers by the Regulator.

Regulator

The Regulator is responsible for the entire energy sector. It is appointed by the Croatian Parliament on the Government's proposal and financed from the price of electricity and other energy products. In the field of electricity, the main tasks of the Regulator include: issuing licences to energy undertakings for carrying out electricity activities, ensuring proper functioning of the electricity market, and meeting public service obligations. The Regulator performs these functions by controlling free access to the network, approving construction plans and regulating electricity prices for tariff customers and the prices of individual infrastructure services. The Regulator has been appointed and is gradually taking charge of its functions.

Competition in generation

The construction of new generating capacity in Croatia can be realized either through the tendering process for the supply of electricity to tariff customers or through the licensing process for supply via the electricity market. The Regulator carries out tendering and licensing procedures.

Unbundling

In the event that one energy undertaking carries out more than one energy activity, accounting separation between the activities is a minimum requirement. As regards HEP, it has been established that individual core electricity activities will be organized in legally independent, associated companies integrated into the HEP Group.

Unbundling of transmission system operator

It has been established that the activities related to power system operation and electricity market activities will be organized according to the ISMO model, separate from the electricity transmission activity. A separate company for performing such activities (CISMO) has already been established and is gradually taking charge of the activities related to system operation and electricity market organization.

Tariff setting

The Government of the Republic of Croatia is still setting electricity prices. Basic price adjustments, ie general price rises and the establishment of fair relations between consumption categories (today households pay less than industry), will be regulated by a Governmental resolution, and subsequent control over prices will rest with the Regulator.

Renewable energy and energy efficiency

Improving energy efficiency in the generation and use of energy, and the utilization of renewable energy resources (RES) are among the objectives of HEP's environmental and development policy. Apart from the traditional use of hydroelectric power (over half of installed capacity), HEP is actively promoting private investment in small RES, co-generation and energy consumption services. Activities started in 1994 with the voluntary decision to buy electricity from small RES and co-generation plants, up to 5 MW, at favourable rates, based on the average electricity sales price. HEP currently has Power Production Agreements with two small hydroelectric power plants, one co-generation power plant and one wind farm, with interest from many other developers keen to invest in RES technologies in Croatia.

The future policy will comply with National Energy Programmes (1997), the Energy Strategy of Croatia and the Energy Law. The Law on Electricity Market gives priority to energy from co-generation and renewable sources.

The main proposed financial instrument to date for promoting renewable energy and energy efficiency is the Environmental Protection and Energy Efficiency Fund Bill. It is intended to raise money from various sources (eg taxes on emissions) to create a fund that can support programmes to improve energy efficiency and the use of RES.

With the World Bank loan and the GEF (Global Environmental Facility) grant, the HEP subsidiary HEP Esco has been established, which will provide commercial services for energy efficiency improvements in all sectors of energy use. HEP has also actively participated in the development of the World Bank/GEF Croatia Renewable Energy Resources Project, which will provide support in developing secondary RES legislation, as well as initial finance for project development and investment, thus stimulating development of a sustainable RES market in Croatia.

JEDINSTVO D.D. KRAPINA – CROATIA

ACCOMMODATION CONTAINERS

- offices
- sleeping rooms
- shops
- storages
- workshops
- schools
- containerized objects

ABLUTION CONTAINERS

- container with shower cabins
- container with toilet cabins
- toilet container male/female
- with shower and toilet cabins

PREFABRICATED OBJECTS, STEEL CONSTRUCTIONS AND STEEL BUILDINGS

- storages, industrial areas, workshops, shops, etc.
- prefabricated steel buildings; fast and easy for building system
- executing of camps, sleeping rooms, administrative areas, kitchens, laundries, recreation facilities, common rooms
- all elements and materials are made in accordance with EURO norms

MOBILE HOUSES FOR TOURIST CAMPS

Other products: profiled steel sheets for roofs and facades, cold formed profiles, road equipment, pay toll houses, sound proffing barriers, wire fences, steel guard rails, gantries, road and border crossings, petrol stations, building executing on domestic market.

JEDINSTVO d.d., Mihaljekov Jarek 33, HR-49000 KRAPINA
Tel: 385 49 370 567, 370 505, 370 539   Fax: 385 49 370 546, 371 429
E-mail: pmd-jedinstvo@kr.htnet.hr   http://www.jedinstvo.com
jedinstvo1@kr.htnet.hr   http://www.container-object.com

JEDINSTVO d.d. Krapina is a company with 50 years long tradition in metal production, especially in production of accommodation containers, profiled steel sheets and steel constructions.
JEDINSTVO d.d. has over 400 employees and is situated at 136.000 m² of land area, 34.000 m² of them are production, warehouse and office area.

We are interested in exporting our products to foreign markets, cooperation with foreign companies; joint investments in machinery and production, product developing, technology transfer, mutual exporting to new markets.

We have free capacity of land area and over 20.000 m² production and warehouse area. This area is free for the letting and it is very good traffic binding.

We would also like to mention possibility of cooperation in the free zone area located next to our firm. There are possibilities for production, storing, finishing and other activities. Exports and imports procedures are very simplified.

2.12

Industrial Sector Case Study:
Kaplast of Karlovac

Mario Dombos, Kaplast Company; and Marat Terterov

Introduction

Kaplast is a company engaged in the production of injection-moulded products made from plastic. This is a well-known technology and has been in use for over 50 years. Products made from this technology are employed in virtually all spheres of human life – from very basic sectors such as food production, to the extremely high-tech space industry. More specifically, Kaplast specializes in the production of all kinds of plastic crates: crates for agricultural products, the fish and meat industry and the bread industry, multifunctional crates, crates for beverages, internal transport crates, crates for post, etc.

During the last few years Kaplast has specifically focused on the production of crates for beverages (soft drinks, beer, mineral water, etc). These crates are a relatively complex line of production, with the numerous ribs that keep bottles in position during transport. These internal ribs bring additional complexity to the hardware and software of the crates' production process. Not every company in the industry is able to manufacture this product line because of this complexity. Kaplast's success in this respect is based largely on the input of the company's employees, their experience, knowledge and enthusiasm.

Kaplast produces other plastic products too, including those suitable for production with injection moulding technology, such as cans, cases for electrical equipment, and other parts for the electrical industry. Furthermore, Kaplast owns two additional technologies: silkscreen printing, and hydrographical decoration. Silk screens are printed in four colours and used for decoration on the crates; for example each brewery may have its own logo on the crates. Hydrographical decoration is decorating electrical switches in the home, etc.

Company history in brief

The Kaplast Group consists of two companies: Kaplast and Kaplast-Eko. Kaplast is responsible for management of the group, providing leadership, marketing and development, sales, purchasing, financial and bookkeeping. It is in essence the head of the entire operation. Kaplast-Eko, on the other hand, is responsible for physical production.

Kaplast is situated in Karlovac, a small town 40 kilometres from Zagreb, the capital of Croatia. Kaplast-Eko is situated in Kupljensko, a small village 30 kilometres from Karlovac. Kaplast has nine employees, while Kaplast-Eko employs 55 people. From time to time, depending on the amount of contracted work, Kaplast-Eko can have up to 100 employees. Most of the employees live in Karlovac and get to and from work on transport provided by the company. Kaplast-Eko is situated outside of the city of Karlovac because it was originally a state-owned firm established to generate employment and growth in an economically underdeveloped area. It is doubtful whether the production side of Kaplast's business would have been located in Kupljensko had the company been founded under free market conditions.

Kaplast d.d. was established on 9 July 1992, being privatized and legally created on the foundations of a former state-owned enterprise. It is the legal successor of OOUR Plastika (Osnovna Organizacija Udruzenog Rada – Basic Organization for Associated Work), which was founded in 1971 and operated under the state holding company Ivo Marinkovic. At the end of the 1970s Plastika became a part of a big and complex corporation, Jugoturbina, and from OOUR it became RU (Radna Organizacija – Work Organization). In 1986 it became an independent organization, d.p. Kaplast. Kaplast d.d. is a joint-stock company, registered by the trade court in Karlovac; it was the first company to be established through privatization in Karlovac. During the privatization Kaplast shares were freely sold on the market: 22,717 shares were created with the nominal value of DM100. International accounting standards are employed in the Kaplast company.

On 14 January 1997 Kaplast d.d. founded the subsidiary Kaplast-Eko d.o.o. in the town of Vojnic. The new company was a joint venture between Kaplast d.d. and the Italian company Genaral Plast, which acquired a 25 per cent stake in Kaplast-Eko (it provided the production equipment for the new enterprise, which was valued as being equivalent to 25 per cent of the worth of the company). It invested in the company with a view to planned deals with Kaplast-Eko, though these did not develop as readily as first hoped. Kaplast has recently been in discussion with the multinational company Electrolux over the production of refrigerator parts.

Kaplast d.d. is a private closed joint-stock company with more than 50 per cent of the stock being owned by one person. This concentrated ownership structure is good for Kaplast according to the company management – good because it is clear 'who is in charge' and 'who is the boss'. Several examples exist in Croatia where the ownership structure of a company is not clear, or non-conclusive cross-ownership exists between the public sector and private shareholders. In such cases the decision-making processes at the company can become hazy, leading to uncertain management strategies and a dubious corporate governance environment.

Product line

Kaplast produces approximately 2,400,000 crates per year and the company's clients include all the breweries in the region. The market for the company's product is growing, due to the overall tendency of economic liberalization taking place in the market. The company's main clients include:

- Interbrew – Belgium/Zagrebacka pivovara – Zagreb.
- Carlsberg – Denmark/Panonska pivovara – Koprivnica.
- Jamnica – Zagreb.
- Karlovacka pivovara – Karlovac.
- Osjecka pivovara – Osijek.
- Sarajevska pivara – Sarajevo, BIH.
- Uniline – Grude, BIH – member of Interbrew.
- Coca-Cola – Croatia.
- Koncar N.N. – Zagreb.

It is obvious that within the context of Croatia's relatively small market of 4.5 million people, it is the beverages industry that places the greatest demand on Kaplast products. It requires Kaplast crates for the storage and transport of its glass bottles. Each individual brewery can occasionally require up to 100,000–200,000 crates, and together the Croatian market requires some 1 million crates per year. Kaplast is by far and away Croatia's dominant player in the production of this type of plastic crate, holding nearly 100 per cent of the market. Competition does arise from time to time and, in theory, any company that has an injection moulding production capability is a competitor. In practice, Kaplast has remained the dominant player in the market to this point. Kaplast's business is further strengthened by its cooperation with a licensing partner from Germany, Scholer Wavin System. The German firm owns almost all the sophisticated moulds for the production of crates and Kaplast rents them from Scholer Wavin System.

The market for non-beverages industry crates (vegetable and food industry crates, multifunctional crates) is problematic for Kaplast due to the small and fragmented nature of the Croatian market. Kaplast occasionally receives requests for the purchase of small quantities of such crates, usually for 200 to 300 units. However, producing less than 50,000 units makes no economical sense for Kaplast. As a result, and bearing in mind Kaplast's virtual monopoly on domestic crate production, the Croatian market tends to be full of imported non-beverages industry crate products (especially those from Germany and Italy). Given that the needs of the Croatian market are relatively small, when the foreign companies produce the various crates for their own much larger markets, it is easy for them to produce an additional 2,000–3,000 extra units for export to the Croatian market. Kaplast management, in an attempt to mount stronger competition to the foreign companies in the non-beverages sector, is contemplating an adjustment in strategy which would involve production of, for example, 100,000 units of such crates, which would be stored and then sold to order. The merits of this strategy are currently being debated by the company management, since storage costs have to be taken into account and to produce this number of crates will involve an investment of several hundred thousand euros (which, in effect, would be an investment in future customers). With proper marketing strategies, however, it is possible that such an investment may still be worthwhile for the company.

Similar problems to those experienced with the non-beverages sector crates also apply to other goods manufactured from plastic, particularly in the case of smaller products. Such products can be produced in smaller, even family-run factories, competing with which is difficult for firms like Kaplast. For Kaplast to win market share in this segment it must invest in very fast and sophisticated modern machines, which means again a large investment with a relatively high risk.

Marketing

Kaplast recently established a marketing and development department, the main function of which is to support Kaplast in all aspects of the company's physical production, to research and investigate the market, and in general to help the company innovate and compete effectively, thereby ensuring a decent profit for shareholders. Kaplast management is seeking to collect as much know-how as possible with regard to the relevant plastics industry production process. It is seeking to demonstrate the company's production possibilities and for its line plastic products to be acclaimed in Croatia and beyond. The marketing department is striving to create an environment where clients approach the company with simple but potentially profitable enquiries such as: 'Can you produce this?' This strategy requires the following:

- good marketing with a constant eye on the market and customer, and fresh ideas;

- a good development department capable of designing almost anything, using computers, including production of complete technical documentation for products and tools;

- good production techniques capable of self-maintenance and the development of new tools;

- taking advantage of Croatia's geo-economical position, its relatively low costs, and the quality of its workforce.

Kaplast's products are predominantly sold in Croatia, Slovenia and Bosnia and Herzegovina. The company is looking to expand business into other former-Yugoslavian countries, particularly Serbia and Montenegro, although this is currently progressing slowly. If Croatia enters the European Union, Kaplast management believes that the company would have much to gain. The company (and for that matter many of the other enterprises operating in the country) would no longer have to invest time and resources in imports and exports of all kinds of products and tools. Saving money on transactions costs related to international trade would also allow the company to reap the benefits of Croatia's cheaper labour costs and would force the Croatian government to pass more open and flexible laws.

Doing business with Croatia

As far as the country's investment climate is concerned, it cannot be said that Croatia has a perfect business environment. There is a lot of room for improvement. However, on a positive note, the country is improving in this sphere day by day and is learning from some of the mistakes made by others in Europe, including the other transitional economies. New legislation in support of improvements in the business climate takes some time to be implemented, which tends to fuel the country's large internal debt. There are still far too many policy-makers in the country used to the ways of socialist economic planning. Furthermore, other policy-makers engaged in the privatization process are encouraging a 'quick profit' mentality among entrepreneurs, rather than thinking long term about the companies in their portfolio. The socialist regime was in place in Croatia for virtually half a century and it is high time to replace it with a well-regulated market-oriented system.

As well as the advantages for a company like Kaplast in operating a business based in Croatia, there are some disadvantages, including: relatively high taxes, which make production more expensive; a small market, which makes investment in production and development questionable; and some problems with infrastructure (the cost and distribution of energy, roads, etc), some of which are a consequence of the recent war.

In a broader, historical context, Kaplast management sees Croatia as geo-socially central, between the ancient Greek and Roman empires – the cradle of European civilization. There is something special about Croatia – the mixture of sun and clouds, water and colours, wine and smells, summers not too hot and winters not too long. The mixture of the earth's basic elements influences the Croatian people in a most positive way, and the work ethic of this Euro-Mediterranean nation is one of 'wanting to work, but also wanting to live'. Croatians are close enough to the 'west and the north' to make them industrious, but also enough to the south to gear them towards the 'good things' – a relaxed, low-stress, high-quality lifestyle.

Karlovac is located right in the middle of Croatia and the city's residents benefit from having to spend a minimum amount of time and energy when travelling around the country. Karlovac is close enough to Zagreb, the Croatian capital, to enjoy its benefits, but far enough out to 'avoid the crowd'. Karlovac is close enough to the Croatian seaside and port cities to enable it to be connected with the outside world, but it is also surrounded by hills and countryside, and four beautiful rivers run through the city.

As a final note, Kaplast management wishes to point out that, in the final analysis, everything depends on people. People are the key ingredient for success or failure:

> We find that positive energy is very important. People with more life, time and space experience more of this 'positive energy'. We are well satisfied that we have a good team to work with: Kaplast. We owe much of this team success to the people employed in our company, as well as a little bit of luck that has brought all the elements together to their right positions in our company. The professors of plastic technology from the University of Zagreb (Croatia's largest university) are frequently praising the general manager of our company. Furthermore, throughout its history, Kaplast's factories have managed to avoid serious disruptions to their business and the company has maintained a stable, production cycle over the years. These factors jointly tell us that that the name Kaplast is truly a recognizable one when it come to doing business with Croatia.

Kaplast's annual turnover for 1999–2002, in euros (source: Kaplast Company) was:

1999	2,043,417
2000	2,662,689
2001	5,851,400
2002	6,224,000.

Part Three

The Taxation and Legal Environment

3.1

The Legal Framework for Doing Business with Croatia

S Miroslav, Deloitte & Touche Zagreb

Introduction to the Croatian legal system

The legal system of the Republic of Croatia is by its nature a part of the legal systems of the countries of continental Europe.

The elements of the Croatian legal systems are regulations, legal customs, court practice and jurisprudence. Regulations represent a substantive legal source in the Republic of Croatia, as they contain written legal rules applied on a day-to-day basis. They are in hierarchical order: the Constitution of the Republic of Croatia, laws and regulations.

The Constitution, being the fundamental and organic Act, governs the basic framework of the legal, political and economic systems of the Republic of Croatia as a modern European democracy. Thus, the basic provisions declare the inviolability of ownership as a high value of the constitutional order of the Republic of Croatia. Rights of ownership and of succession are guaranteed; however, the ownership right is binding for its holders and beneficiaries in terms of their contribution to the general welfare.

Further, entrepreneurial and market freedoms are guaranteed, and monopolies are forbidden. Exceptionally, entrepreneurial freedom and right of ownership may be legally restricted to protect the interests and security of the state, nature, the human environment and public health. As regards the protection of foreign investments, the Constitution specifies that rights acquired on the basis of the investment of foreign capital cannot be diminished by law, or by any other legal Act. Repatriation of profits and the capital invested is guaranteed.

Constitutional provisions are further explicated by appropriate laws, which represent the foundation of individual legal institutes. The legal system of the Republic of Croatia is based on the codification of legal institutes in the tradition of Continental Europe. The legal rules of contractual, ownership and commercial relations are codified by the Law on Property and Other Proprietary Rights, the Law on Obligations and the Companies Law.

By signing the Stabilization and Association Agreement with the European Union in 2001, the Republic of Croatia assumed, among others, the obligation to reconcile its legislation with EU laws. Thus, the Croatian legislation should be complemented by new acts governing various areas such as interest rates, savings deposit insurance, copyrights and other related rights, e-commerce, etc.

Regulations govern the implementation of laws; however, certain regulations may exceptionally override the legal force of laws. These are primarily the directives issued by the Croatian prime minister, which govern individual legal issues on an exceptional basis.

Reference to legal customs as the source of legal systems is made only if the customs are based on a legal right. In the law of obligations, legal customs serve as a supplementary source of law, in particular of commercial and contract law, the so-called commercial customs.

Commercial customs are also codified, forming commercial practice. One distinguishes between general and specific commercial practice, depending on whether it applies to trade in all kinds of goods and services, or only to certain goods and services.

The governing principle underlying the Croatian law of obligations is that commercial practice applies only if the parties have agreed to apply it, or if the circumstances imply that they actually wanted to apply it.

Since the legal system of the Republic of Croatia is based on legal right, the court practice in Croatia represents an indirect rather than a direct source of law. In Croatia, a decision of a higher court affects a decision issued by a lower court only by force of conviction. As a result, compilations of court decisions have a positive impact in standardizing court practice.

The courts in the Republic of Croatia are the Constitutional Court, the Supreme Court, county courts and municipal courts. The Constitutional Court is not a part of the judiciary but rather a separate court, whose activities are aimed at protecting the constitutionality and legality of Croatia's judicial system. The Supreme Court of the Republic of Croatia is the highest judiciary body issuing final rulings in appellate court proceedings. County courts judge in appellate proceedings in civil matters and represent a first-instance court in criminal proceedings. Municipal courts are first-instance courts in first-instance civil proceedings.

Regulatory incentives to promote investments in Croatia

Investment incentives

The Investment Promotion Law, enacted in 2000, provides an institutional framework for incentives to domestic and foreign investors, legal entities and individuals, to promote economic growth, development and a more intense participation in international trade by enhancing exports and the competitiveness of the Croatian economy.

The Investment Promotion Law was conceived as a system of incentives, tax and customs benefits to investors under the following prerequisites. Investors are entitled to incentives when they establish applicable new companies in the Republic of Croatia (except for investments in the tourist trade, where the Croatian Government may accept an existing company as the beneficiary of incentives and benefit receiver on the basis of the proposal of the Ministry of Finance). Investments comprise the value of items, rights and obligations, as defined by international accounting standards, which have to be invested in the initial capital of the incentives beneficiary. Investments in land, buildings older than one year and previously used equipment are not recognized as investments. To be able to exercise the right to incentives, the investor has to make an investment of at least HRK4 million.

Incentives comprise co-financing of new jobs, professional training and retraining of workers, and other specific benefits, such as the lease, use, purchase and sale of properties or other infrastructure facilities under commercial or favourable terms and conditions, with or without a consideration.

The existing legislation emphasizes the role of tax benefits to investors, consisting in a lowered corporate income tax rate, or even tax exemption during a certain period, depending on the amount of investment and the number of new employees at the incentives' beneficiary. The reduced corporate income tax rate ranges from 13 per cent to zero rate, ie full tax relief. For example, for an investment of a minimum of HRK10 million, corporate income tax will be paid at a 7 per cent rate over a period of 10 years from the beginning of the investment, provided that a minimum of 30 new staff are employed during the period.

The incentives' beneficiaries who make an investment of a minimum HRK60 million will have a 10 per cent corporate income tax rate over 10 years from the beginning of investment, provided that a minimum of 75 new employees are taken on during the period.

Customs benefits are in the form of customs duty exemptions on imported equipment for the purposes of the business for which customs benefits otherwise apply.

To be able to obtain incentives, tax and customs benefits, first the incentives procedure has to be initiated. However, there is also the obligation of regular annual reporting to the Ministry of Economy and the Ministry of Finance of the Republic of Croatia. The procedure for obtaining incentives, tax and customs benefits is initiated by submitting an application to the Croatian Ministry of Economy and the Ministry of Finance.

Concessions

The legal framework for concessions in Croatia is defined by the Law on Concessions, which has been in force since December 1992. Thus, a foreign and/or a domestic legal entity or individual may acquire the following on the basis of a concession: the legal right for economic use of natural and other resources that are designated as objects of interest for the Republic of Croatia by a separate legal act; the right to carry out a business activity of interest to the Republic of Croatia and to construct and use facilities and plants necessary for this purpose. Concessions cannot be granted for forests and forest land in Croatia.

The law has enabled a transparent procedure for granting concessions in Croatia on the basis of public tender. Participants in granting concessions are, in addition to executive bodies (the Croatian Government) and legislative bodies (the Croatian Parliament – Sabor), the executive bodies of the units of local administration and local self-government (towns, cities, municipalities or counties) in whose territory the subject of the concession is located. They give a prior opinion to the Croatian Government, which then forwards the proposal to the Croatian Parliament as the final decision-making body.

Concessions are granted by the Croatian Government on the basis of the following criteria:

● business reputation of the bidder;

● ability of the bidder to qualify for the concession;

● favourableness of the bid (technical and financial);

● environmental impact of the concession.

The rights and obligations between the government authorities, ie local authorities, and the bidders are governed by a concession contract, which may be concluded for a maximum period of 99 years, except for a concession contract for agricultural land, which is concluded for a maximum period of 40 years.

The concession contract as a legal transaction should provide appropriate guarantees that the granted concession will meet the economic purpose of the concession and are in line with the interests of the Republic of Croatia. Concession contracts are entered in the register of concessions, which is maintained by the Croatian Ministry of Finance.

A frequent clash of local interests represented by local authorities and those of the government authorities means that this Law has created problems in practice. For this reason, a new legal solution is expected in the near future, which would provide an efficient resolution of any potential conflict between the interested parties, along with measures to ensure an efficient concessions process.

Free zones

Free zone regulations are a major portion of the Croatian legislation aimed at promoting investment and economic development. The Free Zones Law, in force as of June 1996, defined free zones as separate, distinctly marked parts of the Croatian territory in which economic activities are carried out under favourable conditions.

Free zones may be established in seaports, airports, river ports, along international roads, or in other areas suitable for their operations. Free zone users may be the founders of a particular free zone, but also other domestic and foreign persons who carry out their businesses in the zone on the basis of an adequate agreement concluded with the zone founder. The following activities may be performed in duty-free zones:

- manufacturing of goods;

- finishing works;

- wholesale trade and trade mediation;

- services;

- banking and other monetary transactions if connected with the manufacturing of goods or provision of services;

- property and personal insurance and reinsurance if connected with the manufacturing of goods or provision of services.

A special benefit for free zone users is that they pay corporate tax at 50 per cent of the prescribed rate (currently 20 per cent). The free zone users involved, directly or indirectly, in infrastructure construction in the free zone valued at over HRK1 million are exempt from paying corporate income tax in the first five years of operating the business in the zone.

The following free zones have been established in the Republic of Croatia:

- Krapinsko-Zagorska Free Zone, Krapina;

- Free Zone Kukuljanovo, Rijeka;

- Free Zone Osijek;

- Free Zone Podi, Sibenik;

- Port of Rijeka;
- Free Zone Zagreb;
- Free Zone Obrovac;
- Free Zone Split;
- Splitsko-Dalmatinska County Free Zone;
- Free Zone Ploce;
- Free Zone Pula;
- Free Zone Buje;
- Free Zone 'Duro Dakovic', Slavonski Brod.

3.2

Business Entities in Croatia

Vanja Markovic, LLM, Tax and Legal Consultant, Deloitte & Touche Zagreb

Introduction

The basic statute regulating business organizations in the Republic of Croatia is the Law on Commercial Companies (*Narodne Novine*, No 111/93), which came into force on 1 January 1995. (hereinafter referred as the 'Company Law').

Croatian company law was modelled on the laws and legal practice of the Central European countries, based on German company law. Since 1995, when the Company Law came into force, the law has not been significantly amended, except with the ruling of the Constitutional Court of the Republic of Croatia (Decision n. U-I-945/99 dated 10 May 2001), which abolished the prerequisite that at least one member of the management board of a company has to be employed by the same company. Provisions of the Company Law were harmonized with the solutions applied in the European Union at that time.

Recently, the Parliament introduced comprehensive amendments to the Company Law (*Narodne Novine*, No 118/03), which will apply from January 1, 2004. In the preamble of the Governmental proposal to the Parliament, several reasons were given for the adoption of the amendments:

- to correct the mistakes of the Company Law currently in force;

- to introduce changes in the Croatian legal system based on the achievements in corporate law of developed countries adopted since 1993, eg closely held corporations, no par value shares, restrictions regarding acquisition of treasury shares, strengthening the position of minority shareholders, information flow in corporations, and supervision of company operations, more protection for stakeholders, giving more responsibility to managers and the supervisory board, etc;

- to harmonize provisions of the Company Law with other statutes that took effect after the Company Law entered into force, eg Law on Enforcement, Bankruptcy Act, Securities Act and Law for the take-over of joint-stock companies;

- to continue harmonization of the Company Law with the provisions on the European Business Interest Grouping in accordance with EU Directives;

- to make certain provisions of the Company Law more clear and to give legal solutions necessary to ascertain uniform application of the Company Law by the courts, which is in accordance with the common practice in the member states of the EU.

A short list of major changes to the Company Law is included at the end of this chapter.

Foreign investments

The equal treatment of domestic and foreign entrepreneurs is pro-claimed in The Constitution of the Republic of Croatia. In addition, the Constitution grants to foreign entrepreneurs the right of free movement (transfer) of profit and invested capital. The Company Law defines the term 'foreign company' and grants to foreign investors equal treatment in the territory of the Republic of Croatia. Pursuant to article 619 of the Company Law, foreign investors are deemed to be those legal persons, whose principal place of business is not registered in the Republic of Croatia, and every natural person that is a foreign citizen, refugee or without citizenship, or Croatian citizen having permanent residency outside of Croatia, that is acquiring a stake or shares or is investing in a company on a contractual basis. From the notion of the foreign investor it derives that investments are limited to corporations, eg join-stock companies and limited liability companies; meanwhile partnerships are partially excluded. In fact, the law prescribes foreign entrepreneurs investing in partnerships to have the legal form of a corporation (joint-stock company or limited liability company) and to have at least one Croatian partner (natural or legal person) personally responsible for the obligations of the partnership.

In accordance with the Croatian Company Law, foreign persons are allowed to organize their business activities in the following manner:

- open a representative office;
- organize a branch office;

- establish a company with other foreign or domestic partners, or acquire shares or stakes in an existing company;

- conclude entrepreneurial agreements.

Representative office

Provisions of the Decree on Conditions for the Establishment and Operation of Foreign Representative Offices in the Republic of Croatia (*Narodne Novine*, No 7/1997) will apply if there is reciprocity between Croatia and the country where the founder of a representative office has a registered principal place of business. A representative office is defined as a non-profit organization, which is not allowed to carry out any commercial activity on behalf of its founder or to conclude contracts on the founder's behalf. The exception applies to representative offices of foreign air carriers in accordance with international treaties signed by the Croatian State. Foreign companies and national or international business organizations are allowed to open representative offices in Croatia. Pursuant to the applicable regulations, a foreign representative office in the Republic of Croatia can be engaged in the following field of work only:

- advertising;

- local market research activities;

- carrying on promotion and information-gathering activities and marketing.

Such activities might consist of:

- developing possibilities for the founder's activity in Croatia;

- communicating with customers;

- providing business partners in Croatia;

- providing consultancy services and imparting instructions to customers in Croatia on a 'free of charge' basis;

- collecting and analysing market data for the purpose of business planning, etc.

Under Croatian law, a representative office does not have a separate legal personality. A representation office is considered to be a part of the founder, and therefore is deemed to carry out activities on behalf of the founder and under the founder's name, though excluding commercial activities. For the latter reason, representative offices are not corporate income tax payers and are not VAT registrants. However, for personal income tax purposes, the representative office is considered as any other separate legal entity in Croatia. In accordance with the personal income tax laws, the representative office is required to remit income tax for employees. The representative office is also required to remit all applicable social contributions, such as health, pension and others, for both employees and employer portions.

From the accounting standpoint, the representative office does not have to keep complete and formal accounts. The assets of the representative office are kept on the books of the founder. However, the representative office should keep evidence regarding expenses that occur in the course of its operation and have evidence of payroll taxes.

It is important to note that all payments to and from the founder and a representative office in Croatia are effected through a non-resident account. The account can be opened with any commercial bank in Croatia that is licensed to perform foreign transactions. In addition, these accounts can be used by the representative office for the receipt of payments from which it can cover the costs of its business operations, such as wages, rent, advertisements, etc.

A representative office will exist once it has been registered with the Registry of Representative Offices of Foreign Entities in the Ministry of Economy. In order to register a representative office in Croatia, the founder has to provide the following documents:

- excerpt from the company register of the founder;

- copy of the latest balance sheet of the founder;

- request for the establishment of the representative office to the Ministry of Economy of the Republic of Croatia;

- resolution on the appointment of the representative office manager (person responsible for operations of the representative office in Croatia);

- copy of the payment slip proving the payment of taxes in the amount of HRKK30,000;

- statement of the founder accepting responsibility for all obligations incurred by the representative office;

- resolution of the founder on the establishment of the representative office in Croatia.

The Ministry has to decide on the registration within 30 days after the submission of the application.

In the course of its business operations, the representative office would be obliged to act in accordance with applicable Croatian Labour Law; ie with respect to its Croatian employees the rules of the Croatian Labour Law are applicable, and foreign employees must obtain Croatian work permits.

Branch office

A branch office is not a separate legal entity and is deemed to be a part of the foreign founder. Consequently, its rights and obligations pertain to the mother company or to the individual merchant and not to the branch office itself. Business operations of a branch office are not limited to a definite list of activities as is the case with representative offices.

The establishment of a branch office in the Republic of Croatia is regulated by the Company Law. The first prerequisite for foreign companies or individual merchants to open a branch office in Croatia is reciprocity with their country of origin. The founder will be able to start business operations through its Croatian branch once it is registered in the commercial court registry with the authority in the area where the branch office will be situated.

When submitting the request for the registration of a branch office, the founder has to include the following documents translated into Croatian by the certified court translator:

- excerpt from the company register of the founder (evidence of its business form and date of incorporation);

- resolution to open a branch office;

- certified copy of the articles of association of the founder;

- certified copy of the latest balance sheet of the founder;

- resolution on the appointment of the person authorized to represent the branch office.

Working relations are regulated in the same manner as for representative offices. In fact, the working relations of Croatian employees are regulated by provisions of Croatian Labour Law and other related provisions.

From the accounting and tax standpoint, the branch office is treated as a separate legal entity. Based on its financial statements, which have to be prepared and kept in accordance with the Croatian laws, a branch is required to calculate and pay corporate income tax in Croatia for the income earned in Croatia.

Business organizations

The Company Law is not the only law on the establishment and legal structure of business organizations in Croatia. There are several special laws that regulate particular fields of business such as banking, insurance, brokerage and the labour market that have to be taken into consideration when investing in Croatia. However, the basic provisions on the structure and organization of businesses are included in the Company Law.

Pursuant to the Company Law, where a foreign investor decides to operate in the Croatian market through a legal entity independent of the mother company, ie obligations incurred by a Croatian company are not the responsibility of the founder as is the case of a representative office or branch, this can be accomplished in two ways: a) by acquisition of shares in existing Croatian companies or other contractual bases; b) a foreign founder has to organize a partnership or a company in Croatia.

Partnerships
Croatian Company Law provides for different types of partnerships and leaves ample room for autonomous regulation of relations within an organization. Foreign investors can participate in the following forms partnership provided by Croatian law:

- general partnership (javno trgovacko drustvo);

- limited partnership (komanditno drusvo);

- economic interest grouping (gospodarsko interesno udruzenje);

- silent partnership (tajno drustvo);

- joint venture (zajednicki pothvat).

General partnerships   A general partnership is a business organization of at least two people formed for the purpose of permanently performing business activities under a joint company name, where the partners are jointly liable for obligations of the partnership with all their assets. Partners in a general partnership may be domestic legal and natural persons, or domestic and foreign legal persons. In fact, for foreign companies willing to form a general partnership in Croatia, the law prescribes the need to have at least one Croatian partner (natural or legal person) in the partnership. A partner can dispose of his or her interest in the partnership only with the consent of all other partners.

Every partner is authorized to manage the ordinary work of a partnership, but partners are free to determine different structures in the memorandum of association, which is the basic document required for its formation. For actions that go beyond the normal course of business, it is necessary to obtain the consent of all partners.

The memorandum of association has to include the following data for registration with the Commercial Court Registry:

- company name and address of companies participating in the partnership;

- partnership name and address of the general partnership to be established in Croatia;

- scope of business;

- obligations of the companies participating in the partnership, and other data relevant to the operation of the partnership.

Limited partnerships   A limited partnership is a business organization of at least two people whose liability is limited only to the amount of their capital contribution in the limited partnership. For foreign investors, the same limitation applies as for other forms of business. There has to be at least one domestic legal or natural person personally liable for all of the assets of the obligations of the partnership. The name of the firm must include the name of one or more general partners and letters 'i dr.' (cro and others).

A limited partnership has a legal personality and has to be registered with the Commercial Court Registry.

Economic interest groupings   The provisions on economic interest groupings (EIG) have been taken from the law of the European Union. The Company Law defines an EIG as a legal person set up by two or more individuals or legal persons for the purpose of facilitating and promoting their business activities and of promoting or increasing the effect of these activities, with a limitation that a grouping may not earn profits for itself.

The law provides that members of an EIG may be natural or legal businesspersons, ie persons who carry on business activities, or those following an independent profession, eg lawyers and dentists. Members of the EIG are personally liable for the obligations of the grouping. The law does not provide for any kind of limitation based on country of registration for members of an EIG, as is the case in the EU, where the form is available to people registered in EU countries only.

A member may transfer its interest only with the approval of all members. The consent of all members is also required for the accession of a new member.

An EIG is formed based on a memorandum of association and has to be registered in the Commercial Court Registry.

Silent partnerships   The contract by which a person (entrepreneur) invests certain assets in the enterprise of another person and thereby acquires the right to participate in sharing profits and the obligation to share losses of the undertaking is known as a 'silent partnership'. However, the parties can determine differently in the agreement and provide for the silent partner to be excluded from covering any losses.

A silent partnership is founded on a contractual relationship and is not considered a separate legal entity, ie it does not have a company name and it is not registered with the Commercial Court Registry. It derives that a contract does not have effect in relation to third parties and that it does not have its own property.

Joint ventures   A joint venture is a particular type of partnership, which is internationally accepted as a type of direct investment of capital in international business operations. Croatian provisions on joint ventures are included in the chapter on partnerships in the Law on Contracts. In joint ventures, parties to the contract agree on contributing capital and participating in profits earned or losses incurred in undertakings of common interest.

The business operations of a joint venture partnership are based on the agreement – joint venture agreement, shareholder agreement, etc – concluded between the parties. Usually, the agreement is very detailed and includes provisions on common interests, project development, participation and transfer of profit, the capital contributions of the parties, management of the partnership, transfer of know-how, etc. Pursuant to Croatian law, a joint venture is not deemed a separate legal entity, and therefore partners are held personally liable for the obligations of the partnership. In fact, if the shareholder agreement does not provide for a specific arrangement to represent the partnership, each partner will have the right to approach third parties.

Under Croatian law, a joint venture may operate as either a contractual joint venture or an equity joint venture. In the case of a contractual joint venture, the undertaking is limited to the contractual relationship between the parties, excluding the incorporation of a new company for the management of the venture. In an equity joint venture, partners to the venture will organize a company (usually a limited liability company or joint-stock company) to establish the undertaking. Anti-trust provisions apply.

Corporations

Pursuant to Croatian law, a limited liability company and a joint-stock company are two types of business organizations whose main feature is that the capital of the company is divided, respectively, in stakes and shares. Accordingly, the rights of a stakeholder in the company will derive from the value of his or her contribution in the share capital. The transfer of stakes in corporations is free, except for limitations made in the association agreement. In that respect, Croatian law allows 'vinkulacija', the term used when the articles of association of a joint-stock company (or a limited liability company) provide that shares may not be transferred without the consent of the corporation.

Limited liability company   A limited liability company is defined as a company in which one or more individuals or legal persons (members of the company) invest their property and thereby participate in the previously agreed share capital. The corporate name must include the letters 'd.o.o.', which indicate that the company is structured as a limited liability company in Croatia.

Members of the limited liability company are not held personally liable for obligations incurred by the company. Share capital of a limited liability company is divided in stakes, whereby a single investor may not hold more that one stake when establishing a company. If the founder of the company is a single investor, the basic document for such an organization will be the founder's statement, or in case of more founders, the basic document will be a memorandum of association, both of them in the form of a notary public document.

Pursuant to the Company Law, a limited liability company is composed of the management and the general assembly. A supervisory board consisting of at least three members is mandatory for companies with more than 300 employees. Members of the supervisory board are elected by a vote by the members in the general meeting of the company. All stakeholders of the company are represented in the assembly of the company. Members of the company have votes in proportion to their contribution in the share capital.

The management board is composed of one or more members. There are no restrictions with respect to appointment of a foreign national as a director. Members of the board have the authority to represent and manage the company. Members of the assembly may recall the management board of the company 'at any time'. From that perspective, the position of the members of the management board is less independent than that of the directors in joint-stock companies. The idea of the limited liability company is to have a close relationship between partners who are actively involved in the management of the company.

Formation   The fundamental document for incorporation of a limited liability company is a memorandum of association, or statement of the founder where the incorporation is accomplished by a single founder only. This agreement must be signed by all shareholders and certified by a notary public.

The law provides for a minimal share capital that can be executed in cash or in kind, which is the equivalent of €2,500 (approximately HRK2,600 after January 1, 2004). If contributions are made in cash, the investor should make a transfer on the temporary account of any financial institution in Croatia. If the contribution is in kind, than it has to be fully rendered. In addition, investors have to agree on the members of the management board. Investors are free to determine in the memorandum of association if they want to have a supervisory board as well.

Under Croatian law, a company will acquire its legal personality once it has been registered with the Commercial Court Registry in the district where the company is going to have its permanent place of business.

A foreign investor has to provide the following documents when submitting an application to the Commercial Court Registry for organizing a limited liability company in Croatia: original excerpt from the company registry of the founder, resolution of the founder to establish a company including the name of the company and its address in Croatia, the scope of the business, and the share capital.

The application for registration will be submitted after the company agreement has been signed, the shares paid in compliance with the company agreement and one or more members of the company management board appointed. The application for registration will include the following items:

● company name, address and scope of business;

● share capital;

● statement of the management board members on their obligation to provide all information to the court;

● names of the company members and, if company members are physical persons, their registration numbers.

Further, the following documents have to be enclosed with the application:

● a copy of the memorandum of association;

● a list of members/founders;

● a certificate issued by a relevant financial institution that they received the payment of the share capital;

● a guarantee where the company is being founded by one founder only;

● reports on revision of the company's incorporation when the share capital consists of contributions in kind;

● a list of people authorized to conduct business operations, the scope of authorizations and their statements of acceptance of the given assignments before a notary public;

● approval of the state body;

● signatures of members of the management board.

Joint-stock companies
A joint-stock company is a business organization in which share capital is divided into shares and shareholders are not personally liable for the obligations of the company. The company name of joint-stock companies has to include the letters 'd.d.', which stand for joint-stock company (hrv. dionicko drustvo).

The law provides for the minimal share capital of DM30,000 (approximately €15,000) for setting up the company if the registration is accomplished before January 1, 2004 and HRK200,000 (approximately €26,000) after January 1, 2004. In any case, the amount of the share capital expressed in Croatian Kuna must be a multiple of HRK100. Other laws provide for higher amounts of share capital for particular business activities such as banking, securities trading, etc.

The minimal nominal (par) value of shares is the HRK100. However, with the recent amendments of the Company Law it will be possible to issue shares with no par value or to have shares with the par value of HRK10. There can be two types of shares: registered name-shares and bearer shares. Share issues before payment of full par value have to be name-shares. In principle, shares are freely transferable, but share-holders may stipulate in the articles of association restrictions with respect to registered shares requiring the consent of the management board for their transfer. Joint-stock companies are allowed to have treasury shares in cases strictly determined by law.

Pursuant to Company Law, a joint-stock company is composed of a management board, a supervisory board and the general assembly. The management board is appointed by the supervisory board for a maximum period of five years and may be re-elected. Members of the board may be discharged from their duty by the supervisory board if there is an important reason for this. The management is in charge of the management of the corporation. Members of the management board cannot be influenced by the supervisory board in taking business decisions. However, the articles of association may include provisions on mandatory consent of the supervisory board for certain decisions. Currently, the Company Law does not mandate representation on the management board for particular groups of stakeholders.

The supervisory board is composed of at least three members that cannot be members of the management board of the same company at the same time. They are elected by the general assembly of shareholders for a term of four years and can be re-elected. Shareholders may stipulate in the articles of association that no more than one-third of the members are nominated by shareholders. The supervisory board has a duty to supervise the management of the corporation. The general shareholders meeting of a joint-stock company is the principle forum through which shareholders exercise their rights.

A joint-stock company can be formed by simultaneous incorporation and by incorporation in stages. A simultaneous incorporation consists of:

- the founders adopting and signing the articles of association;

- the founders giving the statement to a notary public on setting up the corporation;

- adopting all outstanding shares;

- payment for adopted shares;

- appointment of the supervisory board and the auditor, and having a supervisory board to appoint the management board;

- report on the establishment of corporation.

A joint-stock company has to be registered with a commercial court.

If a corporation is set up by incorporation in stages, the founders of the corporation must adopt the articles of association, subscribe part of the shares and issue a prospectus for subscription of the remaining shares (to be subscribed in the following three months).

Acquisition of shares and takeover law

A company may decide to invest in Croatia by acquisition of shares in an existing joint-stock company. There are two fundamental statutes to be observed in this case: the Company Law and the Law for the Takeover of Joint-stock Companies (*Narodne Novine*, No 84/02). The Law on Securities (*Narodne Novine*, No 84/02) contains provisions on the Croatian Securities Commission and Central Depository Agency and provisions concerning the protection of investors, issuance and transfer of securities, etc.

Pursuant to the Law on Takeover, an investor is required to publish a tender offer for the remaining shares in a company in the following situations:

- When a person procures more than 25 per cent of the total number of votes in the main assembly of the issuer, they shall be obliged to report the acquisition to the Securities Commission of the Republic of Croatia (hereinafter the Commission), the Issuer and the public, and to publish the tender offer following the procedure prescribed by the Law.

- When a person, by means of a tender offer, has achieved less than 75 per cent ownership of voting shares, they are obliged to publish a tender offer in case of any further procurement of shares from the same issuer.

- When a person by means of a tender offer procures the ownership of 75 per cent or more of all voting shares, they are obliged to publish a tender offer when procuring additional voting shares of the same issuers in the following situations:

  - when after the tender offer has been accomplished they acquire an additional 5 per cent of voting shares;

- after 18 months following the acquisition of shares at the completion of the previous tender offer.

The price for tendered shares cannot be lower than the highest price paid by the tender for shares acquired in the period following the previous tender offer.

Before the publication of the tender offer for the takeover, those making the offer must place in a separate account the monetary assets necessary to pay for all shares that are the subject of the tender offer for the takeover, or enter into an agreement with the bank on approved credit for that purpose, or originate a bank guarantee for first rights in favour of the shareholder and for the amount necessary to pay for all shares concerned.

In addition, before the publication of the tender offer for the takeover, those making the offer must enter into an agreement with a depositary institution on the deposit of the shares concerned.

Within 30 days after the obligation for the mandatory tender offer has arisen, those making the offer are required to request the approval of the Croatian Securities Commission to publish the takeover, and the offer and documentation as stated in Article 12 of the Takeover Law. If all the requirements prescribed by the law have been observed, the Securities Commission is obliged to give approval within 14 days of receiving the duly submitted request. Those making the offer are obliged to publish the tender offer in the *Croatian National Gazette* (Narodne Novine) and in one of the daily newspapers regularly distributed throughout Croatia.

The offer is binding for 30 days starting from the day it was made public. In the case of a hostile bid, another term of 30 days will start to run. The law does not provide for a maximum number or duration of extensions. After expiration of the term, those making the offer have an obligation to acquire all deposited (tendered) shares.

Mergers and acquisitions

It has become a frequent practice in the business world to concentrate capital, technologies, finance and labour in order to strengthen the position of a company in the market. This practice should be even more evident in Croatia and other Central and Eastern European countries, which are aware of the significant impact the European Common Market will have on their business operations. The most common procedure provided by the Company Law to effect this aim is a procedure of merger by acquisition. Under the Company Law a merger by acquisition is defined as a procedure by which one or more legal entities transfer all their assets to another company against shares (a stake) of the other company. Acquired entities cease to exist without effecting the liquidation procedure. A merger is where two or more entities form a third company to which all of their assets will be transferred. To perform a merger Croatian law prescribes that all merging companies must have been in existence for at least 2 years (this to be ascertained in the Commercial Court Registry of legal persons) if they are both joint-stock companies. Where a merger is effected between a joint-stock company and a limited liability company, the restriction does not apply. Provisions on mergers and mergers by acquisition apply to limited liability companies and joint-stock companies only.

The Company Law provides for several provisions related to the protection of the rights and interests of shareholders/stakeholders participating in the merger. In fact, the law mandates for the minimal content of the merger agreement that management boards have a duty to prepare a comprehensive report on the merger and inform the shareholders, that there has to be a revision of the merger, that all companies participating in the merger have to approve the merger with a majority of 75 per cent of members of the assembly, etc. Special attention has to be given to the share exchange ratio of the merging companies. The ratio must be related to the net asset value of the respective companies.

Minority shareholders freeze-outs
The present Company Law does not provide for the case where majority shareholders may in certain cases buy out other shareholders. The recent amendments to the Company Law provide for shareholders of a joint-stock company having at least 95 per cent of all shares in the company to buy out minority shareholders by giving them an adequate price for their shares.

Entrepreneurial contracts
The relationship between the subsidiary and the parent can be of different intensity. The entrepreneurial agreements represent a type of relationship between two companies where one of them (the dependant) renounces in favour to the other company (the parent) one of the main features of the company, which is to make profit and to act in the interests of its stakeholders. There are two types of entrepreneurial contracts: agreement on conducting business operations, and agreement on transfer of profit.

Agreement on conducting business operations is the contract by which a company agrees to transfer the conduct of its business operations to another company, while in the agreement on transfer of profit, a company agrees to transfer all its profit to another company. Due to the importance of such a decision, the law prescribes a majority of at least 75 per cent of votes present at the shareholders assembly of both parties to the agreement.

The controlling company will be responsible for debts of the dependent and has to provide for the severance payment of the minority shareholders at the value of the estimated annual dividend.

The amendments to the Company Law (Narodne Novine 118/03)

The Croatian Parliament introduced important amendments on the Company Law of 1993, in order to harmonize those provisions with EU Directives and other Croatian legislation adopted after 1993, such as the Law on Enforcement, the Bankruptcy Act, the Law for the Takeover of Joint-stock Companies, etc.

Foreign investors in Croatia should be aware of the following amendments that were made to the Company Law.

Share capital

The share capital will be expressed in the local currency, and the minimum share capital was raised from DM30,000 (approximately €15,000) to HRK200,000 (approximately €26,000) for joint-stock companies, while it remains basically unchanged for limited liability companies (HRK20,000 or approximately €2,600). Corporations (d.o.o. and d.d.) established before the proposed amendments enter into force may continue to work in line with the current regulations. Corporations will have to comply with the new provisions when changing bylaws on legal share capital or the par value of shares for the first time after the amendments to the Company Law become effective.

Par value of shares

Pursuant to the Government's amendments it will be possible to issue shares with no par value. However, a minimal par value will be HRK10 instead of HRK100, as it is today.

Approval of financial statements

The management board has the obligation to prepare financial statements in accordance with accounting regulations, which will be transmitted to the supervisory board for inspection and approval. If approved, the statements will be passed to the shareholders' assembly. In this manner the board is held responsible for the accuracy of the statements prepared.

Dividend payment

The amendment provides for a clear distribution of income. Before a dividend can be paid to shareholders, a joint-stock company will have to cover the losses from previous years and cover the legal reserves. The remaining profits may be used for treasury shares, and finally to cover statutory reserves if any. It will be impossible to pay dividends if, pursuant to the latest financial statement, the income of a company is lower than the legal share capital increased by the reserves that cannot be paid to the shareholders.

3.3

The Taxation System

Deloitte & Touche Zagreb

Taxes in Croatia

A new Corporate Income Tax and Value Added Tax Law was introduced on 1 January 2001 so as to create a transparent and modern tax system in Croatia that is comparable with European standards.

The Croatian tax system is based on taxing income and sales rather than capital. Business income is generally subject to corporate income tax, while income earned by individuals is subject to personal income tax. Most domestic sales and imports are subject to VAT and this is augmented by a number of excise and other taxes and fees levied on specific transactions.

The taxation system is based on a set of direct and indirect taxes:

- basic direct taxes:

  - Corporate Income Tax (CIT),

  - Personal Income Tax (PIT),

  - surtax (levied on personal income tax);

- basic indirect taxes:

  - Value Added Tax (VAT),

  - excise taxes,

  - real estate sales tax.

The taxation system is uniform across the state and only small differences may occur in local taxes. Generally, foreign companies and individuals pay the same taxes as Croatian legal or natural persons. The exception to this rule applies where taxation is regulated by international treaties concluded by Croatia. Croatia honours all double taxation agreements made between the former Yugoslavia and other countries, and has already signed new agreements on avoiding double taxation with numerous other countries.

www.deloittece.com

Who applies global solutions locally?

Deloitte & Touche

Deloitte Touche Tohmatsu

Deloitte&Touche – Company Profile

Founded in 1997, Deloitte&Touche Croatia today has 100 employees in three Croatian cities (Zagreb, Osijek, and Split) and uses extensive knowledge of the local market and best practices from around the world in providing various services to its clients.

We at Deloitte understand our clients expect the highest professional standards of their independent auditor. But in addition to annual audits, which provide us with a good starting point, our experts also express their opinion on clients' financial statements, help our clients achieve business objectives, strengthen risk management and improve profitability. Through the use of advanced proprietary technology, we can help them to reduce their costs by maximizing the efficiencies, minimizing the disruption and improving the effectiveness of their audit process. What we offer in scope of audit and advisory services is credibility, assurance and independence.

Enterprise risk services help our clients build trust and enhance performance by enabling them to measure business risk and control throughout the enterprise. Enterprise risk services offer a comprehensive array of services designed to help our clients understand business risks, determine acceptable levels of exposure, implement controls and provide ongoing measurement and monitoring of the risk environment and compliance.

Since every transaction has a tax effect, we at Deloitte&Touche work very hard to help our clients minimize the tax effect for all transactions they undertake. International tax specialists actively assist in strategic tax planning for cross-border transactions. Our domestic corporate specialists help clients deal effectively with the tax authorities, while minimizing the burden on their tax departments. Our indirect tax specialists (VAT and Costumes Duty) assist in planning to minimize the impact of these taxes. Our individual tax specialists help minimize personal income tax and also assist expatriates and clients with local filing obligations. We help our clients comply with the local tax regulations wherever they operate in the world.

Management Consulting Services provide integrated consulting services focused on large national entities, multi-national corporations, growth organizations and public sector. In this area we provide the following services: corporate and business planning, IT Strategy and Selection, Financial Management, Performance and Cost Management, Business Process Improvement, Electronic Commerce, Systems Design and Development, Supply Chain Management, Systems Assessment and Assurance, Package Implementation, Technology Infrastructure, Maintenance Services and Environmental Services.

Our Financial Advisory Services can help you in privatization strategies, cross-border acquisitions, corporate finance transactions, development and venture capital, business and asset valuations, value epnhancement strategies, corporate recovery or fraud investigations.

Our mission is to help our clients and our people excel. We help our clients meet the challenge of demonstrating globally responsible business practices while balancing social, environmental and financial performance.

An interview with
Ivica Smiljan, Chairman of
Deloitte&Touche in Croatia

Could you tell us some facts about your company?

Deloitte is one of the world's leading professional services organizations. The member firms of Deloitte deliver world-class assurance and advisory, tax, and consulting services. With more than 119,000 people in more than 140 countries, the member firms serve over one-half of the world's largest companies, as well as large national enterprises, public institutions and successful, fast-growing global growth companies. Our internationally experienced professionals strive to deliver seamless, consistent services wherever our clients operate. Our mission is to help our clients and our people excel.

Through our advisory role to governments and local and foreign businesses we have has played an integral part in Central Europe's transition. In 1997 we integrated our national practices to form Deloitte Central Europe because we realized that to best serve our clients, we needed to be able to share our knowledge, expertise and manpower throughout the whole of our geography. Our integration has allowed us to manage regionally and deliver locally, adding value to our services and allowing them to be performed in the most efficient manner. Today Deloitte Central Europe employs more than 2000 people, has 27 offices in 16 countries and has annual revenues exceeding 140 million US$. Nevertheless the company operates as one cohesive organization.

Can you start off with some background about the Croatian practice? When was the practice established?

Deloitte has been present in Croatia since 1997. We started a bit late, compared with our competition, but soon we became one of the best quality consulting companies in the market. Today we employ a staff of over 100 professionals, including expatriates from around the world. Firm's main office is in Zagreb and beside that, in our efforts to serve our clients in the best possible way, we have two regional offices, in Split and Osijek. Among our clients today are many of the largest national and international companies and banks. We blend both national and international expertise, thus offering Croatian clients guaranteed access to international state-of-the-art know-how and global best practices.

What is your company's main line of business in Croatia?

At Deloitte we offer more than simple accounting and auditing services. We help our clients achieve their business objectives, strengthen risk management and improve profitability. Our primary objective is to be our clients' trusted business adviser. We achieve this by developing an in-depth understanding of their business processes and strategies. This understanding is the basis on which our audit plans are developed and executed.

Additionally our tax practitioners work hard to help our clients increase their bottom line. We deliver a full range of tax services that minimize the effect of the many taxes our clients face. In addition, we consult our clients how to comply with local tax regulations.

Over the last 13 years Croatia has experienced the war and the regression that comes with it, then stagnation and than a period of slow growth. Croatian economy is now growing at a steady pace and Croatian companies are constantly improving their competitiveness, to be able to compete successfully in the EU market. That opens a window of opportunity for our Management Consulting services in Croatia. Our aim is to combine our expertise, business knowledge and pragmatic approach to offer our clients practical solutions in a complex environment. Our activities encompass a range of consulting services, including business planning, electronic commerce, information systems implementation, financial management, operations services and environmental consulting.

For the past 13 years governments throughout Central Europe have dramatically reformed their economies by moving commercial enterprises from state control to private ownership. We offer a broad range of Financial Advisory Service such as privatization strategies, cross-border acquisitions, corporate finance transactions, development and venture capital, business and asset valuations, value enhancement strategies, corporate recovery or fraud investigations.

The potential for growth is significant, but Croatia and the region also present unique challenges not found in developed markets. So the main objective of our team is to help our clients successfully surmount challenges and eventual obstacles.

What are the biggest challenges for the Croatian practice?

Croatia is in a very unique period of time. After a period of war and regression, the country is now facing the EU accession project. The fact that Croatia has applied for EU presents a great opportunity for all our services. We will pay due consideration to the consequences of the legal adjustment to the EU standards' requirements, that set new goals for Croatian companies. Croatia must continue its reforms and prepare its companies for improved export results to cover the negative score in foreign trade balance sheet. With our methodology and professional quality services we at Deloitte can make this process easier and shorter.

What is your strategic vision for your company in the future?

A: Increasingly our clients demand comprehensive services that take into account best practices as well as market and industry trends from around the world. To support our commitment to innovation and top quality service, we will continue to invest heavily in technology and in our people. We will be at the forefront in using, developing and implementing the latest that the world has to offer. We strive to establish Deloitte in Croatia as the provider of the full range of best quality services.

Entering the new millennium, we continue to set the pace in the professional services sector. The region has faced many challenges and experienced many changes over the last ten years. However our firm has shown an unrivalled ability to adapt, develop and improve. And we will continue in the same way.

Tax system and administration

Tax authority

The Croatian tax administration comprises the Tax Administration located within the Ministry of Finance. The central Tax Administration office is located in Zagreb, and there are 20 regional offices with 120 branches throughout Croatia. The Central office of Tax Administration is responsible for monitoring and implementing uniform compliance with tax obligations throughout the country and plays an important role in the formulation of tax policy and tax-related regulations.

General Tax Law

The General Tax Law systematically, integrally and uniformly regulates the legal relations of taxpayers and tax authorities that are common to all taxes. The General Tax Law deals with the broad issues relating to taxation procedure and the application of tax provisions, payment, reimbursement, forced payment, evidence and dispute resolution. Furthermore this Law defines the main taxation principles. The new provisions of this law extend the rights of taxpayers, clearly defining the relationship between debtors, creditors and successors in the payment, disbursement, guarantee, compensation and compounding of tax obligations or claims proceedings. It also clearly defines the relationship in proceedings of pledging, ceding and impounding of assets or rights.

Returns and assessments

In most cases taxes are levied by self-assessments. Taxpayers must file a return and make any payment by the due date stipulated by Law without waiting for a formal assessment from the tax administration.

If the tax is not paid in time, interest is charged at the rate of 15 per cent per annum. The period for the calculation of interest starts from the day when the tax should have been paid and goes on to the day when it is actually paid.

There are no group registration provisions in Croatia for tax purposes.

Corporate Income Tax

Taxpayers

Those liable to pay profit tax are companies or other legal entities engaged in an economic activity for the purpose of making profits. The resident business branch of a non-resident entrepreneur is also a taxpayer. A non-resident entrepreneur is one who does not have a headquarters or management in Croatia. A representative office does not fall within the ambit of the corporate profit tax law unless it is engaged in an agency capacity in the airline or another travel industry generating income from tickets sold in Croatia.

Tax rates

Corporate tax is levied at a single rate of 20 per cent on taxable income.

Taxable base

The taxable base is the profit (difference between revenues and expenditures of the firm) defined as profit increase or decrease according to the corporate profit tax law and regulations. The tax base for a resident taxpayer is the total profit made in Croatia and abroad. The tax base for non-resident taxpayers is the profit earned in Croatia. Any profit made during a liquidation procedure is also included in the taxable base.

Tax calculation

The law defines separately all items that increase or reduce profit.

The corporate profit tax base is increased for any depreciation charged in excess of the highest tax-deductible amount. It is also increased for 70 per cent of entertainment costs, the costs of fines and penalties, 30 per cent of expenses related to personal transport, gifts and donations greater than 2 per cent of revenues made in the previous year, and hidden profits payments or transfer pricing.

The corporate profit tax base can be reduced by the earnings from dividends and shares in profit, by depreciation charges that were not allowed in earlier periods and by employment incentives (the amount of the gross salary costs of newly engaged labour).

Transfer pricing

If through business between a resident branch of a non-resident entrepreneur and a founding company, or between a resident subsidiary company and a non-resident parent company, the expenditures of the resident taxpayer are increased because of expenses for the procurement of goods and services, management services, intellectual services, trademarks, patents, licences, loans and/or various fees, and the tax base of the resident taxpayer is decreased in other ways, and if a hidden profit transfer is made, the said transactions shall be calculated at the market prices that would be achieved for a comparable transaction on the comparable market in the same or similar circumstances among persons who are not connected. The same relates to hidden payment of profit via reduction in the revenue of the resident taxpayer.

For differences determined in this manner the profit tax base of the resident taxpayer will be increased accordingly.

Relief, exemptions and incentives

The Corporate Income Tax provides financial incentives to companies in the form of reductions in the corporate rate or additional reductions in the tax base itself.

In order to claim the tax incentive, the company must prove that it is involved in an incentive measure as defined by the Investment Promotion Law. An incentive measure includes the introduction of new equipment/modern technologies, the employment and education of employees and the modernization and improvement of the business.

Corporate Tax Reductions

Corporate Tax Reductions are available where new employees are employed and funds are invested in Croatia. The tax rate reduction itself is contingent on both the amount invested (in Croatian Kuna) and the number of employees.

Benefits may be given only to newly established companies for a period of 10 years from the beginning of the investment. However, for an investment in tourism the existing company may be the beneficiary of tax benefits. The incentives presently available in Croatia are as follows:

- The corporate tax rate will be reduced to 7 per cent for a 10-year period, beginning in the year of investment, where a company invests at least HRK10 million in the business and employs a minimum of 30 employees.

- The corporate tax rate will be reduced to 3 per cent for a 10-year period, beginning in the year of investment, where a company invests at least HRK20 million in the business and employs a minimum of 50 employees.

- The corporate tax rate will be reduced to 0 per cent for a 10-year period, beginning in the year of investment, where a company invests at least HRK60 million in the business and employs a minimum of 75 employees.

Employment incentives

Employment incentives exist which effectively allow a double deduction to be claimed in respect of wages paid to new employees. A new employee is an employee with whom an indefinite employment contract has been drawn up, and who has been secured employment after being registered as unemployed for a minimum period of a month, or who has given up the right to retire or who is being employed for the first time.

The additional reduction in the tax base can only be claimed for one year from the date that the employee was employed, or for a three-year period if the employee is disabled.

Creation of new employment positions
If an entrepreneur creates new jobs or employment positions, they may be granted up to HRK15,000 for each employee to cover the cost of job creation. It should be noted that when calculating the number of newly created jobs the number of other job terminations will be taken into consideration.

Retraining
Retraining costs can be reduced by virtue of the incentives and assistance available. For instance, when an employer invests in the vocational training or retraining of employees, the Fund for the Stimulation of New Job Creation and Retraining of employees may contribute funds to cover 50 per cent of the costs.

Relief for taxpayers in areas of special national concern
Taxpayers who carry on their business in an area of special national concern and employ more than five people, with more than 50 per cent of the employees having their domicile and being resident in the area of special national concern, will pay profit tax at a rate of between 25 and 75 per cent of the prescribed tax rate, depending on the area classification.

Relief and exemptions for taxpayers in the area of the City of Vukovar
Taxpayers that carry on their business in the area of the city of Vukovar and employ more than five people with more than 50 per cent of the employees having their domicile and residing in the area of the city of Vukovar will be exempted from paying profit tax in the years 2000 to 2005, and after that will pay profit tax at 25 per cent of the prescribed rate.

Relief and exemptions for taxpayers who do business in Free Zones
Users of Free Zones as defined by the Free Zones Act will pay profit tax at 50 per cent of the prescribed rate (10 per cent).

Tax losses

Tax losses can be carried forward for five years from the year the tax loss was incurred. If losses are not utilized within this time, the loss will expire. Accordingly, losses should be utilized on a 'first in first out' basis. Until 1 January 2001 tax losses were multiplied by an applicable protective interest rate. From 1 January 2001 protective interest was abolished.

Statute of limitations

The relative period for the statute of limitations is three years. The absolute period for the statute of limitations for establishment of tax debt and interest, the filing of offence procedures, the collection of taxes, interest, costs of execution and fines, and the right of the taxpayer to a refund of taxation, interest, costs of execution and fines is six years, counting from the date when the statute of limitations for tax purposes came into effect. Both relative and absolute periods on the whole begin with the elapse of the year in which the tax return was due.

Assessment

The Corporate Profit Tax in Croatia is assessed for the business year, which corresponds to the calendar year. The tax return must be submitted to the tax administration within four months after the end of the tax period for which the profit tax is being assessed, which is normally by the end of April for the preceding business year.

The Croatian Corporate Profit Tax stipulates that the corporate taxpayer pay monthly advance payments, based on the previous year's corporate profit tax return. Any shortfall at year-end must be self-assessed and paid by the corporate profit taxpayer. If corporate profit taxes have been overpaid during the business year, the surplus tax paid shall be returned upon request or it can be taken forward into the next taxable period.

Withholding tax

Taxpayers who pay compensation to foreign legal entities for the use of intellectual ownership rights, market research services, tax consulting, auditing services, dividends, profit shares and interest rates, are obliged to calculate and pay profit tax at the rate of 15 per cent. The withholding tax is not paid on interest rates for selling equipment on credit, tied loans and loans granted by a foreign bank. However, if Croatia has a double tax treaty avoidance agreement with the country where the compensation beneficiary is resident, then the provisions of such a treaty will apply.

Value Added Tax (VAT)

VAT was introduced in Croatia on 1 January 1998, replacing sales tax on goods and services. The VAT system is harmonized with Croatian Direct Tax Law (ie The Profit Tax Act) and is modelled on the EU Sixth Directive.

The scope and rates of VAT

Scope

The following transactions are subject to VAT unless they are exempt from VAT or 'VAT free' (which is equivalent to being zero-rated or exempt with credits for related costs):

- goods or services provided for payment;

- imports of goods;

- entertainment and the use of personal vehicles and other means of personal transport which are not tax deductible; and

- supplies made to company owners (this refers to supplies for the benefit of shareholders and members of their immediate families, if the recipients of these supplies are not required to provide any payment or if a personal discount is provided).

Rates

The standard rate of VAT is 22 per cent. There is no higher rate and no reduced rate.

Place of supply

Goods

Where goods are not transported, the place of supply is taken to be the location of the goods at the time of supply. Where goods are transported, the place of supply is taken to be the location of the goods at the time transportation begins. If goods are installed or assembled by or on behalf of a supplier, the place of supply is deemed to be the place where the goods are installed or assembled for use.

Services

As a general rule the place of supply for services is taken to be the registered office of the person performing the service. If a particular business unit performs services, the place of performance is considered to be the headquarters of that business unit. Where this cannot be determined, the place of performance is taken to be the temporary or permanent residence of the person performing the service.

The following exceptions to the above general rule exist and are similar to those listed in the EU Sixth Directive:

- The place of supply is taken to be the place where the recipient is located for the following services:

  - the transfer, cession and use of copyrights, patents, licences, trademarks and similar rights, and renunciation of such rights;

– promotional services, including intermediation in such services;

– services performed by engineers, lawyers, auditors, accountants, interpreters, translators, and other providers of consultancy services;

– automated data processing services;

– cession of information, including information on business procedures and know-how;

– banking, insurance and re-insurance services; and cession of employees.

● The place of supply is taken to be the place where the services are supplied for the following services:

– transport services and services ancillary to transport;

– artistic, scientific, sporting, entertainment or educational services; and

– services (repairs, maintenance and valuation) on movable property.

The place of supply for services relating to land (such as leasing, construction and real estate) is taken to be where the land is located.

Time of supply

Goods
Goods are taken to be supplied at the time the goods are placed at the disposal of the buyer or end-user. The VAT liability on imports of goods arises on the day customs duties are due and payable.

Services
Services are supplied at the time of performance. Where a service is performed over two successive accounting periods, the service is taken to be supplied and VAT is charged in the second accounting period. Where services are performed over more than two successive accounting periods, VAT must be charged and accounted for in each accounting period regardless of when the final invoice is issued.

Value of supply

The taxable value of a supply is the payment provided for the good or service exclusive of VAT. Where no payment is provided or where the parties are not dealing with each other on an arms-length basis (which includes supplies to employees), the value of a product for VAT purposes is taken to be its fair market value.

The taxable value of an import is its customs value increased by the amount of any customs duties and any other taxes or charges payable.

Registration

Every resident or non-resident company conducting business operations in Croatia (eg a branch office or limited liability company) must register its legal entity in the Croatian Company Register at the Commercial Court before it commences business operations. This means that a non-resident company must establish a Croatian registered legal entity before it can register for VAT.

The Croatian VAT Act provides that a taxable person is any person or entity supplying goods or services that are subject to VAT. This includes entrepreneurs delivering goods or performing services, issuers of invoices and non-profit organizations that make taxable supplies with the intention of deriving profit.

Compulsory registration

A taxable person must register for VAT if their turnover in any calendar year exceeds the compulsory registration threshold of HRK85,000 (approximately €11,350). Turnover, for this purpose, is defined as the total value of delivered goods and services including VAT, which includes the value of zero-rated supplies but not exempt supplies.

A person whose turnover does not exceed the compulsory registration threshold can apply to be registered voluntarily.

Export transactions

As exports are exempt from VAT, there is no requirement to issue a VAT invoice in respect of them. However, an invoice issued in respect of an export should clearly state that VAT has not been included.

VAT returns

The VAT year is the calendar year. A taxable person with an annual turnover (inclusive of VAT) exceeding HRK300,000 (approximately €40,360) is required to file a monthly VAT return. Where a taxable person's annual turnover is below this amount, the taxable person can choose to adopt either a monthly or quarterly VAT period. VAT returns are due by the end of the month following the VAT period.

A taxable person must also file an annual VAT return. The taxable person is required to disclose his or her annual turnover when completing the annual VAT return. It is also the final adjustment period for any partial exemption calculation and all other adjustments relating to the tax period. Where a taxable person submits monthly VAT returns, the annual VAT return must be submitted by the end of April of the following year. Where a company submits quarterly returns, the annual VAT return must be submitted by the end of February of the following year. The annual VAT period is always the calendar year.

Payments

VAT is payable when lodging a VAT return and must be made by bank transfer or cheque to an account stipulated by the Minister of Finance.

Refunds

Where a taxable person's input tax credits exceed the VAT liability the taxable person is entitled to a VAT refund. The person can either request to receive an actual cash refund or can elect to treat the excess as a VAT prepayment. The tax refund is indicated on the usual VAT return and the tax authority must pay the refund within 15 days after the tax return is filed.

Exemptions

Exemptions without credit

In Croatia supplies that are exempt from VAT without credit are similar to those contained in the EU Sixth Directive and include:

- rental of residential property;

- goods and services rendered by banks, savings institutions, savings and loan institutions and insurance institutions;

- medical services, including services conducted by doctors, dentists, nurses, physiotherapists, and biochemistry laboratories engaged in private practice;

- services of medical care performed in healthcare institutions (primary healthcare institutions, casualty medical care institutions, policlinics, general and specialized hospitals and clinics, end-services of medical care performed by institutions specializing in health care at home and deliveries of goods made by the above institutions);

- services and deliveries of goods by social care institutions;

- services and deliveries of goods by institutions of child and adolescent care;

- services and deliveries of goods by nursery, primary and secondary schools, universities and student catering and boarding institutions;

- services and deliveries of goods by religious communities and institutions;

- services and deliveries of goods by public institutions in the field of culture, such as museums, galleries, archives, libraries and theatres;

- winnings from special games of chance in casinos, slot machine clubs and other gambling;

- supplies of gold by the central bank;

- supplies of domestic and foreign legal tender;

- company securities and shares;

- supplies of real estate (land, buildings, parts of buildings, housing premises and other structures), with the exception of newly built buildings; and

- temporary imports of goods that are exempt from customs duty.

Exempt supplies with credit
Strictly, the following supplies are zero-rated or 'VAT free' under Croatian VAT legislation:

- bread and milk;

- books of a scholarly, scientific, artistic, cultural or educational character as well as school textbooks (primary, secondary and tertiary education, including materials printed on paper and other media, such as CD-ROMs, video cassettes and audio tapes);

- certain medicines and surgical implants;

- scientific journals;

- services rendered by cinemas; and

- holiday packages paid for from abroad (accommodation or accommodation with breakfast, full or half board in all kinds of commercial hospitality facilities).

Exports of goods and services are exempt with credit.

VAT recovery

Generally a taxable person has the right to recover VAT costs incurred in the course of conducting his or her ordinary business activities. This includes making taxable supplies and 'VAT free' supplies. Input VAT cannot be recovered in respect of purchases made in the process of providing VAT exempt supplies, supplies made abroad which would be exempt if in Croatia, and supplies made free of charge, which would be exempt if paid for.

VAT cannot be claimed on the following expenses as these expenses are taken to be private in nature and are not deductible for Croatian Profit Tax purposes: 70 per cent of entertainment expenditures, and 30 per cent of expenses incurred in connection with a person's own or rented personal motor vehicles and other means of personal transport for entrepreneurs, management and other staff.

Expenditure relating partly to exempt or non-business activities must be distinguished and input tax may be partially deducted.

VAT recovery adjustment

If the tax treatment governing tax exemption of certain goods that was effective in a certain year is changed within five years from the beginning of the use of the assets, then the tax credit adjustment must be effected for the period after the change became effective. In the case of real estate, the period of adjustment of initial VAT recovery is 10 years. The initial deduction is adjusted on a one-off basis upon the change of taxable status. Where the value of VAT does not exceed HRK2,000 (approximately €270) per item the adjustment is not effected.

Imports of good and services

Only a registered Croatian entity (eg a branch or company) is entitled to make a customs declaration in respect of imported goods. A non-resident must, therefore, appoint a Croatian resident agent to complete the customs declaration on his or her behalf.

Goods
VAT is calculated on the total value of imported goods inclusive of custom and excise duties. VAT is payable at the time the goods are imported and is collected by the Customs Authority.

Services
The Croatian VAT legislation contains a 'reverse charge' rule which requires resident taxable persons to account for VAT at a rate of 22 per cent for certain supplies received from abroad.

The reverse charge rule applies to those services that are taxed according to the place where the registered office of the service recipient is located (see 'Place of supply' p 229).

Exports of goods and services

Only a registered Croatian entity (eg a branch or company) is entitled to make a customs declaration in respect of exported goods. A non-resident making exports from Croatia must, therefore, appoint a Croatian resident agent to complete the customs declaration on his or her behalf.

Goods
Exports (including transport and forwarding service costs) are exempt from VAT and the supplier is entitled to claim input tax credits for the VAT paid in the process of providing the goods.

Services

Where a Croatian business provides services and the place of supply is outside Croatia, the supplies are treated as exempt from Croatian VAT rather than being outside of its scope. However, the supplier is generally entitled to recover input tax credits in relation to these supplies of services unless a domestic supply of the service would be exempt.

Notwithstanding that a supply is made in Croatia, the supply may be deemed to have been made abroad (ie considered to be an export) in the following cases:

- deliveries of goods to a customs free zone, customs free and bonded warehouses and deliveries of goods within a customs free zone;

- deliveries of goods to diplomatic and consular missions provided that a reciprocal arrangement exists with the appropriate country;

- deliveries of goods to humanitarian organizations, healthcare, educational, cultural, scholarly, scientific, religious and welfare institutions, amateur sports clubs and bodies of national and local government and self-government that are paid for from foreign monetary donations; and

- services provided by a Croatian taxable person in Croatia to a non-resident person that provides air, river and/or sea transport.

Property

The sale of real estate including buildings, parts of buildings, housing premises and other structures and parts of structures is exempt from VAT with the exception of the first supply of a 'new' building. A building is deemed to be 'new' if it was built after 31 December 1997.

The leasing and letting of residential property is exempt from VAT, except for the letting of temporary accommodation to non-permanent guests (eg hotel accommodation). The leasing of commercial property is always subject to VAT.

It is not possible to opt to waive exemption from VAT in relation to exempt supplies (both sales and leases) of real estate.

Refunds to tourists

Tourists are entitled to reclaim VAT on goods purchased and taken out of Croatia. This is on condition that the goods have not been used and that their invoiced value exceeds HRK500. A PDV-P form has to be provided by the supplier and stamped at the border. The tourist must claim the VAT refund within six months of the day the invoice was issued. VAT refunds are not available for oil derivatives.

Refunds to foreign entities

A foreign entity is generally not entitled to a VAT refund unless it has a permanent establishment in Croatia and is registered for VAT.

A foreign entity participating in Croatian Trade Fairs may be entitled to claim a VAT refund in respect of costs incurred in Croatia. This is on condition that it does not have a residence, business management, branch or any other form of business entity in Croatia. A refund is also available to foreign entities who exhibit at Trade Fairs and who do not have a representative office in Croatia and who would not otherwise be eligible to claim a VAT refund in Croatia.

Foreign exhibitors may be entitled to a VAT refund for the following goods and services: rental of the exhibited area; the costs associated with the exhibited area (electricity, water, gas, heating and cooling facilities and telecommunication services); the construction and mainte-nance (including materials) of the exhibited area; and parking expenses.

An application for a VAT refund can be lodged in the name of the foreign entity by a Croatian tax resident who has authorization from the foreign entity. An application for a VAT refund must be submitted as part of the ZP-PDV form (VAT application on the tax return) and must be lodged within six months of the end of the calendar year in which the conditions for a VAT refund have been met. VAT refunds are only relevant for amounts in total value above HRK1,000.

3.4

Personal Income Tax and Social Security Contributions

Mihela Maodus, Deloitte & Touche Zagreb

Resident individuals are taxable in Croatia on their worldwide income. Non-residents are taxable only on their Croatian-source income. An individual is considered resident if he or she maintains a permanent or temporary residence in Croatia for at least 183 days. Other individuals are considered non-resident.

Taxable income

Taxable income includes employment income, business or self-employment income, income from property and property rights, income from capital and income from insurance.

Salary and wage income, pensions, benefits (whether in cash or in kind, paid to the employee in relation to current, previous or future work, in various forms, such as through the use of cars, favourable interest on loans and the like) and employment-related awards are included in employment income. Benefits in kind are taxed on the basis of their market value.

The tax base for business or self-employment income is total revenue less expenses. Losses may be carried forward for five years. Certain individuals pay profits tax instead of personal income tax on their business or self-employment income.

Income from property and property rights includes rental income from real estate and movable property, copyright royalties, and income from industrial property rights. Gains from disposals of property and property rights are also included, unless the property or rights have been held for at least three years. Taxpayers are allowed to deduct 30 per cent of real estate rental income or 50 per cent in certain circumstances.

Income from capital includes dividends and shares in the profits according to the share in capital and interests. In addition, withdrawals of assets and use of services by the owners of companies for private purposes shall be deemed dividends and shares in the profits.

Tax return, personal assessments and payments

The tax year is the calendar year. Tax on employment income is withheld at source by the (local) employer.

Self-employed individuals should make monthly advance payments, which are based on the amount of income tax payable in the previous year.

Advance payments must be made in case of rental income, income from capital and income from insurance. On income from capital, income from insurance and in certain situations on rental income, advance payments are made by the employer/persons paying out the income.

A taxpayer who is employed or performs jobs under contract with a non-resident entity in Croatia is liable to calculate tax on his or her salary and pay it within eight days from the date of the salary payment. Calculation and payment of tax within eight days from payday may instead be carried out by a non-resident (employer) salary payer.

An annual tax return is due by the end of February for the previous tax year. The tax authorities will review the return and issue an assessment/resolution for any tax still due after advance payments and employer withholdings. Overpayments will be refunded.

Tax rates

Current personal income tax rates (applicable since 1 January 2003) are shown in Table 3.4.1.

Table 3.4.1 Income tax rates (from 1 January 2003)

Income tax rates (%)	Income tax bands/per month
15	Up to HRK3,000
25	HRK3,000 – 6,750
35	HRK6,750 – 21,000
45	Above HRK21,000

Personal income tax is further increased by surtax, ie city tax, which can vary from town to town, the highest rate being 18 per cent, in Zagreb.

Rates for advance tax payment on rental income, income from capital and income from insurance range from 15 to 35 per cent.

The monthly personal allowance is set at HRK1,500. Additional allowances are available for dependent spouses and children, aid received from legal and natural persons for health purposes ie operations, medical treatments, drugs and orthopaedic aid, expenses incurred in buying or building a flat or house and investment maintenance on an existing flat or house up to HRK1,000, and gifts in cash and kind for cultural, educational, scientific, health, humanitarian, sport and religious purposes to special organizations of up to 2 per cent pa of the income earned in the previous year.

Foreign taxes paid abroad on foreign-source income may be offset against Croatian tax liability in the form of a tax credit. However, Croatian personal income tax law recognizes the rules of treaties on avoidance of double taxation, which Croatia has signed, or honours those signed by the former Yugoslavia. Currently Croatia applies treaties on avoidance of double taxation with 35 countries.

Social Security contributions

For employees working under Croatian terms and conditions, the employer is required to pay all applicable employer's social contributions, including health and pension contributions, and to remit employees' social contributions to the appropriate authorities, on a monthly basis. Social Security contribution rates are shown in Table 3.4.2.

For individuals aged below 40, pension insurance is paid in two pillars: 15 per cent to the general savings fund and 5 per cent to the special fund chosen by the individual.

Table 3.4.2 Social security contribution rates (from 1 January 2003)

| | Rate | |
Type of Contribution	Employer (%)	Employee (%)
Pension insurance	–	20.00
Health insurance	15.00	–
Additional health insurance	0.50	–
Unemployment insurance	1.70	–

Entities paying self-employed individuals on the basis of special 'service contracts' are obliged to withhold Social Security contributions from pay as follows: 15 per cent to the general pensions savings fund; 5 per cent to the special fund (as above); and health insurance 15 per cent.

Generally, treaties on social contributions, which Croatia has signed with 30 countries, define the liabilities of foreigners working in Croatia for such contributions.

3.5

Auditing and Accounting

Deloitte and Touche Zagreb

Legal framework

The Accounting Law and the Law on Auditing, published in the *Official Gazette* (NN), No 90, 1992, constitute the legal framework for audits and accounting issues applicable to companies. These laws have been in effect since 1 January 2003, without any subsequent modifications.

Under the law, companies (entrepreneurs) with a registered office in the Republic of Croatia are to maintain their accounting records and prepare their financial statements in accordance with the fundamental principles of bookkeeping, ie so as to enable insight into the transactions and the assets of a company.

Parent companies and their domestic or foreign-related and/or associated companies prepare consolidated financial statements, presenting the group as a single entity.

The financial statements are prepared in accordance with international accounting standards as published in the *Official Gazette*.

Definition of an entrepreneur

For the purposes of the Accounting Law, an entrepreneur is a legal person carrying out an economic activity to generate profit. An entrepreneur may also be a natural person carrying out a business activity independently for the purpose of earning profit if such a person has been defined as a corporate income taxpayer under specific regulations.

The Law also applies to foreign organizational units of an entrepreneur, unless the foreign regulations impose obligations on such a unit to maintain accounting records and prepare financial statements. Finally, the Law is obligatory for organizational units of foreign entrepreneurs whose office is registered abroad and who carry out a business activity in the Republic of Croatia (not applicable to representation offices).

Classification of entrepreneurs

Under the Law, entrepreneurs that have the obligation to maintain accounting records and prepare financial statements are classified into three categories: small, medium and large entrepreneurs.

Small entrepreneurs

Small entrepreneurs are those who do not exceed the limits set by two of the following three criteria:

1. Balance sheet total after deduction of loss presented in assets is equivalent to DM2 million.

2. Income for the 12 months prior to the balance sheet date is equivalent to DM4 million.

3. The annual average number of employees is 50.

Medium-sized entrepreneurs

Medium-sized entrepreneurs are those who do not exceed two of the three criteria applicable to small entrepreneurs and never exceed two of the following three criteria:

1. Balance sheet total after deduction of loss presented in assets is equivalent to DM8 million.

2. Income for the 12 months prior to the balance sheet date is equivalent to DM16 million.

3. The annual average number of employees is 250.

Large entrepreneurs

Large entrepreneurs are those who do not exceed two of the three criteria applicable to medium-sized entrepreneurs.

For the purposes of the Accounting Law, banks, financial institutions and insurance and reinsurance companies are classified as large entrepreneurs.

Accounting records

Accounting records have to be kept in accordance with double-entry bookkeeping principles, and consist of the following:

- journal – a business record serving to enter transactions in chronological order, classified into balance sheet and off-balance sheet items;

- general ledger – represents a systematic accounting evidence of changes in assets, liabilities, capital, expenses, income and operating results; consists of balance sheet and off-balance sheet entries;

- subsidiary ledgers – they are, as a rule, set up separately.

Keeping and filing of accounting records

Accounting records are maintained for a business year, which is the calendar year. The general ledger and the journal are to be filed for a minimum of ten years, and the auxiliary ledgers for at least five years.

Chart of accounts

Transactions are classified as per a pre-defined chart of accounts (which includes the account description/number), based on the prescribed structure of the balance sheet, the income statement and off-balance sheet items.

Accounts in the chart of accounts are further itemized according to the specific needs of the entrepreneur, taking into account that balance sheet and income statement items as specified by the Law are included. The content of the chart of accounts for banks is defined by the first six digits of individual items as provided by law.

Applicable accounting standards

International accounting standards (IAS) as published in the *Official Gazette* represent the accounting standards applicable in the Republic of Croatia. The Accounting Law (as well as IAS) additionally defines the fundamental accounting assumptions used in the preparation of the financial statements, which are as follows:

- going concern;

- consistency;

- accrual basis.

When preparing the financial statements, the following fundamental principles of measuring individual positions in the financial statements are to be observed:

- prudence;

- substance over form;

- materiality;

- individual measurement;

- time connection of balance sheet items.

Statutory financial statements

The statutory financial statements comprise:

- a balance sheet;
- an income statement (profit and loss account);
- a statement of changes in financial position;
- notes to the financial statements.

The statutory financial statements have to give a true, reliable and fair view of the assets, liabilities, capital, cash flows, and profit or loss for the period, and should be signed by a legal representative of the enterprise concerned.

Preparation and disclosure of financial statements

The statutory financial statements are prepared for a financial year. Accounting records and financial statements are kept, ie prepared in the Croatian language, using the Croatian national currency.

All large and medium-sized enterprises have an obligation to publish their financial statement if they are incorporated as a joint-stock company. A report of an auditor is published together with the financial statement.

Audit of the financial statements

Once a year, the financial statements of all large enterprises are subject to an audit, as well as those of medium-sized enterprises if they are set up as joint-stock companies.

Small enterprises incorporated as joint-stock companies are subject to a statutory review of operations every three years.

Presentation of the financial statements and of the annual report to shareholders

Large enterprises are obliged to present the financial statements and the annual report to their owners within six months of the end of a business year.

Medium-sized enterprises and small enterprises have to present to their owners the financial statements and the annual report within four months of the end of a business year.

A group of entities preparing consolidated financial statements has to present the consolidated financial statements and the annual report to its owners within nine months of the end of a business year.

Audit firms

An audit firm is a legal entity registered to carry out audits. An audit firm may, in addition to audits, perform other services from the area of accounting, tax consultancy, financial analysis and controls.

Audits may be performed by a foreign audit firm registered in the Republic of Croatia, or jointly by an audit firm registered in Croatia and a foreign audit firm.

An audit is carried out in accordance with the procedures established by the international standards on auditing.

Responsibilities of company management and of auditors

The objective and the fundamental principles governing an audit of the financial statements are to enable the auditor to express an opinion on whether the financial statements, in all material respects, comply with international accounting standards, in accordance with the Croatian Accounting Law.

The auditor is responsible for forming and expressing an opinion on the financial statements, and the management of the entity concerned is responsible for the preparation and disclosure of the financial statements.

An audit of the financial statements does not reduce the responsibility of the management.

Availability of information to the auditor

The auditor has a legal right to access the reports, accounts, evidence and other information as required for the purpose of an audit and issuing the audit report.

If an enterprise limits the scope of investigation, or disables application of certain audit procedures, the certified auditor is to draw attention to these matters in the audit report according to the Audit Guidelines.

Contents of an audit report

An audit report contains the report of the certified auditor, and the financial statements subject to audit and notes to the financial statements.

The auditor's report is signed by a certified auditor.

Indemnification

An audit firm that has deliberately or negligently incurred damage as a result of the audit carried out is to indemnify the enterprise concerned. The indemnification per audit is limited to DM50,000, to which extent an audit firm has the obligation to provide professional liability insurance coverage.

Corporate management trends and resulting audit implications

Large-scale bankruptcies among companies are often filed in relation to the financial reporting issues and have resulted in legal actions, criminal charges and loss of reputation, affecting in this way the management, auditors and employees involved in the company.

These trends inspired the promulgation of new regulations around the world, such as:

- the Sarbanes-Oxley Act (USA);

- reform of the Companies Act and the Higgs Review (UK);

- the Winter Report (European Union).

The new regulations propose a greater responsibility on the part of the management and staff involved in corporate governance, including responsibilities for the financial statements and control over the audit as defined by law, as well as higher penalties or more rigid sentences for non-compliance.

None of the regulations has a direct impact on the Republic of Croatia and enterprises registered and operating in Croatia; however:

- international guidelines will definitely have an impact on the expectations of foreign investors and, consequently, may affect the future legal framework in Croatia;

- the penal provisions, currently effective under Croatian law, may be more frequently used in the future;

- investors increasingly tend to associate poor corporate governance standards with high investment risk;

- the interest of the broader public in corporate governance standards may be increased.

As a result, it is in the best interests of the managing bodies of an enterprise to ensure:

- appropriate emphasis by management on a reliable accounting and internal controls system;

- appropriate audit arrangements to achieve efficient audits;

- adequate focus on the decision-making process and the segregation of duties;

- setting up various committees by the management or supervisory boards (such as an Audit Committee, Performance Appraisal Committee, Environmental Commission, etc).

Part Four

Business Development

4.1

Real Estate in Croatia

Visnja Bojanic, Deloitte & Touche Zagreb

Introduction

Efficient use of land is fundamental for a market-based economy, and all successful economies in the world have efficiently run, well-organized real estate markets. An open and dynamic real estate market is a major contribution to GDP, while services related to the real estate business represent a huge source of employment. By contrast, in Croatia, and in other countries of Eastern Europe and the CIS countries, real estate markets are not dynamic, land is under-utilized and undervalued as an asset, and trading and investing in real estate are limited.

Gradual liberalization of real estate purchases

By signing the Stabilization and Association Agreement, Croatia has assumed the obligation to gradually liberalize regulations for foreign natural and legal persons in relation to real estate purchases, ie to reduce the level of restrictions for the acquisition of real estate. Currently, the position of foreign natural and legal persons with regard to real estate is defined by the Law on Ownership and Other Property Rights.

Unless the applicable regulations or international contracts stipulate otherwise, the Law provides equal treatment of domestic and foreign persons. Thus, foreign persons as bearers of proprietary rights on real estate are not treated differently from domestic persons with regard to their factual and legal disposition of real estate. Apart from ownership rights, they are also equal with regard to the acquisition of property and contractual obligations, and the realization and protection of these rights; ie a foreign person can acquire property and real property liens, the right to build and a mortgage.

The equal position of foreign persons in real estate transactions has also been corroborated by the adoption of the Law on Obligations (obligatory rights) for real estate, which empowers the bearer of rights to private and economic use of real estate, such as rent, lease and concession. Conditions for foreign persons in acquiring obligatory rights on real estate do not differ from those that apply to domestic persons. The equal position of foreign and domestic persons from the legal point of view is particularly evident in granting concessions for the economic use of certain real estate in public (state) ownership and of those properties that are considered a public good. In fact, concession is often the only way in which foreign legal persons can make use of such real estate (Law on Concession).

The biggest difference between a foreign and a domestic person in real estate transactions is linked to the acquisition of the ownership right. Special conditions under which foreign persons can obtain ownership (title) of real estate in Croatia are specified by the Law on Ownership (Article 355–357).

Besides general conditions that apply to both domestic and foreign persons, additional requirements are imposed on foreign persons. These are provided by the Law on Ownership and Other Property Rights, which apply unless they are overridden by special regulations or international treaties.

Ownership right on the basis of inheritance

A foreign person – both private and legal – can acquire ownership of real estate on the basis of an inheritance document, providing there is a reciprocal agreement with the person's country of residence. If this is the case, the foreign person becomes the owner at the moment of testament, ie of the death of testator. A foreign person may request, on the basis of a legally valid testament, the registration of ownership in the register of property.

There are no quantitative restrictions with regard to ownership rights on real estate. However, there are some qualitative limitations; for instance, a foreign person cannot acquire certain real estate in an area that has been declared as an area of a special importance to the state. In that case, a foreign person is entitled to compensation for the inherited real estate in such an area, as provided by the dispossession provisions.

Ownership on the basis of legal transaction

When a foreign person acquires ownership on the basis of a legal transaction (eg on the basis of law, decree of competent authorities), two conditions are to be met according to the Ownership Law: reciprocity and consent by the Minister of Foreign Affairs of the Republic of Croatia. The Minister decides at his discretion, based on the opinion of the

Ministry of Justice. Foreign persons may, if they are not satisfied with the decision, institute applicable administrative proceedings at the competent court.

However, the requirements of reciprocity and consent by the Minister of Foreign Affairs do not apply to those foreign persons who were Croatian citizens at the effective date of the Law on Amendments to the Law on Compensation for Property Expropriated During the Yugoslav Communist Regime (effective until 1996). According to the Law, such persons are fully entitled to ownership.

The current situation with regard to foreign ownership of real estate in Croatia

According to the records of the Consular Department of the Ministry of Foreign Affairs, between 1995 and July 2003, 2,934 Croatian real-estate ownership applications filed by foreign nationals were approved and 467 were rejected. German and Austrian nationals own most of such titles in Croatia, while US nationals own houses on the Adriatic coast, the majority of which are located around Dubrovnik. Other foreign investors who also purchased real estate in Croatia are from Hungary, The Netherlands, Finland, Bosnia and Herzegovina, Switzerland, France, the UK, Italy, Sweden, Canada, China, Venezuela and Belize. Altogether 1,937,993 square meters have been bought, most of which are concentrated in Istarska county, Primorsko-Goranska county and Splitsko-Dalmatinska county.

Before making any purchase, a potential foreign buyer should check whether his or her country has a reciprocity agreement with Croatia. So far, Croatia has signed such agreements with Austria (different agreements with each region), Belgium, the UK, Canada, Germany, France, The Netherlands, the USA and Australia. A limited reciprocity has been agreed upon with Switzerland, Italy, Bosnia and Herzegovina, and Slovakia (under the condition of permanent residency of the real estate buyer or registered business activity). For purchasers from Macedonia and Bulgaria, reciprocity is limited so that, for buying real estate, they have to have permanent residence in Croatia, or a registered business activity, while citizens of Poland, can only buy apartments. Agreements are in process with the Scandinavian countries (Sweden, Finland and Norway), as well as with the Russian Confederation (on an individual basis, with each Confederation member). Since Hungary and Austria have left the regulation of real estate issues to their particular counties, comparisons with the regulations of respective counties/regions are being made, ie a citizen from Hungary or Austria can buy real estate in Croatia, providing a mandatory statement of a particular county has been provided.

Although the purchase of real estate is straightforward, it is nevertheless advisable to seek professional advice from a real estate agency or an attorney. The usual fee for their services is 2 to 3 per cent of the purchase price and is paid both by the seller and the buyer. The selected agency or attorney reviews and analyses documents regarding the title of the proprietor to the real estate, identifies potential legal risks and exposures in respect of the transfer of ownership and assesses the market value of the real estate.

After the agency or attorney has prepared a contract, the parties sign it and have it certified by a notary public. Only then can the potential buyer initiate the procedure for obtaining consent from the Ministry of Foreign Affairs, which is a requirement under the Croatian Law on Ownership and legislation in respect of other real estate rights for foreign individuals and business organizations who wish to become owners of real estate in Croatia. The application will be accepted if there is a reciprocity agreement between the Republic of Croatia and the applicant's country of origin.

To apply for the consent, applicants must submit a request, together with the following documents written in Croatian, either personally or through an attorney, to the Ministry of Foreign Affairs, Consular Department in Zagreb, (originals or copies certified by a notary public and not more than six months old):

- the basis on which the property was acquired (purchasing contract, gift contract, inheritance paper);

- proof of title (land registry certificate, etc);

- certificate issued by the authorized authorities for urban planning that proves that the particular real estate is located within the zone in which construction is allowed, according to the zoning plan;

- proof of the buyer's citizenship (legalized copy of passport);

- power of attorney for the attorney;

- photocopies of each of the above documents.

For further details on the consent procedure, see the Web site of the Ministry of Foreign Affairs: http://www.mvp.hr/index-en.htm.

Only after the Ministry issues the respective approval to the customer can the buyer register the real estate in his name in the Land Registry as the ultimate evidence of his title on that specific property. The local courts will not allow a foreign national to be entered in the Land Books without the approval of the Ministry of Foreign Affairs.

After the contract has been approved, the customer has to register the purchase with the competent tax authority within 30 days from the day of conclusion of the contract. The customer also has to pay real estate purchase tax within 15 days from the day of receipt of the decision from the tax authorities stipulating the exact tax amount. Tax on all real estate transactions in Croatia is 5 per cent of the transaction value. The tax is calculated based on the price of the real estate as per the sales contract and the value as estimated by the tax authority for the area in which the real estate is located. Tax can be paid either by the purchaser or by the seller on behalf of the customer, if the parties so agree. If this tax is not paid on time, penalty interest is charged for every day of delay.

The usual down payment for purchasing real estate is 10 per cent of the sales price, or as agreed between the contractual parties.

All foreign natural and legal persons can sell their real estate in Croatia without restrictions. However, if they decide to sell the acquired property at a higher price within three years of acquisition, they are subject to income tax, ie tax on the price difference at the rate of 35 per cent, plus surtax, depending on the taxpayer's place of residence in Croatia.

For a foreign entity, there is no difference between buying an old house or a new apartment, ie the buyer is equally subject to the 5 per cent real estate tax. Value Added Tax (VAT) of 22 per cent is imposed on transactions involving new structures, and is paid either by the seller or, more usually, is included in the price of the new real estate. When buying an old property, it is necessary to verify whether it is a protected cultural monument; if it is, it has to be offered first to the authorities (Republic of Croatia, Municipality, City, or County). If they decline to exercise their pre-emptive right, the property may be offered to foreign citizens and enterprises (Law on Protecting and Preserving Cultural Monuments). It is also worth mentioning that there are no restrictions on the acquisition of ownership of real estate by foreign persons with respect to the number and the size of real estate holdings.

A potential buyer of real estate in Croatia can conclude a sales contract and have it authenticated abroad in a Croatian embassy or consulate, provided that the notary's authentication is translated into the Croatian language by a certified court interpreter.

Those who cannot obtain approval from the Ministry of Foreign Affairs for any reason, or have no time to wait for the completion of the purchase formalities (the process for getting approval from the Ministry of Foreign Affairs can take from several months to a year) may effect the purchase by establishing a company in Croatia. All the necessary procedures for establishing a company in Croatia can be completed within approximately one month, and the minimum initial capital for a limited liability company is €2,500. A company owned by a foreign person in the Republic of Croatia is considered to be a Croatian legal entity and, as such, may acquire real estate ownership rights without any restrictions and irrespective of whether the real estate is acquired for business or for other purposes.

If consent for the acquisition of ownership of real estate has been refused by the Ministry of Foreign Affairs, a foreign person cannot repeat the request for the same property within five years from the day when the request was submitted. Foreign citizens and enterprises cannot acquire ownership of agricultural land (Law on Agricultural Land) or of forests or forest land (Law on Forests).

Business premises market

The development of the business premises market over the last few years has been strongly influenced by a rising number of new foreign offices, the restitution of a large number of properties in cities as per the Law on Amendments to the Law on Compensation for Property Expropriated During the Yugoslav Communist Regime (effective until 1996), the privatization of state and municipal properties, and the rapidly emerging new business and shopping centres.

Foreign legal persons usually rent office space; buying business premises is not so frequent and is contingent upon the efficiency and the prospects of the business. Rents for office space in the 'A' zone (city centre, either new or renovated buildings) range from €14 to €30 per square metre, whereas those for offices located in the suburban 'B' zone, which are, as a rule, new modern business centres, range from €5 to €20 per square metre. However, along with the increasing number of new business centres in the 'B' zone and because of growing demand for space, the prices in the suburban area of Zagreb (notably, Buzin, where the American embassy has recently relocated) are showing a slow but steady increase. The increased interest in office space has boosted the property development business, so that the sale or rent of office space by investors, even before construction has begun, is now a common practice.

4.2

Visas and Work Permits for Foreigners – Expatriates Working in Croatia

Mihela Maodus, Deloitte & Touche Zagreb

Currently, procedures for investors and expatriates to enter Croatia and perform certain business activities are covered by several regulations. Changes that should make the regulations more transparent and Croatia more attractive for investors and highly skilled professionals are expected in the near future.

The Law on Entry and Residence of Foreign Nationals and the Law on the Employment of Foreign Nationals are the principal legislation defining the status of expatriates in Croatia.

Two types of visas are of particular concern to foreign investors and expatriates: the business visa and the employment visa. In addition, a work permit is required for foreign nationals working in Croatia.

Visas

A business visa can be granted to a foreign national for the following purposes:

- performing economic activities provided by the regulations on foreign investment and foreign trade;

- performing work based on agreements on business and technical cooperation, long-term production cooperation, transfer of technology and foreign investment; and

- to owners/members of the management/supervisory board of a company established in Croatia.

The employment visa, officially called the 'Entry Visa for the Purpose of Employment', is applied for in all other cases of work/employment in Croatia.

Before applying for either of the visas, a prior consent by the Croatian Ministry of Labour should be obtained, which usually takes up to two weeks. Application for both types of visas should be made at the Croatian diplomatic mission or consulate closest to the current place of the foreign national's residence before arriving in Croatia.

Business visa

The application for a business visa is submitted to the nearest Croatian consulate abroad at least one month prior to the planned arrival to Croatia.

In addition to an administrative fee of approximately €60, the following documents are required to obtain the business visa:

- a completed application form, which is available in the Croatian diplomatic missions and consulates;

- a passport;

- a copy of the ID page of the applicant's passport;

- two passport-size photographs;

- an excerpt from the court registry of the foreign founder;

- an excerpt from the court registry for the entity in Croatia, or a copy of the resolution of the Ministry of Economy on the establishment of a representative office;

- the decision of the foreign founder on the appointment of the applicant to the relevant position in the Croatian entity (translated into the Croatian language, with both the original and the translation being submitted);

- a letter by the Croatian entity or the foreign founder for whom the applicant will be working, addressed to the Croatian consulate, specifying the purpose of the engagement of the foreign national in Croatia and the planned duration of work in Croatia (translated into the Croatian language);

- consent of the Croatian Ministry of Labour.

Once approved, the business visa is stamped into the passport of the foreign national and needs to be validated on the first entry into Croatia. A valid business visa represents a residence permit and is usually granted for a period of one year. Visa extensions can be obtained in Croatia and should be applied for one month prior to expiry.

Business visa registration

After having arrived in Croatia, foreign nationals are required to register their business visas at the Ministry of Internal Affairs. The documents required for business visa registration include:

- a copy of the passport – ID page and the business visa stamp;

- two passport-size photographs;

- a letter by the Croatian entity or the foreign founder for whom the applicant will be working, addressed to the Croatian consulate, specifying the purpose of the engagement of the foreign national in Croatia and the planned duration of work in Croatia (in the Croatian language);

- an excerpt from the court registry of the Croatian entity for which the foreign national will be working.

Foreign nationals should be personally present at the Ministry of Internal Affairs for the purpose of the business visa registration. After the registration, the Croatian ID number for the foreign national (MBS) is issued.

Registration of address in Croatia

Each foreign person has to register the address of his or her residence in Croatia within 24 hours of arriving in Croatia. If a foreign national stays at a hotel, the hotel will do the registration and the person should register (at the Ministry of Internal Affairs) his or her private residential address once the address is known.

The registration procedure, for which a fee of HRK20 is imposed, requires the following documentation:

- a registration form;

- a passport (including visa);

- the ID card of the landlord (owner of the rented flat/house) or the person authorized to represent the landlord;

- evidence of the landlord's ownership of the flat (purchase agreement or excerpt from the land registry);

- the rental agreement.

Employment visa

The employment visa is required for all foreign nationals who are employees not covered by a business visa. The application can be made at the Croatian diplomatic mission or consulate and it generally takes four to six weeks to receive the 'entry visa for the purpose of employment'. The following documents should be submitted:

- a completed application form;
- a passport;
- a notarized copy of the ID page of the applicant's passport;
- two passport-size photographs;
- the assignment letter (translated into Croatian);
- a letter by the applicant's employer, with a short explanation of the visa applicant's qualifications for the post and justification for employing a foreign national rather than a Croatian.

Residence permit

The residence permit, or the 'extended residence permit', is necessary for all foreign nationals arriving in Croatia with an 'entry visa for the purpose of employment'. The permit is applied for at the Ministry of Internal Affairs on the same day as registering the address in Croatia (see above). The following documentation is needed for obtaining the 'extended residence permit':

- a completed application form;
- a passport;
- a copy of the ID page and entry visa page in the passport;
- two passport-size photographs;
- the statement of accounts of the Croatian company in which the foreign national will work issued by the Croatian Financial Agency (FINA) upon arrival of the assignee in Croatia;
- an excerpt from the court registry of the Croatian company for which the foreign national will be working;
- a letter from the Croatian company in which the foreign national will be working, with a description of the foreign person's position, the duration of stay and justification for engaging a foreign national rather than a Croatian;
- a a copy of any university diploma or other relevant certificate regarding the educational background of the applicant;
- copy of the assignment letter by the current foreign employer outside Croatia.

In addition, a fee of HRK150 is imposed.

It takes approximately two weeks to obtain a residence permit and the permit is granted for a maximum period of one year. A foreign national should apply for an extension of the permit in Croatia one month prior to its expiry.

Croatian ID number for foreign nationals

A Croatian ID number for foreign nationals (MBS) is allocated to each foreign national in possession of either a business visa or an extended residence permit. To obtain a certificate with an ID number, an application should be submitted to the Ministry of Internal Affairs in the place of residence. Documentation required for this procedure is as follows:

- a completed application form (obtained at the Ministry of Internal Affairs);

- a passport;

- a copy of the passport – ID page and extended residence permit page;

- two passport-size photographs – needed only if a foreign national wishes to obtain a Croatian ID card (not obligatory);

- a letter requesting issuance of an ID number and ID card (if applicable) and the purpose of the issuance.

The minimum fee amounts to HRK40, which is higher if an ID card is requested.

Work permits

Prior to the start of work/employment in Croatia, a foreign national should obtain a work permit. There are two types of work permits for which foreign nationals can apply once they have obtained a business visa or extended residence permit.

Work permit requested by the employer

The Croatian employer submits the application to the Croatian Employment Bureau. This type of work permit may be applied for on the basis of a valid business or employment visa. A work permit is issued for the maximum period of validity of the business visa/extended residence permit.

Personal work permit

A personal work permit is issued on the personal request of the individual and on the basis of a valid business visa under the same terms and conditions as for a business visa, as well as to foreign nationals having permanent residence in Croatia. In most cases, the personal work permit is granted to foreign nationals whose work is not performed in, or directly related to, another Croatian company. The application is submitted to the Croatian Employment Bureau. Documentation required for the work permit includes:

- a completed application form, signed and stamped by the Croatian employer and the applicant;

- notarized copies of the ID page and the page with the entry visa and registered business visa or extended residence permit in the passport;

- a letter from the Croatian company in which the foreign national will be working (or company abroad, depending on the circumstances), stating his or her position, justifying the necessity of engaging a foreign national and the duration of the work in Croatia;

- a copy of the excerpt from the court registry of the entity in which the foreign national will be working in Croatia;

- if requesting a personal work permit, a written opinion of the Ministry of Labour on satisfying the conditions for issuing a business visa and, if applicable, the relevant documentation on business and technical cooperation.

A fee of HRK70 is imposed.

It takes approximately two to six weeks for the work permit to be granted. To extend the work permit, the applicant should first extend the business visa/extended residence permit and then (while the work permit is still valid) apply for the renewal of the work permit. An extension should be granted within two weeks.

Procedures after receiving a work permit

Provided that a foreign national works at the Croatian entity on the basis of an employment contract with that entity, the person should also obtain a 'workbook'. The workbook is endorsed by the City Economic Department and the following documentation needs to be submitted:

- a completed application form;

- the company's request to employ the foreign national, with justifications;

- a workbook (prepared by the employer);

- a copy of foreign national's ID card;

- a copy of the work permit;

- a copy of the passport (containing the extended residency permit).

Upon satisfactory completion of this procedure the employee is in a position to sign a formal employment contract with his employer.

Finally, the foreign national must apply for a 'tax card'. Documents that need to be submitted to the Tax Authority are the request for the tax card and the foreign national's ID (MBS) number.

The entire process of acquiring all the necessary work-related visas and permits generally takes around three months. In order to facilitate the procedure and further boost foreign investment opportunities, the Government is currently preparing a new set of regulations that should simplify and shorten the procedure.

4.3

Intellectual Property

Markovic & Pliso Law Firm

General

After gaining its independence and introducing a market economy, the Republic of Croatia started building its national system of intellectual property in harmony with requirements set out by international agreements and treaties, as well as standards imposed by European Union directives.

As a first step, it was determined by the Constitutional Resolution on Sovereignty and Independence that all international treaties and conventions concluded or accessed by the Socialist Federative Republic of Yugoslavia shall be applicable in the Republic of Croatia, unless contrary to the Constitution of the Republic of Croatia or its public order. In that sense, the Government of the Republic of Croatia deposited on 28 July 1992 with the World Intellectual Property Organization (WIPO) an instrument by which it manifests its intention to be considered as a contracting party of the following international conventions:

- the 1967 Convention establishing the World Intellectual Property Organization (WIPO Convention);
- the 1891 Madrid Agreement Concerning the International Registration of Marks;
- the 1957 Nice Agreement Concerning the International Classification of Goods and Services for the Purposes of the Registration of Marks;
- the 1883 Paris Convention for the Protection of Industrial Property;
- the 1968 Locarno Agreement Establishing an International Classification for Industrial Designs;
- the 1886 Berne Convention for the Protection of Literary and Artistic Works.

It is also important to stress that during 1998 the Republic of Croatia also acceded to the 1970 Patent Cooperation Treaty (PCT).

As a second step, the Croatian Constitution set up a legal framework for establishing a system of intellectual property protection. Under the section 'Basic Freedoms and Rights of a Man and Citizen, Chapter Economical, Social, and Cultural Rights', the protection and guarantee of certain rights and freedoms relating to intellectual property were inserted. The provision of Article 68 is the most important, as it establishes that:

> the freedom of scientific, cultural and artistic creativity is guaranteed, Republic of Croatia encourages and helps development of science, culture and arts, Republic of Croatia protects the scientific, cultural and artistic goods as spiritual national values and protection of moral and material rights emanating from scientific, cultural, artistic, intellectual and other ways of creativity is guaranteed.

Finally, in 1999 completely new intellectual property legislation was adopted by the Croatian Parliament, entering into force on 1 January 2000 and reflecting legislative solutions proposed by international standards that have been adopted by the countries with more developed market economies. In this legislative initiative the following laws were adopted: the Patent Law, the Trademark Law, the Industrial Designs Law, the Law on Geographical Appellations of Origin of Goods and Services, and the Law on Protection of Integrated Circuit Layouts. By enactment of these laws the system of intellectual property regulations was completed.

As a main state institution in the field of intellectual property, the Croatian State Intellectual Property Office was founded on 31 December 1991 under the name of Republic Office for the Industrial Property. The State Patent Office assumed authority for copyright protection and changed its name to the Croatian State Intellectual Property Office (CSIPO). The CSIPO is in charge of all administrative and expert matters in relation to protection of copyright and industrial property. It also carries out all activities concerning collecting, administrating and publishing relevant data. On the international level it cooperates with the WIPO and related offices in other countries, and participates in the preparation and conclusion of multilateral and bilateral treaties and agreements.

Copyright

In 1999 the Republic of Croatia took on the former Yugoslav Copyright Law (*Official Gazette*, Nos 19/78 and 53/91), which is still in force. The provisions were, however, significantly amended throughout 1993 and 1999 (*Official Gazette*, Nos 58/93, 76/99 and 127/99) and phonogram producers and broadcasting organizations' rights were introduced, along with some other innovations.

The Law is drafted in line with the guidelines set forth by the Bern Convention for the Protection of Literary and Artistic Works and the Rome Convention for the Protection of Performers, Producers of Phonograms and Broadcasting Organizations. The 1999 amendments explicitly defined computer programs as works of literary art, thereby removing any doubts about their nature.

Patents

This aspect of intellectual property is regulated by the provisions of the Patent Law (*Official Gazette*, Nos 78/99 and 127/99), and the Patent Regulation (*Official Gazette*, No 146/99), wherein the patent registration procedure is prescribed.

This national system of patent protection is in compliance with the relevant international conventions and treaties, which are also ratified by the Republic of Croatia. They are the Paris Convention for the Protection of Industrial Property, the Strasbourg Agreement Concerning the International Patent Classification, the Patent Cooperation Treaty (PCT), and the Budapest Treaty on the International Recognition of the Deposit of Microorganisms for the Purposes of Patent Procedure.

For the purposes of the Law, a patent is defined as a right protecting the patent holder in the sense of economical utilization of his or her invention. When defining the object of the protection, along the lines of patent provisions in other laws, the Law determines that a patent shall be granted only for an invention that is new, contains an innovative dimension and is industrially applicable. The patent holder is either the inventor or his or her legal successor.

The CSIPO carries out the patent registration procedure proscribed by the Law. Applications for patent registrations are published in the official gazette of the CSIPO, the *Croatian Intellectual Property Gazette*. Patent registration can also be performed on the basis of an international patent application that is made in accordance with the PCT. The Patent Law also allows for a 'consensual patent application', which enables patent registration without performing a complete patent application examination.

Trademarks

In the Republic of Croatia the system of trademark protection is regulated by the Trademark Law (*Official Gazette*, Nos 78/99 and 127/99) and Trademark Regulation (*Official Gazette*, No 146/99), which defines the trademark application procedure.

National trademark regulations comply with the following international conventions and treaties: the Paris Convention for the Protection of Industrial Property, the Madrid Agreement Concerning the International Registration of Marks, the Nice Agreement Concerning the International Classification of Goods and Services for the Purposes of the Registration of Marks, and the Vienna Agreement Establishing an International Classification of the Figurative Elements of Marks.

The Law defines as an object of trademark protection a mark that can be shown graphically and is suitable for distinguishing the goods and services of one merchant from those originating from another merchant. A mark is considered to be distinctive if it provides a special and distinctive character to the goods and services in comparison to otherwise similar goods and services of another merchant.

The CSIPO carries out an administrative procedure for trademark registration. The Office is also in charge of the national stage in the international registration procedure according to the Madrid Agreement Concerning the International Registration of Marks.

Industrial designs

The main national source of law, the Industrial Designs Law (*Official Gazette*, No 78/99) complies with the relevant international instruments in the field of industrial designs protection, notably the Paris Convention for the Protection of Industrial Property and the Locarno Agreement Establishing an International Classification for Industrial Designs.

The Law determines that by an industrial design one protects a three-dimensional or two-dimensional shape of the product or part of the product, in so far as it conforms to the conditions of novelty and specificity set out by the Law.

Again, in this aspect of IP law, the Republic of Croatia chose the most common solution for compliance with the obligations imposed under the Paris Convention for the Protection of Industrial Property and provided a special system of protection of industrial designs by registration of industrial designs with the CSIPO.

Appellations of origin

Along with other IP laws the Law on Geographical Indications of Origin of Goods and Services (*Official Gazette*, No 78/99), applied from 1 January 2000. The Law, following the tradition of certain special treaties, distinguishes two concepts, notably the appellation of origin and an indication of source, anticipating legal protection for both of them.

Under the indication of source, the Law considers and protects any name that refers to a locality or, in exceptional cases, any name that refers to a given country. It has the effect of conveying the notion that goods bearing the indication originate in that country or locality. On the other hand, under a more limited concept of appellation of origin the Law protects the geographical name of a place which serves to designate the product originating from there, the quality and characteristics of which are due to the geographical environment, inclusive of natural and human factors.

Protection of appellations of origin and indications of source is granted upon entry of the respective right in the registry of appellations of origin or indications of source, which are held by CSIPO.

Integrated circuit layouts

Before enactment of the Law on Protection of Integrated Circuit Layouts (*Official Gazette*, No 78/99) in 1999, this subject matter had not been regulated by the Croatian intellectual property legislation, nor did the Republic of Croatia take any responsibility at the international level. The Law regulates the notion of topography, the right to legal protection, the conditions and procedure for gaining protection, the effects and limitations of protection, and the duration of protection. The Patent Law applies to any matters not regulated by the Law on integrated circuit layouts.

4.4

Arbitration and Dispute Resolution

Markovic & Pliso Law Firm

General

Disputes in Croatia may be settled either before the Croatian courts or before a tribunal, where arbitration may be institutional or informal (ad hoc). The provisions dealing with these matters are set out in Croatian legislation and in the applicable international conventions that Croatia is a party to. Needless to say, there are no obstacles for any Croatian entity or individual to enter and to be bound by the arbitration clause that agrees on the jurisdiction of the Arbitral Tribunal seated out of Croatian territory, as well.

The most notable domestic sources of law in this respect are provisions of the Law on Civil Litigation (*Official Gazette*, Nos 53/91, 91/91 and 112/99) and the Law on Arbitration (*Official Gazette*, No 88/01), as well as the Rules on Arbitration of the Permanent Arbitration Court Attached to the Croatian Chamber of Commerce ('The Zagreb Rules') (*Official Gazette*, No 150/02) and the Rules on Conciliation (*Official Gazette*, No 81/01). Thus, following the provision of Article 34 of the Zagreb Rules, the Management Committee of the Croatian Chamber of Commerce is authorized to enact the bylaws related to the reimbursement of the arbitration costs.

According to the Constitutional Resolution on Sovereignty and Independence that was enacted on 25 June 1991, all international conventions that were in force in former Yugoslavia also apply in Croatia, provided that they do not contravene the Constitution or the general provisions of its legal system. Consequently, almost all important multilateral treaties on arbitration that former Yugoslavia was a party to were taken over or adopted by the Republic of Croatia. The most important are:

- the 1958 New York Convention on the Recognition and Enforcement of Foreign Arbitral Awards;

- the 1923 Geneva Protocol on Arbitration Clauses;

- the 1927 Geneva Convention on the Execution of Foreign Arbitral Awards;

- the 1961 (Geneva) European Convention on International Commercial Arbitration;

- the 1965 Washington Convention on Settlement of Investment Disputes between States and Nationals of Other States.

So far, no legislation dealing with mediation or alternative dispute resolution has been enacted in the Croatian legal system, although this is expected to change shortly, when these modern means of dispute settlement will be introduced to the domestic legal and business community.

The provisions of the Rules on Conciliation envisage activity of the Conciliation Centre, which is also attached to the Croatian Chamber of Commerce and where one or more conciliators may act as an intermediary, to a certain extent, between the parties in a dispute. The conciliation proceedings may end either through settlement, thereby finally resolving the case (unless certain claims remained uncomprehended by the conciliation), or by a Decree on adjournment of the proceedings if it is established that the conciliation proceedings may not be successfully pursued any more.

Enforcement

The recently enacted Croatian Law on Arbitration expressly provides Article 40, Paragraphs 1 and 2, that any foreign arbitral award shall be recognized and executed in the Republic of Croatia, unless the court finds upon the other part's objection that certain criteria have not been met. These are cases where a) certain obstacles defined in provisions of Paragraph 2 of the Article 36 exist, or b) where the award did not become legally binding, or c) where the court of jurisdiction where it was rendered has annulled or postponed the legal effects.

According to the provision of Paragraph 2 of Article 36, the application for a recognition and/or execution of a foreign award shall be dismissed if the court establishes: a) that the matter in dispute may not be subject to arbitration pursuant to the laws of the Republic of Croatia, or b) that the recognition or enforcement of the award would be contrary to the public order (*ordre public*) of the Republic of Croatia.

Since according to the Law on Arbitration, an arbitral award originates in the state on whose territory it was rendered, foreign arbitral awards are executed in the same manner as are domestic awards. In other words, that is by adhering to the procedural provisions of the Law on Arbitration and attaching the original or a certified translation of the award, the agreement containing the arbitration clause and the eventual translation thereof. However, foreign awards have to be first recognized in separate court proceedings, where the court shall explicitly examine whether any of the aforementioned negative presumptions was priory met. Interestingly, the Law explicitly allows the parties bound by the arbitral award to request the court to rule that there are no grounds for challenging the award, thereby effectively preventing the other party from doing so (provided, however, that the pertinent applicant possesses adequate legal grounds for such a motion).

Thus, the Law explicitly allows the court to informally re-examine the merits of the case and to request clarification from the arbitral tribunal itself or the parties involved in the proceedings. It is also entitled, on its own discretion, to postpone the proceedings at either the stage of recognition or enforcement, should separate annulment proceedings or an application for stoppage of recognition be initiated or filed.

When the matter comes to the stage where the recognition or even execution measures are to be made by the court, the Law imposes an obligation on the court to grant the parties an opportunity to respond with their own views on the merits of the case, thereby somehow starting to settle the dispute again. It is due to the fact that the arbitral award slightly differs in its legal nature from the court judgement, and a duty to apply special enforcement rules contained in the Law on Arbitration. Namely, pertinent Decrees on recognition and execution of the arbitral and execution of the arbitral award have to contain a legally argumentation.

As regards jurisdiction, to resolve on the jurisdiction of the arbitral tribunal itself, the deposition of the award, a complaint on annulment of the arbitral award and a request to recognize and/or execute the award, the Commercial Court in Zagreb is entitled to deal with these issues where they fall within its competence, and the District Court in Zagreb for all other issues. A court whose competence relates to the subject matter is defined by a special Law (Law on Courts, *Official Gazette*, Nos 3/94, 100/96, 131/97 and 129/00) shall have the jurisdiction to pursue the execution proceedings, as well as to resolve any interim measure. Consequently, in certain cases provisions of the Law on Arbitration shall derogate and overlap the application of the provisions of the Law on Execution during the enforcement of an arbitral award (*Official Gazette,* Nos 57/96 and 29/99).

4.5

Small and Medium-sized Enterprises (SMEs) in Croatia:
A Foreigner's Perspective

Hayley Alexander, Deloitte & Touche Zagreb

Relevance to foreign investors

Individuals and companies considering the Croatian market as a target for potential investment might ask the entirely rational question: why is the SME sector relevant to me as a potential investor in Croatia? There are at least three answers.

While SMEs are less likely targets of foreign direct investment than large enterprises, they are nonetheless often as viable. This is particularly true for mid-sized investors unable to take on the debt and complicated restructuring efforts that are characteristically required for large and/or formerly state-owned enterprises.

SMEs tend to lead the economic recovery process in transitional or emerging countries. Their prospects for growth and development thereby serve as a useful barometer to gauge the pace of a country's structural reform and its ability to create a business-friendly environment. The more an investor understands about the structural reforms being undertaken in support of SMEs, the better the chance to anticipate structural business and regulatory hazards in the broader sense.

SMEs form the basis of second-tier suppliers in any business environment. The strength of a country's enterprises, regardless of size, is at least partially reliant on the availability of a dependable supplier network.

Addressing SMEs as a unified sector is always a risky proposition, due to their diverse nature, widely varying management and technological proficiencies, and disparate markets served. Any attempt to evaluate SMEs at the macro level is, consequently, best focused on aspects common to all. Two of the most important of these are the enabling environment and related government policies. Identification of trends among the most rudimentary SME performance indicators is also important. In most countries (Croatia included) the most widely available and relevant SME performance indicators are compiled annually and include annual sales growth, employment figures, numbers of registered companies and export sales revenues. These are addressed below.

Croatian SME sector: vital statistics

SMEs cannot be ignored in Croatia. They represent well over half, and by some estimates nearly two-thirds, of total employment in the country. In terms of businesses registered, they comprise over 95 per cent of all legally registered concerns and are responsible for approximately 55 per cent of GDP. While large enterprises continue to shed employees – losing approximately 30 per cent during the past two to three years – SMEs are maintaining their numbers and making a substantial contribution to keeping the economy on track. The Croatian government has become increasingly aware of the role SMEs play in economic development, a fact evidenced by the elevation of SME issues on the political agenda in recent years.

The Croatian business-enabling environment

Since the creation of the Ministry for Small and Medium Enterprises in 2000, the Croatian business-enabling environment has improved substantially. Prior to its formation, SME concerns were lumped together with all other general economic and business policy issues under the Ministry of the Economy. In their decision to form the Ministry for SMEs, Croatian policy-makers correctly assessed the need for special treatment of the one sector of the economy most likely to lead it out of severe recession, which had peaked in 1998.

On the down side, a legacy of overlapping business laws and regulations (promulgated before and since the war) remains to be dealt with. Newly formulated laws and regulations affecting the business climate, when viewed in the context of an already complicated legal framework, are often confusing at best, and contradictory at worst. Separate sets of laws are imposed to address cooperatives, craftspeople and companies, while SMEs in particular have been under the purview of yet another law, The Law on Accountancy. In fact, no fewer than 14 individual laws figure prominently in the daily lives of Croatian enterprise managers. Simply put, the process to unravel the legal and regulatory requirements, for business investments or start-ups, can be daunting for domestic and foreign concerns alike.

The existence of a complicated legal structure is not, however, a situation unique to Croatia. Legal and regulatory complexity could be characterized as endemic in post-socialist economies, a consequence that might be expected in the wake of dismantled and partially restructured institutions. In this respect, Croatia is no worse than most other countries in transition, and with appropriate legal assistance, investment decisions can generally be made with a reasonable degree of transparency.

One of the main problems facing Croatia's SMEs and foreign investors is the lack of a centralized property register to establish clear title for due diligence in purchase transactions, and to verify collateral in support of financing proposals. Perhaps more troublesome, especially from the standpoint of foreign investors, is the backlog of claims in the court system and the resulting inability for timely conflict resolution through legal due process.

For those already familiar with the risks of investment in transitional economies, Croatia offers many positive features. In the couple of years since the Social Democrats achieved a majority over Tudjman's HDZ party (in 2000), the country has demonstrated a clear predisposition towards economic reform and tackling corruption. One by one, business constraints are being dealt with. Business registration, for instance, formerly a key impediment to SME creation, has been greatly simplified. And the measures to create a more friendly business climate, largely in pursuit of increased employment, are working. Foreign direct investment (FDI), led by Germany, Austria, the UK, the USA, Italy and Luxembourg, is increasing. In 2001, nearly $1.5 billion flowed into the country, mostly in the form of privatization investments. A great opportunity remains for foreign companies looking for strategic partners in Croatia. SMEs should figure prominently in this respect and provide an excellent means with which to establish production and distribution bases. Those in first will gain a foothold into South-East Europe, a region whose pent-up demand for products and services is expected to yield substantial increases in consumer and industrial markets.

A factor further enhancing Croatia's attractiveness to foreign investors interested in SMEs is the existence of some very useful institutions to aid them in their search. These are led by the Ministry of SMEs, which is motivated to assist investors to locate enterprises for collaboration or investment. Depending on the nature of the partnership, the Ministry may also be able to assist SMEs to finance new technology or acquire know-how.

These are important programmes, because the willingness of banks to lend money to SMEs has been evolving at an unacceptably slow pace. Much of the banking sector is now foreign-owned (largely Austrian), a benefit of which has been the infusion of more sophisticated lending instruments. These notwithstanding, the absence of a fully functioning property register and the difficulty in processing claims through the courts are strong disincentives to lend on any basis other than heavy collateralization. Even relatively small loans offered to Croatian enterprises typically impose liens on a disproportionately large amount of their assets which severely restrict their ability to obtain critical additional financing. Future cash flow is still generally recognized by financiers in the provision of bank loans. Despite governmental loan and loan guarantee programmes designed to stimulate financing for SMEs, the amount of bank lending is still low in relation to demand. In 2000, only one-third of government funding provided to commercial banks for this purpose was actually lent to SMEs as intended.

The advent of relatively near-term European accession and the fiscal discipline this implies further reinforces Croatia's need to strengthen its SME sector, as a reliable tax base and generator of employment. For these reasons and those already mentioned, a continuation in the positive trends already witnessed in Croatia may be expected: an easing regulatory burden (including tax relief) and further stimulation of banking sector involvement in SME financing.

SME key sectors

Croatia's overall GDP growth during the past four years has been surprisingly strong, averaging in excess of 3.5 per cent. A significant portion of this was directly attributable to the tourism sector, which continues to rebound after the devastation caused by the Balkans wars. Tourism in Croatia remains largely an SME activity, with small and medium-sized hotels, restaurants and tour operators at the core of the industry. Such establishments, especially in the medium-sized category, present interesting opportunities for investors. The widely anticipated growth in foreign tourists visiting Croatia, if the sector is sensibly managed and adheres to sustainable development practices, is likely to attract a large amount of investor interest within the next two to three years. Information technology, business services (package delivery, management training, catering, etc) and food processing also offer attractive SME investment possibilities.

Croatia is poised to begin more seriously accommodating foreign investors interested in SMEs. The country's structural impediments have thus far prevented a rapid influx of capital; however, once the flow of investment begins in earnest, available opportunities will be rapidly seized. Investors with even a marginal interest in Croatia are best advised to begin their research into this intriguing market now.

4.6

Corruption in Croatia:
Risks and Actions

Josip Kregar

Corruption, in different forms, is eternal. Corruption was tolerated as a systemic part of ancient (pre-modern) government. Not any longer: corruption we now understand is economically harmful and ethically intolerable. In modern democracies it brings uncertainty; rights are not guaranteed, obligations not fulfilled. The justice system and courts are inefficient; the government incapable; market competition, business and enterprise inert. The biggest harm is distortion of criteria and priorities in political and economic decision-making and the devastation of public responsibility and morale.

The risk of corruption

The present situation in Croatia encourages corruption. The risks arise from the economy (mass privatization, denationalization, unregulated market rules) but also from the general weakness of institutions (clientism, nepotism, formalism, primitive bureaucracy) and the general instability of social norms (an explosion of consumption and aspirations, social anomie, lack of orientation). The phenomenon of corruption reflecting the growing pains of a new democracy are not an incident but a permanent obstacle and part of the system.

Public opinion surveys in the Republic of Croatia show, without exception, that the respondents perceive and consider that corruption is widespread (extensively widespread 65.8 per cent, widespread 32.9 per cent, while 55 to 82 per cent condemn it).

International surveys reveal slow progress. According to the Corruption Perception Index (CPI) of Transparency International, the Republic of Croatia is in 51st place. In comparison with the 1999 report, which covers the time of the previous regime of Franjo Tujman, Croatia has shown a significant advance, since it used to be in 74th place. Compared with neighbouring countries and other countries in transition (Ukraine,

Russia, Albania and Moldavia), the Republic of Croatia has been assessed relatively lowly and from 1999 to 2003 the positive perception has prevailed. This was the fastest improvement since the beginning of international comparisons. Now Croatia is in the same group (with minimal differences) as the Czech Republic, Bulgaria and Lithuania.

Studies carried out by the World Bank show that the Republic of Croatia, according to surveys conducted at the end of 1999, can be categorized in the intermediate group of transitional countries. The data indicates a relatively low total index, particularly in Administrative Corruption (low, petty corruption), but a high level of corruption at the level of political decision-making (State Capture Index), and the judiciary (Judiciary Capture Index). The study shows weak social and political responsibility – which is both a sign of and a condition for corruption – and also shows the existence of strong social groups that are ready to impede social reforms.

Recent public opinion research (Transparency International Croatia, May 2003) pointed out that 85.9 per cent of respondents perceive corruption as an existing problem in Croatian society (49.0 per cent 'very much', 37.9 'widespread'). In Gallup research (June 2003) 69.5 per cent respondents were of the opinion that corruption is present in the economy (69.5 per cent) and politics (65 per cent).

In spite of methodological controversy, it is a fact that people's perceptions and economic analysis indicate the same: corruption is a serious threat to economic and political development. The fact that we cannot measure exactly how widespread corruption is in the Republic of Croatia does not mean that we do not know for sure that it obstructs business and that the impression of its extensiveness puts off foreign investors and Croatian entrepreneurs. Moreover, relativization is extremely damaging because it creates a potential excuse for a lack of political decisiveness in taking action: the important thing is what is being done to eliminate corruption. Everyone doing business in Croatia has to be aware of the traces left behind by previous political regimes (particularly their dark sides: the privileges given to those who are obedient, the possibility to steal in the name of high ideals, the fact that everything can be done through connections and influence, that for those in power loyalty and obedience mean more than work and innovations).

Legal regulation

In March 2001, the Croatian parliament adopted a National Programme for the Fight against Corruption with an Action Plan for Fighting Corruption (the National Strategy). The National Strategy was developed in broad consultation with non-governmental organizations (which actually initiated the process) and has been supported by the consensus of all political parties. According to the Action Plan, there are priority areas: the administration of criminal justice, public administration, and financial responsibility, promoting political and civil responsibility and enhancing international activity.

In the National Strategy corruption is defined as 'Every form of abuse of public authority in order to achieve personal benefit'. This is a sociological and political definition, useful for analysis of phenomena such as misuse of public authority, organized and economic crime, and poor governance and its consequences. The elements of the definition – and this is a major point – are changeable. This reflects an increase of public sensitivity towards politicians and government. Some incidents, such as conflict of interest, unauthorized use of public property, and benefits for functionaries and leaders, which were ignored and tolerated just few years ago, are now strongly condemned by the public.

The emphasis of the National Strategy is on preventive measures, improvement of good governance, legal reforms of public administration and the judiciary, local self-government and decentralization, an active role for a free and independent media and civil society. Respecting the legislative optimism of government, and their (relative) achievements against corruption, what we need most is new legal initiatives on conflict of interest, access to information, public procurement and political parties financing legislation.

There is no single definition of 'corruption' in the Croatian legal system. Conventionally it is regarded as offering and accepting bribes (347, 348 – Criminal Code (CC)), illegal intercession/trading in influence (343 CC), abuse in performing governmental duties (338 CC), abuse of office and official authority (337 CC), concluding a prejudicial contract (294 CC), the disclosure of an official secret (351 CC), and the unauthorized procurement and disclosure of a business secret (295 CC). Corruption is sanctioned regardless of the form of the bribe; it can be a gift or any other benefit, whether pecuniary or non-pecuniary, real or personal, tangible or non-tangible. Bribes given or promised for the purpose of obtaining both commissions and omissions of public officials are covered. A person who promises or gives a bribe and has been solicited by a public official to do so, and has reported the act to the competent law enforcement authority before the crime was detected, can be exempted from the sanction. Sanctions for active bribery range from three months to three years imprisonment and for passive bribery from six months to five years imprisonment for active bribery.

Corruption in the private sector (private–private corruption) is also criminalized. The new legislation provides also for the criminal liability of legal entities. Until recently, all corruption offences fell under the jurisdiction of the Municipal Courts (since the prescribed sanctions for all these offences are below 10 years imprisonment). This has changed with the adoption of the Law on USKOK (the State Office for Prevention of Corruption and Organized Crime). The law stipulates that all corruptive criminal offences will be adjudicated by four major County Courts.

The statistics for criminal offences do not mirror the actual behaviour and incidence of corruption. These statistics suggest that there are very few people who have been reported, accused and convicted of the criminal offence of corruption. In the period from 1992 to 1997, a total of 3,316 criminal offences were reported. In the same period, 1,408 indictments were issued, and 570 people were convicted on the basis of a final judgement. Therefore, a kind of filtering of the affairs of corruption seems to occur during the criminal procedure, so that only 17.2 per cent of reported offences result in a conviction, and only 13, or 0.0392 per cent, end with a non-suspended prison sentence. Besides the fact that these figures should be treated with caution – because false reports are possible – they primarily represent a warning that there is a conflict between the public perception of the extent of this pheno-menon and public opinion about it. *Quod non est in actis non est in mundo* (what is not in files is not real!) is a dangerous bureaucratic trick.

Croatia ratified various international legal instruments to fight corruption (Criminal Convention Against Corruption, 2001, Civil Convention against Corruption, 2003, Convention on Money Launder-ing, Search, Seizure and Confiscation of Proceeds of Crime). Croatia is a part of the GRECO programme. In the Stability Pact, Croatia actively promotes the 'Anti-corruption Initiative for SEE', developing regional leadership for such programmes. The Government publicly declared its willingness to instigate OECD conventions against bribery.

Institutions

The main institutions to combat corruption are the repressive state institutions: police, state prosecution, and the specialized investigative body, USKOK.

The Croatian police conduct preliminary investigations into corrup-tion crimes. Croatia has a single centralized police service, which is responsible for public order and the detection and investigation of criminal offences. The police are organized as a special service (the Police Directorate) within the Ministry of the Interior. The police also have a specialized Department for Economic Crime and Corruption. Such organizational specialization for combating new forms of white-collar crimes (and corruption) were established in order to improve the level of expertise of the investigators.

Criminal proceedings against corruption and economic crimes are conducted on the request of the public prosecutor. Prosecution as an institution is perceived as independent – the National Council of Public Prosecutions has the final authority over the appointment, dismissal and control of the performance of duties by individual prosecutors, but is rather inefficient in the proceedings against powerful organizations, gangs or corrupt officials. That was a major reason for forming USKOK as a legally powerful and organizationally competent institution.

USKOK is formally within the system of the Public Prosecutor's Office. All USKOK personnel are subjected to security checks, have to be competent, and have previous professional experience (a minimum of eight years in the police or judiciary). The USKOK has intelligence, investigative, prosecutorial and preventive functions. USKOK prosecutors direct the work of the police and other bodies in detecting and investigating corruption and organized crime, cooperate with competent authorities in other countries and with international organizations, and initiate procedures relating to the seizure and confiscation of proceeds from crime. They have the right to use special investigative means, such as covert surveillance and recording, use of undercover investigators, simulated offering of bribery, and supervised transport and delivery of objects. USKOK's structure and competences are designed for it to become the leading state authority in the prevention and repression of corruption in Croatia.

Various measures of financial control have been put in place. The Anti-Money Laundering Office was established in 1997. The Office is responsible for gathering and processing reports on suspicious transactions from banks and other institutions, which could be indicative of laundering of the proceeds of crime, including proceeds of corruption. The Office has limited authority for investigations, but a large database and research software for analysing and recording evidence.

The State Audit Office is responsible for auditing the use of public finances and those of local self-government, including all state-owned companies and funds, such as health and pension funds.

Concluding remarks

Actions against corruption are not only the political gestures, nor a warning signal to entrepreneurs, but also an instruction to state institutions to act, and a request to society to condemn and mobilize. It has to be commonly accepted and acknowledged that corruption in Croatia is systemic and endemic. Corruption is endemic as a part of tradition crystallized in the collective memory and values of people. Corruption is not an imported phenomenon. It is not a relic of the communist past or oriental or Balkan traditions. It derives and is reproduced from the very system.

Corruption does not have a single cause, but many contingencies – weak institutions, a hungry market, conspicuous elite traditions and values incompatible with an open society. For this reason it is even more important to invest additional efforts to combat corruption. Orthodox measures should be taken: reform of the judiciary, a decrease in bureaucratic procedures, voluntarism and discretion, serious measures to establish standards in public life, and the abolition of party state elements. The new beginning has been good and improvement fast. The greatest difficulty was that corruption prior to 2000 was ignored.

It may be that Croatia has substantial and bigger problems, but investment and business will not prosper in a corrupt society with greedy politics. Good governance and open and honest government have to abate corruption.

4.7

A Final Thought on Doing Business:
Foundation 2020 and three likely scenarios for future Croatian development

Professor P Turkovic, Foundation 2020

The Civic Scenario Project, 'Croatia's Creatia 2010'

Foundation 2020 (Zagreb, Croatia) was established in November 1999 in order to contribute to the development of Croatia as a democratic and modern European country during the coming 20 years. Foundation 2020 stands for basic values to be the grounds of the Croatian state in the 21st century: human rights, civil society, freedom and the responsibility of individuals, entrepreneurs and local communities, overcoming of ethical, moral, communication and management crises, and, finally, the democratic and global context through the creation of the framework for dialogue within Croatia and with the rest of the world. Foundation 2020 gathers together a number of well established and recognized scientists, managers, artists, politicians, journalists, members of NGOs, musicians, lawyers, consultants, etc, from Croatia and abroad.

Similar to several other countries' scenario planning projects carried out in the last decade (The Mont Fleur Scenarios, JAR, 1992, The Future of Northern Ireland, 1996, Scenarios for Cyprus, 1996, etc), Foundation 2020 designed Croatian development scenarios for the 2001–2010 period.

The purpose of the project was to create and explore an understanding of possible developments and opportunities for Croatia among larger groups of stakeholders in the country. Also, the project shows that although the future is determined by where we are today, it could turn many different ways when directed by different events or powers. The work process used scenario methodology. The scenario approach was applied in order to create important new learning and shared views – results that would lead to new and inclusive national strategies.

The eight months' work of the multidisciplinary project group facilitated by Nextwork consultants from Sweden resulted in three possible Croatian future scenarios. The scenarios were determined by two major coordinates. One coordinate was dichotomized about the concept of organization (of society, state, institutions…), with the inclination towards traditional forms of organization on the one hand and the acceptance of new forms of organization on the other. The other coordinate was related to the integration concept with the dichotomy of inclusion and exclusion in all main aspects of the concept, be it the cooperative atmosphere, communication, openness and awareness, trust, shared ideas and vision, elite vs shared society, etc.

Although the coordinates divided the outcome into four starting scenarios, two of them were joined together because of their low dissimilarity. The three final scenarios (described below) were named: Do It Yourself!, with the motto 'Croatian heritage and pride'; Hurry Up, with the motto 'Networked Euro Croatia', and Emperor's New Clothes, whose motto was 'Croatia repeats itself'.

After producing the three possible scenarios of Croatia's future, the Puls marketing and public opinion research agency carried out a survey of the scenarios based on a sample of 1,000 respondents. The 'liking' and the 'probability' of each scenario was tested and measured in terms of respondents' attitudes. The results have clearly demonstrated a high preference for the Hurry Up scenario, with the Emperor's New Clothes the least popular. On the probability scale, however, the difference was statistically less evident, but the opinion that the most liked scenario has the least chance of happening was the prevailing one. Also, respondents claimed that the least preferred scenario, Emperors New Clothes, is already happening.

The scenarios and the public opinion research were presented at the third Foundation 2020 international conference in Cavtat, as well as on a number of relevant occasions in Croatia, in order to provide the context for discussing the future of Croatia.

Three Croatian future scenarios – an overview

The different ways to the future are represented in a simplified manner in Figure 4.7.1. The drawing illustrates how different triggers and social circumstances could lead the future to very different directions and outcomes.

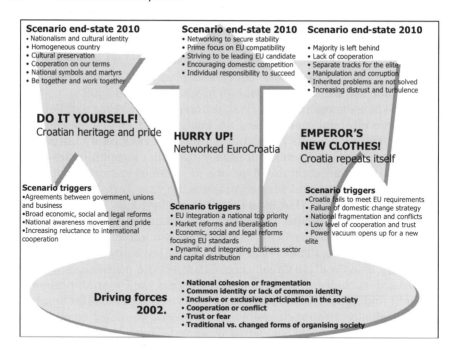

Figure 4.7.1 Three future scenarios

The first scenario: Do It Yourself!

Croatia is proceeding slowly with regard to European integration. The negotiations about entering the EU are not successfully concluded yet. There are many obstacles to that. Foreigners can still not purchase property on the coast. The 12-mile economic zone on the Adriatic has been declared and is being strongly protested by the Italians and other EU states. The obligatory pilotage act for all tankers in our waters has been decreed. The EU is still not satisfied with how we are cooperating with the Hague tribunal and how little we have done to return the Serb citizens who fled after the war in Croatia. The euro was declared a national currency, however.

Croatian interests are still our only political focus, with special care for the Adriatic and our natural resources. On the symbolic main-value coordinates of organization and cohesion, this scenario is positioned high on the national cohesion axis and low on the organizational changes axis. The nation has reached cohesion as to the main national goals and values, but it is not ready to leave behind the old organizational patterns and traditions.

As a result of a relatively poor performance in catching up with the ways of the EU, Croatia is turning to its own sources and with rather good results. Although the goals proclaimed in 2000 have not been attained, the overall situation is acceptable to the population. GDP did not grow at the level of 7 per cent per year, but at 3 to 4 per cent. The unemployment rate is not 6 per cent as planned but 12 per cent, which is double the EU average, but half of what it was in 2002.

The pension reform and privatization process has been implemented within a minimal consensus of the government, employers and syndicates. The economy is characterized by a prevalence of multinational companies. Newly opened mid-size and smaller companies are centred on the Croatian capital. There are an increasing number of foreign workers in lesser-paid jobs. Sometimes they are harassed by marginal groups (Skinheads, Bad Blue Boys, etc) under racist slogans.

Pension and health insurance is permeated by the principle of solidarity, but the quality of the services is markedly different for the rich and the poor. The civil sector does not have any real influence on politics. The Croatian Greens are registered as a political party so as to strengthen their influence and have entered the Croatian parliament. Right and left coalitions are taking turns at power. Popular heroes are sportsmen and entertainers.

The judicial system has clearly improved. There is a stronger regional approach in the administration and budget spending. The problem of corruption has 'moved' to the regions, following the shift of administrative power. Trade and traffic relations inside Croatia and with neighbouring states have been improved.

Croatia is a relatively safe place to live. National awareness and self-confidence are strong. The popular mantra is: 'Well, we are not exactly what we wanted to be, but we are living rather comfortably and safely in this clean and beautiful land and we like it as it is!'

The second scenario: Hurry Up

Public companies are mostly privatized. Stronger and more advanced Croatian companies are active in the regions. The Croatian economy is permeated by entrepreneurship, and the collaboration of foreign, regional and domestic companies has given rise to a strong SME segment. However, development is not uniform.

Accelerated and open development leads to redefining the Croatian identity and the risks involved. The identity is redefined towards greater individualism and open cooperation. Although the entire society is advancing, some social differences are increasing. Progress favours the younger, connected, more enterprising and better educated, and does not favour the old, servile mentality, those who are not connected and the poorly educated. Knowledge, understood as a dynamic possibility of adopting new skills, becomes an important part of personal identity and the most important element of success.

Civil society is flourishing and is setting new standards and values. In that sense, political activity is being redefined and political institutions are becoming significantly more efficient and transparent. Institutions that were an important part of the old identity (church, nation, etc) are networking through non-governmental organizations; they operate in a new way and thus decrease the risk of the involved/not involved division.

The natural environment manages to sustain faster development, and some progress has been attained by more efficient regulation at a local level (ie, the urban planning problem on the Dalmatian coast). However, some parts, such as the Istrian coast, have been sacrificed to 'progress'.

The Hurry Up or Networked EuroCroatia scenario is the one that seems to be extremely positive regarding both coordinates – the organizational changes axis and national cohesion axis. However this is not equally the case throughout the nation. This illustrates the fact that no scenario can be simply described in terms of 'pluses' and 'minuses'. Each of them is positive to some and negative to other social strata.

Croatia has succeeded in EU integration. The legal and economic systems have changed and the state is reaching its goals without delay. We are not Croats any more; we are 'The youngest Europeans' now. Political party members regard their European counterparts as their peers and partners, rather than the members of competing parties in Croatia.

The changes did not happen by accident. Here is a list of some hypothetical triggers and events for the period 2002 to 2004 that bring us to this scenario end-state:

- Slovenian and Hungarian membership in the EU changes our political scenery – we have the EU on our borders now.

- Financial institutions that have reached a sufficient level of stability in 2002 are searching for new investment opportunities.

- New investors are suddenly in the same arena – the funds.

- EU membership becomes the ultimate state target.

- The Croatian and Slovenian stock exchanges are united – the negotiations with Sarajevo and Milan are continuing.

- Two new private faculties are opened in 2004.

- The third TV channel has been privatised, which brings new competition to the media world.

Public enterprises are mostly privatized already and the best of them are becoming strong regional players, mostly in ex-Yugoslav countries.

The Croatian economy is characterized by a strong entrepreneurial spirit and with the support of foreign companies a healthy SME segment has been born.

This sharp development line brings us to a redefinition of Croatian identity and values, but creates new risks as well. The identity and values are switching towards individual responsibilities and openness towards other nations. Everybody is responsible for his or her own destiny. The solidarity that we once knew does not exist any more.

Although society as whole is getting better, there are clear winners and losers in this scenario. The social distance between them is sharp and would be hard to overcome. The winners are young people, net-worked individuals, entrepreneurs and well-educated individuals. The winners are those whose mantra is 'The world is my home'. The losers are small farmers, old households, workers in traditional industries, old-fashioned administration clerks and people with little education.

Civic society is setting the agenda for politicians now. Political activity is redefined because the traditional 'partytocracy' does not live here any more. Traditional social institutions that were the main controllers of society values (the church, national institutions, cultural institutions, etc) now have to accept the new ways. Their activity, together with that of NGOs, is cooling social tensions and lowering the risk of social division and frustration. Natural resources and the environment are preserved by new regulations and national awareness, and some progress has been made on the local level, such as fighting illegal building in the coastal regions. Some areas, such as parts of the Istrian coast, have been sacrificed on the altar of progress, however.

The third scenario: Emperor's New Clothes

Due to the fact that Croatians are not prepared to forgive and forget, what has been dividing Croatians for centuries is still the major issue in political life. Black-and-white type behaviour has finally ended up in deepening the social, economic and political differences among Croatians, causing a serious obstacle for Croatia to meet the standards of the developed world. The Emperor's New Clothes scenario is in a way a recycling of errors from the 1990s. The political environment is evidently changing, so the recycling does not bring us to the same situation as we found in the 1990s.

The different views of the coalition partners regarding EU member-ship, compliance of Croatian laws with EU standards, and support for Croatian business circles integrating with the European and global alliances were the major reasons for the renewal of a political crisis. Political struggles are leading to early elections. The result is a mixture of party coalitions, unable to focus and carry on a consistent political and economic agenda. IMF support is frozen and some existing contracts have been put on hold. Simultaneously, the EU has had a 'crisis of ideas' and that has stopped new applications.

Nationalism is re-emerging and is carried on the social wave; the Rightists' coalition is offering a solution. After the next election they will form the new government, offering new prosperity and modernization. The main political players are more and more dependent on the business elite in the strongest, foreign-owned, companies. The government is becoming more and more technocratic, offering optimistic visions that are in clear contradiction of the facts.

Reforms and incentives for development of the SME sector exist, but are not sufficient to create a strong driver for the Croatian economy. Ordinary citizens find it hard to get a decent level of health protection and care, social welfare and educational services. At the same time the new elite can afford to use small private clinics and private schools, expensive sports resorts, etc. Croatia is becoming more isolated. Its international relationships were based on selected bilateral contacts that created an economy concentrated on serving Croatia.

Society is being directed by 'elitist clubs'. It is clearly a split society, with little social integration or social mobility. The media are serving the elite, promoting the symbols of success, such as occasional sport victories and stars. The civic arena is full of organizations that have no actual impact on politics. The idea of caring for the environment is strongly promoted by NGOs and given public support, but at the same time, the governing structures are ready to abdicate responsibility for the environment in the interest of any profit. Family and religious values are strongly promoted, but the alcohol and drug problem is getting worse. The motto of this scenario is: Croatia is a poor country of rich individuals.

Part Five

Appendices

Appendix 1

The Transport Sector

Croatian Railways

Throughout the past hundred years, the railways have been the biggest means of passenger and goods transport. However, as road, maritime and air traffic began to develop in the mid-1950s, the railways started to lose their dominance as the biggest carrier and nowadays they have become merely one of the competitors in the traffic system. Compared to other traffic branches, railways have a whole range of advantages regarding cost-effectiveness, power consumption and ecological sustainability. Furthermore, rail transport provides a fast, large-scale and economical flow of people and goods. The railways are the synergic backbone of traffic flows and a factor in overall transport development. Positive business results achieved by railway companies nowadays all over Western Europe show that railway traffic is re-establishing itself and is regaining its dominance on the transport market.

Croatian Railways will be able to join in such European trends through high-quality rational business operations, investments in infrastructure and rolling stock capacities, as well as through the introduction of new services. Croatian Railways are situated in an extremely favourable traffic position: the railway network is integrated into the European network and it is included in all the modern railway flows. Croatia acts as an intersection of routes from Europe's west to east and from north to south, being the shortest route between central Europe and the Adriatic and the Mediterranean. This gives additional comparative advantages to the Croatian Railways network.

The intention of Croatian Railways is to create a market-oriented company that will provide passenger and freight transport services in a competitive, safe, reliable, cost-effective and ecologically acceptable way. This can be achieved with a more assertive policy on the domestic market, and the transport markets of surrounding countries, and with an increase in freight transport volume on Pan-European corridors running through Croatia. Croatian Railways' long-term business plan is: the construction of modern infrastructure on lines which are the Croatian sections of the X Pan-European Corridor, as well as on the B and C branches of the V Pan-European corridor (see below); the purchase of high-standard transport equipment; and the establishment of a modern business organization that will enable the provision of modern and high-quality transport services. In a very ambitious but nevertheless necessary Croatian Railways Modernization Project covering the period from 2003 to 2007, investment activities have been planned that will cost HRK15,262.4 million or HRK3,052.5 million on average per year.

Croatian Railways accepts environment protection as a part of its business policy. Environment protection aims are regarded as equally important as all the other development objectives, and contributing to environment protection is an important component of the comparative advantages of Croatian Railways.

Some basic data

Croatian Railways was established as a limited liability company in 100 per cent ownership of the Republic of Croatia on 5 October 1990 pursuant to a resolution brought by the Croatian Parliament. As an independent railway company, Croatian Railways joined the UIC – International Railway Union (Union Internationale des Chemins de Fer), with its headquarters in Paris, as an active member on 10 June 1992. Croatian Railways provides public transport of passengers and freight in domestic and international railway traffic, and the construction and maintenance of the railway infrastructure. It has 16,177 employees. There are 14 non-transport subsidiaries, owned 100 per cent by Croatian Railways, and one subsidiary in 51 per cent ownership, with total staff numbering 5,100.

Croatian Railways' line network is 2,726 kilometres long. Its structure is:

double-track railway line	248 km
single-track railway line	2,478 km
electrified railway line	1,199 km
non-electrified railway line	1,742 km
core main lines	848 km
secondary main lines	695 km
branch lines, category I	577 km
branch lines, category II	606 km

There are three Pan-European corridors running through Croatia, forming the backbone of the railway infrastructure:

1. Pan-European Corridor X, which connects western Europe with Greece, Bulgaria and Turkey. The Croatian section: railway line state border–Savski Marof–Novska–Vinkovci–Tovarnik–state border (total length, 316.4 kilometres).

2. Branches of Pan-European Corridor V, which connects Italy with Ukraine via Slovenia and Hungary, specifically: branch Vb, which connects Budapest via Koprivnica and Zagreb with Rijeka. The Croatian section: railway line state border–Botovo–Zagreb–Karlovac –Rijeka (total length, 328.7 kilometres); and branch Vc, which connects Budapest via Osijek, Dakovo, Samac, Sarajevo and Mostar with Ploce port.

3. The Croatian section: railway line state border–Beli Manastir– Slavonski Samac–state border and state border–Metkovic–Ploce (total length, 122.5 kilometres).

Transport revenues are 36 per cent from passenger transport, and 64 per cent from freight transport. Agencies abroad are in Munich, Vienna, Budapest, and Belgrade.

Passenger transport

About 35 per cent of all people in Croatia who travel by public transport choose the railways and the relative share of passengers transported by the railways is on the increase (see Table A1.1). Domestic transport, namely urban–suburban, local and long-distance (regional) transport, makes up more than 90 per cent of passenger transport provided by Croatian Railways and 260,000 regular passenger trains operate per year, which means there are more than 700 regular trains a day. Along with regular passenger trains, Croatian Railways also provides special trains for excursions, sports fans, cultural events and artistic events, and agency trains.

Table A1.1 Movement of passengers from 1996 to 2002 and projections to 2007

Year	Passengers (000s)
1996	29,102
1997	28,785
1998	28,470
1999	30,463
2000	34,937
2001	36,964
2002	36,238
Projections	
2003	38,077
2004	39,313
2005	39,487
2006	39,663
2007	40,000

The transformation of the national railway operator into a profit-oriented company that is going to be a competitive provider of passenger transport services in the public interest of the Republic of Croatia and its own commercial interest, on domestic as well as on the broader market, is the vision for the future.

Business objectives up to 2007 are:

- 40 million passengers transported in 2007;

- 15,000 transported passengers per employee per annum;

- increase the average passenger route by 30 per cent per annum;

- increase passenger transport by 1.4 per cent per annum on average ;

- increase passengers/kilometres by 2.7 per cent per annum on average;

- positive business results in 2005.

Strategies:

- a proactive approach to the market;

- an orientation to markets that gravitate towards destinations in Croatia in terms of tourism;

- secure the market by one's own sales management, ie through ways of business interconnections with other operators or travel promoters;

- new passenger services: supplementary services at stations, introduction of new special trains (agency and excursion trains), price differentiation, increase of service quality aboard trains (dining cars and buffet coaches, sleeping cars, business compartments, etc), adjusting timetables to the needs of passengers;

- rolling stock optimization (rolling stock capacities) through reconstruction and modernization of existing sleeping cars, first and second class wagons and motor units, as well as procuring new tilting trains and motor units.

The investment programme contains plans to modernize the rolling stock by purchasing 13 sets of new tilting trains (eight DMUs and five EMUs) for domestic regional traffic, and 71 new motor units for suburban and local transport, and by reconstructing 103 passenger wagons (sleeping cars and first- and second-class wagons) and 40 motor units.

Freight transport

The relative share of railway freight transport when compared to the total amount of land freight transport in Croatia (in tons) is about 23 per cent. Of this, 25 per cent is domestic transport and 75 per cent is international transport. The demand for freight transport services by railways on corridor routes has been increasing (see Table A1.2).

Table A1.2 Movement of freight transport (in net ton kilometres – NTKM) from 1996 to 2002 and projections up to 2007

Year	Freight movements (NTKM)
1996	1,717
1997	1,876
1998	2,001
1999	1,849
2000	1,928
2001	2,249
2002	2,420
Projections	
2003	2,390
2004	2,500
2005	2,640
2006	2,782
2007	2,920

The transport of the future is definitely combined transport, with containers, interchangeable truck bodies and Ro-La wagons ('trucks on rails'), and it is the only option for both European and Croatian traffic systems.

Transformation of the national railway operator into a profit-orientated company that is going to be an important regional leader in freight transport organization, and in logistics for consignees from Croatia and Central and South-East Europe, is the vision for cargo transport. Business objectives up to 2007 are:

- 5,000 tons transported freight per employee per annum;

- increase freight transport in tons at an average rate of 3.5 per cent per annum;

- growth of NTKM at an average rate of 4.8 per cent per annum;

- raise average freight routes to over 200 kilometres per annum;

- positive business results in 2005.

Strategies:

- proactive approach to the market: Croatia, Central and South-East Europe, particularly the area of the former Yugoslavia;

- orientation to transport markets where goods gravitate towards Croatian ports, as well as to all the markets on which one can cover the entire route;

- acquire market positions assisted by one's own sales management; acquire companies having a stable market share in land transport and transport organization; found joint companies with other carriers and transport organizers; and found own companies;

- establish distribution centres;

- develop intermodal transport;

- establish joint association and tariffs with other countries;

- introduce international forwarding offices;

- adopt a differentiated approach to prices;

- optimize rolling stock (rolling stock capacities) by reconstructing and modernizing the existing stock and purchasing new freight wagons to decrease maintenance costs and increase operational possibilities in compliance with market demands.

The investment programme includes plans to modernize the rolling stock by purchasing 1,547 new freight wagons (50 eight-axle low-floor Ro-La wagons for transport of trucks with trailers) and by the overhaul and reconstruction of 5,385 existing freight wagons.

The network of roads and motorways

The development of the motorway network in the Republic of Croatia is based on two objectives: better inter-regional connection within Croatian territory and faster, more efficient integration of the Croatian road network into the main European roads. Connections between the Republic of Croatia and Europe are made through European traffic corridors:

1 corridor V^B	Budapest–Gorican–Zagreb–Rijeka–Trieste
2 corridor X^C	Linz–Graz–Maribor–Zagreb–Zadar–Split
3 corridor V^C	Budapest–Osijek–Slavonski Samac–Sarajevo–Mostar–Ploce
4 corridor X	Ljubljana–Zagreb–Belgrade–Skopje
5 Adriatic corridor	Trieste–Rijeka–Zadar–Split–Dubrovnik–Bar–Durahium–Athens

On all these corridors the Republic of Croatia is building high-quality motorways.

The road network of the Republic of Croatia is divided into state roads, county roads and local roads, with a total length of 28,275 kilometres:

Motorways	447 km
Three-lane two-way roads	150 km
State roads (together with motorways and three-lane two-way roads)	7,467 km
County roads	10.510 km
Local roads	10.298 km

Motorway construction

The strategy of traffic development of the Republic of Croatia since 1999 has been to establish a motorway network with a total length of 1,365 kilometres. By 2002, some 447 kilometres of motorways had been built as well as 150 km of three-lane two-way roads (first phase of motorways). The planning period 2001–2005 includes an accelerated programme of motorway construction. In that period it is planned to build 450 kilometres of motorways and 81 kilometres of three-lane two-way roads.

The reorganization of the road sector, necessary for this programme, led to the creation of Croatian Motorways Ltd and Croatian Roads Ltd.

Croatian Motorways was founded in the spring of 2001, and its task is to design, build, finance, control and maintain motorways and other roads where tolls are collected. In the Republic of Croatia, apart from Croatian Motorways, there are also three concession companies that build, control and maintain roads and motorways with toll collection. These are: Bina Istra Ltd, a French–Croatian company founded in 1995; Motorway Rijeka–Zagreb Ltd, founded in 1998 and owned by the Republic of Croatia; and Motorway Zagreb–Macelj Ltd, founded in 2003 and for the present owned by the Republic of Croatia.

All three concession companies carry out defined programmes of motorway construction. Bina Istra has issued bonds, without a government guarantee, for the construction of the 1B phase of the Adriatic motorway. It is the first time that a company from Central and Eastern Europe (the countries whose economies are in transition) has successfully issued bonds for the construction of traffic infrastructure.

The Zagreb–Split motorway and the Zagreb–Rijeka motorway, due to their traffic and economic characteristics, scale and complexity of engineering works, deserve special mention.

Zagreb–Split motorway

The Zagreb–Split motorway, with a total length of 375.7 kilometres, is a prime example of economic development in the Republic of Croatia. The motorway passes through undeveloped areas of the Republic of Croatia (Lika) where it is planned to build a large number of zones for economic development. The construction of the Zagreb–Split motorway will increase the accessibility of the tourist regions of Central and South Adriatic.

Rijeka–Zagreb motorway

The Rijeka–Zagreb motorway is economically a very significant project whose construction opens the way for an inflow of goods to the part of Rijeka. In 2004, when the motorway will be finished (there are 12 kilometres yet to be built), the Rijeka port area will attract cargo from Central European countries. This road connection will also increase the number of tourists in Istria and Primorje.

Appendix 2

Transport and Infrastructure

Minister Roland Zuvanic, Ministry of Maritime Affairs, Transport and Communications

Realizing the significance of the transport sector, the Government adopted a programme containing a series of guidelines and objectives that conform to the Strategy for the Development of the Transport Sector in the Republic of Croatia. Let me mention just a few of them:

- to focus on transport sector development by improving connections between Croatian regions, especially connections between the coastal area and the continent, and with Europe by means of Pan-European traffic corridors;

- to give priority to routes that will contribute to a better economic exploitation of Croatian ports;

- to pay particular attention to the development of maritime transport;

- infrastructure development projects should be aimed at creating concrete possibilities for investment of foreign capital and for credit support by international financial institutions;

- to improve the condition of the existing traffic network through greater investment in improvement programmes;

- to continue with the liberalization of the telecommunications market;

- to attract transit transport by reducing transport costs;

- to improve and harmonize relevant legislation with EU standards.

Taking into account the present situation, we are confronted with demanding tasks. Allow me to briefly expound on what we have achieved in the past three years and on our expectations and strategies.

Roads

Until 2001, the construction and maintenance of national roads was financed from the state budget and motorway tolls, as well as government guaranteed loans. In circumstances of constant public expenditure constraints, budget financing proved to be very uncertain, presenting an unreliable basis for long-term planning, resulting in uneconomical construction and insufficient maintenance of the existing road network.

The Government adopted a plan for the construction and maintenance of public roads in the period 2001–2004, which evaluates actual construction capacities and defines priorities and a realization schedule. Full maintenance standards on the almost 30,000 kilometre long network are to be achieved by 2007. An important innovation is the creation of conditions for the realization of the plan – a new financing model and a new organization of the public road management system. The Croatian Road Authority has been reorganized into two separate state-owned entities: Croatian Roads and Croatian Motorways. The new financing model earmarks 0.60 Kuna per litre out of the fuel price for Croatian Roads and 0.60 for Croatian Motorways.

This has resulted in a safe mode of financing, transparent planning and optimum project management. By the end of 2005, Croatian Motorways are to build about 400 kilometres of new motorways, out of which 39 kilometres are already open to traffic; works are in progress on a further 274 kilometres, while the remaining portion is still at the contracting stage. The works are proceeding according to schedule, which will enable the completion of the remaining sections from Zagreb to the Hungarian border during 2003 and the opening of about 97 km of the Zagreb–Split motorway to traffic also in 2003 (completion of the full length of the motorway is planned for 2005).

About 150 kilometres of motorways will be constructed in Croatia by the end of this year, while the national motorway construction programme adopted by the Government of the Republic of Croatia envisages construction of 541 kilometres of motorways and semi-motorways in the period 2001–2005, which is equal to the total number of kilometres constructed over the past 20 years. Road construction in Croatia has never been so intensive: aside from the above, more than €2.8 billion will be invested in highway construction and maintenance over the next four years.

The Government's motorway construction plan for the period 2001–2005 includes the construction of 532 kilometres of motorways and expressways, out of which 400.15 kilometres will be constructed by Croatian Motorways, that is:

- 312.1 km of the Bosiljevo–Split motorway;

- 11.1 km of the motorway extension from Split to Dubrovnik;

- 23.5 km of the still unfinished sections of the Zagreb–Gorican motorway (from Breznicki Hum to Varazdin);

- 25.95 km of the Zagreb–Lipovac motorway (the Velika Kopanica–Zupanja section);

- 13.00 km of the motorway from Zagreb to Bregana;

- 14.5 km of the motorway from Rupa to Rijeka.

According to plan, Croatian Motorways Ltd has already constructed 39 kilometres of motorways (Velika Kopanica–Zupanja and Zagreb–Bregana), works are underway on a further 274 kilometres, and contracting of the remaining sections is in preparation or in progress.

Besides the construction works already mentioned, the plan also covers preparatory activities to be carried out by Croatian Motorways Ltd (land acquisition, utility removal) for the construction of the 45.5 kilometres of semi-motorway in Istria (the so-called 'Istrian Y') and for construction of the Zagreb–Macelj motorway, including 19.38 kilometres of a full-profile motorway from Krapina to Macelj and 7.4 kilometres of the second carriageway on the Jankomir–Zapresic section. Both motorways are to be constructed according to a concession model.

The plan also envisages preparatory works (designing, land acquisition, mine clearing) to be carried out by Croatian Motorways Ltd by 2004 for the following:

- the Split–Metkovic–Ploce motorway;

- the Zagreb–Lipovac motorway (final section from Zupanja to Lipovac);

- the Beli Manastir/Ploce–BH border motorway;

- the Rupa–Rijeka–Zuta Lokva motorway (section Rijeka–Zuta Lokva).

The construction of these motorway sections is to be covered by the next four-year plan.

The road sector development strategy will insist on a level of quality compatible with European standards, to ensure integration into the European road network, and will ensure polycentric development of Croatia as well as provide an efficient maintenance system for the existing road network. Participation of foreign capital on a commercial basis will certainly be welcome.

Railways

Compared to the situation in the road sector, the problems in the railway sector are much more complex. In early 2000, the already low level of railway transport services recorded an additional decrease and so did the revenues from the provision of such services. Croatian Railways employed about 19,500 people; more than HRK1.5 billion (about 1.1

per cent of GDP) was allocated from the state budget for the railway sector; operational losses were growing; and there was a persistent problem of low economic efficiency and level of investment.

Our objective is to speed up the railway restructuring and modernization process and to make the railways competitive in the transport market, and at the same time decrease the burden on the state budget for financing current operations. It is of primary significance to increase effectiveness and to rationalize operations, reduce costs and increase investment into infrastructure and the modernization of rolling stock.

The Croatian Railways mid-term operational plan was adopted for the period ending in 2007, thus creating conditions for a further transformation of the railways and making them compatible with the European railway system. In the following five years, investment of about HRK10 billion into infrastructure is planned, including extensive reconstruction and construction works, electrification, installation of optical telecommunications and of the remote control system, reconstruction of railway stations, etc.

Most of the investments will be concentrated on Pan-European corridors X, V^b, V^c and the Zagreb–Split railway line. About HRK5 billion will be invested in rolling stock (purchase of modern vehicles and reconstruction of existing ones). The railway restructuring and modernization process would ensure annual traffic of 40 million passengers and 20 million tonnes of goods in the period following 2007 (the present annual traffic is about 35 million passengers and 12 million tonnes of goods).

The Ministry of Maritime Affairs, Transport and Communications submitted into the legislative procedure the new Railway Act. Its entry into force, which is planned in 2005, will ensure that railway transport will be operated in an accessible and non-discriminating manner, in accordance with EU requirements (several licensed transport operators, conditions of access to railway infrastructure, etc).

Appendix 3

Croatia Airlines

Croatia Airlines is a national airline company whose mission is to connect regularly its domicile country and the world and, at the same time, to promote significantly the Republic of Croatia as a tourist country through connecting its capital Zagreb and the Adriatic coast cities with most important European destinations, and through them the rest of the world. Our aspiration is to be a modern mid-size European airline company with a positive turnover, whose success is well recognized in the safety of its flights and the satisfaction of its passengers.

We try to assure our success in the global market by entering partnerships with some of the world's most important airline companies such as Lufthansa, Air France, KLM, Alitalia and others. Our goal is to turn our competition into associates, and we have already developed close cooperation with the German national carrier Lufthansa, a strategic partner with whom we hope in the future to sign a contract on regional association with Star Alliance. We intend to keep adjusting our ways to market needs as much as possible, and to offer our passengers a high-quality service based on flying safely and always on time.

As a national airline company, Croatia Airlines offers strong support to the development of Croatian tourism and the economy in general, especially to the long-term plan of extending the tourist season, which will require an increase in accommodation capacity on the Adriatic coast.

Despite unfavourable conditions, Croatia Airlines last year offered 4 per cent more capacity and had 6 per cent more passengers than in 2001. We have seen an increase in passenger numbers on all our domestic and international lines and on charter flights. We fly to established destinations, and we have managed to increase passenger cabin exploitation; additionally, we have hired new employees, despite negative trends worldwide.

Problems in Croatian air traffic are partly to do with the issue facing all European air traffic – saturation of the air space above Europe. Many experts agree that the saturation has reached such a level that it will be necessary to critically examine the efficiency of Eurocontrol in order to create more favourable conditions for the recuperation of this vital European industry, especially since it's a lengthy process and all forecasts warn of the need for caution in business expectations. Croatia is entering deeper into European integration processes and it is likely that the country will soon sign the Open Sky contract, the legal framework for integral liberalization of the market, based on rights of transport into countries of the European Union. Open Sky allows airlines from any country to transport passengers from the countries of the European Union into any other country that has also signed the contract. Should Croatia sign the contract, transport rights between, for instance, London and Paris would be available to Croatia Airlines and any European airline would be allowed to operate between Zagreb and Split.

The issue here is whether Croatia should sign the contract before it joins the European Union, probably in 2007, for so far no transition country has signed it. A precondition to signing is fulfilment of some legal provisions at the state level. Open Sky being an interstate contract, the Croatian government must decide how such liberalization would affect Croatian air traffic, as well as many other sectors like agriculture, shipbuilding and trade.

The Croatian market has always been open in terms of air traffic, and Croatia Airlines has since the beginning faced much competition, especially in regular international transport, where there are 12 other airline companies flying to Croatia. Domestic transport has also shown some competition, and just recently another airline company has set up in Croatia, in addition to many charter companies exploiting the beauty of the Adriatic coast. In the last couple of years between 40 and 70 charter companies have provided flights to Adriatic destinations.

As strong believers in the need for competition, we welcome all new companies, for they help us build up our survival skills, examine our cost structure and adjust ourselves to market needs. As the Croatian national airline company we see our strength in the quality of our product, understanding our market, cooperation with eminent business partners and our well-trained and skilled employees.

As signing the Open Sky contract implies lower air fares, and low-cost carriers present an additional challenge to tour operators to adjust their cost structure, Croatia Airlines has already taken some first steps. The winter schedule for 2002 saw a new tariff system with nine price classes, the lowest of which can compete with low-cost carriers. It is a long-term tariff model, still being applied with the summer schedule, and whose implementation will be continued in the future. Between the first day of the implementation of this system and 1 August we flew 40 per cent more passengers than last year, the great interest of service users has been recorded, we have increased the average number of passengers on flights, and we have improved the competitiveness of air travel in comparison to other means of transport.

However, the greatest crisis in aviation history, which has seen the collapse of around 40 airline companies worldwide, the loss of hundreds of thousands of jobs, and a range of negative side-effects, has had an impact on Croatia Airlines and the development of the Croatian market.

As a full member of the European and world air traffic community, Croatia Airlines has felt the negative effects of 11 September 2001: profits smaller than planned, higher costs due to unfavourable dollar exchange rates and rising fuel costs. The impact of this crisis has reflected negatively on global tourism, but Croatia, as a tourism-oriented country, still managed to record a more positive business year than most other Mediterranean destinations.

With one of the most modern mid-range fleets in the world, based on sophisticated Airbus A319/320s and with turbo-prop aircraft soon to be replaced with regional aircraft, backed by continuous growth of the Croatian economy, Croatia Airlines aims to achieve an even more important place among European and world air carriers.

Appendix 4

Business Organizations

Croatian Chamber of Economy

With its network of 20 county chambers, the Croatian Chamber of Economy (CCE) is the key national organization in connecting the Croatian and global economies.

The CCE is a non-profit, professional public institution serving the business community with the aim of strengthening and promoting economic growth in Croatia, and thereby contributing to overall social prosperity. The CCE was established in Zagreb in 1852, with the mission to protect and represent the economic interests of its members.

The improvement of economic cooperation with the international business community is a primary task of the CCE. For this purpose, various activities, focused on increasing the exchange of goods and services as well as other forms of economic cooperation with foreign business entities, are in place.

Special attention is given to promotional activities, presenting the Croatian economy in individual countries by informing business partners about Croatian laws and regulations as well as about investment opportunities and incentives. The CCE organizes visits of foreign business partners to Croatia and arranges meetings of Croatian delegations with international business partners, in which specific forms of cooperation are discussed. In this context, the promotion of Croatian export-oriented industries at various distinguished international exhibitions and fairs is an important part of CCE activities.

The CCE, as the principal promoter and organizer of joint participation at fairs and exhibitions, makes it possible for its members to get insight into a particular market, both in financial and organizational terms. This level of service is the result of very good relationships between the CCE and international chambers of commerce and/or other economic institutions, which help Croatian firms establish bilateral relationships with those in a particular country or region. These activities are carried out in cooperation with 20 county chambers, trade associations and other institutions.

The CCE also puts substantial effort into Croatia's global trade liberalization trends and in the process of European integration in order to ensure fair market competition in an export-oriented economy. The

CCE is actively and directly involved in these processes, such as joining the WTO and all activities related to further trade liberalization resulting from membership, signing of the Stabilization and Association Agreement (SAA), joining the EU, free trade negotiations with CEFTA countries, including Croatia's membership of this association, and negotiations with EFTA members and other countries. On the level of multilateral cooperation, the focus is on the EU, Croatia's most important foreign trade partner, owing to the fact that full membership of the Union is the country's long-term strategic goal. The enlargement of the single European Market is being systematically monitored. Its integration is being closely followed, as well as its trade policies and customs regulations, which directly affect the export conditions for Croatia. The CCE is participating in the practical implementation of the Agreement on Trade in Textile Products between Croatia and the EU as well as in a number of regional initiatives – the Stability Pact, the Central European Initiative (CEI), the Adriatic-Ionian Initiative (AII), the Alps-Adriatic Working Community, the SECI and others. So far, the CCE has signed about 40 cooperation agreements with chambers of commerce from all over the world.

The CCE exercises public authority, eg the issuance and verification of various certificates of the Croatian origin of goods (non-preferential origin of goods, Form A certificates of Croatian origin of goods required for preferential treatment – General Scheme of Preference). Other documents required for the export or import of goods are also issued and verified, such as export licences and non-preferential certificates for textile goods, ATA Carnet, documents facilitating customs clearance of temporary import or export of goods intended for personal or professional use, especially for commercial samples, professional equipment, fair exhibits and exhibition objects, fair samples, etc.

In 2000, the CEE became the 34th member of Eurochambres – the Association of European Chambers of Commerce and Industry. Even though it is an affiliated member, the CCE has been included in several initiatives. The European Business Panel (EBP) is a joint initiative of European economic chambers (coordinated by the Eurochambres), involved in opinion polling of member companies on various hot issues. The results are used to strengthen the influence of the European chambers network. The ChamberPass is an initiative of Eurochambres for Internet services to chambers, which has been launched as a response to the need for a higher level of services provided to companies by chambers, both in qualitative and quantitative terms, using new technologies. The Eurochambres Survey provides an overview of the economic situation in Croatia as a separate section in the European Economic Report.

The CCE has been a member of the International Chamber of Commerce in Paris (ICC) since 1995, where it participates in the work of several committees and specialized groups. Within the ICC, chambers from all over the world exchange views and experiences to improve their activities and further develop services relevant to their members. Cooperation with the International Trade Centre – UNCTAD (ICT) in Geneva – plays a prominent role in the promotion of the effects of WTO rules on trade and business systems in general, particularly in transition and developing countries. The CCE is a member of other international organizations:

- ASCAME – the Association of the Chambers of Commerce and Industry of the Mediterranean;

- UEAPME – the European Association of Crafts, Small and Medium-sized Enterprises;

- ECSB – the European Council for Small Business, affiliation of ICSB – the International Council for Small Business, Halmstad;

- TII – the European Association for Technology Transfer, Innovation and Business Information; exchange of technology tenders of the EBEN, TRN and CORDIS networks, Brussels;

- FIATA – the International Federation of Freight Forwarders Associations, Zurich;

- OICA – the International Organization of Motor Vehicle Manufacturers, Paris; and

- EMEC – the European Marine Equipment Council, London.

With the aim of better promoting the interests of the Croatian economy internationally, the leaders of the CCE decided to establish representative offices abroad, whose main task is to facilitate access to, and the competitiveness of CCE members, especially of SMEs, in the international market, by providing timely and high-quality information, finding potential partners and helping them to establish contacts.

The first representative office of the CCE was founded in Sarajevo, Bosnia and Herzegovina, in 1996, and the first civil aircraft to land in Sarajevo was Croatia Airline's plane with Croatian businessmen on board, who were interested in the revival of business relationships with Bosnia and Herzegovina. Shortly after, in 1997, an office was opened in Mostar, and the office in Banja Luka, which was established in 1996, started operations in 2001.

Since some 80 per cent of the total commodity exchange involves EU countries, the CCE established its office in Brussels, the capital of the EU, in 2000. Due to the fact that the members of the chamber expressed great interest in expanding business cooperation with Kosovo and in its reconstruction, the CCE founded an office in Pristina in 2000. In early 2002, its Belgrade office started operations. The office in Kotor, Montenegro, was opened in the first quarter of 2003, and another office in Subotica, Serbia, is also in prospect.

Since 1 January 2002, Croatia has been a member of a large free-trade zone, so the CCE plans to establish offices in Italy, Austria and Germany.

Appendix 5

Useful Web sites

Government

President of the Republic
http://www.predsjednik.hr/

Government of the Republic of Croatia
http://www.vlada.hr/

Parliament of the Republic of Croatia
http://www.sabor.hr/

Ministry of Economy
http://www.mingo.hr/

Ministry of Finance
http://www.mfin.hr/

Ministry of Foreign Affairs
http://www.mvp.hr/

Ministry of Labour and Social Welfare
http://www.mrss.hr/

Ministry of Crafts, Small and Medium Enterprises
http://www.momsp.hr/

Ministry of European Integration
http://www.mei.hr/

Government Agencies

Croatian Information Documentation Referral Agency
http://www.hidra.hr/

Croatian Guarantee Agency
http://www.hga.hr/

State Bureau of Intellectual Property
http://www.dziv.hr/

Croatian Privatization Fund
http://www.hfp.hr/

Others

Croatian Chamber of Commerce
http://www.hgk.hr/komora/eng/eng.htm

Zagreb Stock Exchange
http://www.zse.hr/

Trade Partners UK Croatia Desk
http://www.tradepartners.gov.uk/croatia/profile/index/introduction.shtml

Croatian Employers Federation
http://www.hup.hr/hrvatski/index.asp

Croatian National Bank
http://www.hnb.hr/eindex.htm

Croatian Embassies Overseas

Austria

Joanneumring 18/3
8010 Graz
Tel: (+43/316) 33 82 50
Fax: (+43/316) 33 82 50 14

Belgium

Kunstlaan 50
8ste verdiep – bus 14, 1050
Brussels
Tel: 2500 0920
Fax: 2 512 0338

Canada

229 Chapel Street
Ottawa
Ontario K1N 7Y6
Tel: (613) 562-7820
Fax: (613) 562-7821
E-mail: info@croatiaemb.net

France

39 avenue Georges Mandel
75116 Paris
Tel: 01 5370 0280
Fax: 01 5370 0290
E-mail: secretariat@amb-croatie.fr

United Kingdom

21 Conway Street
London W1P 5HL
Tel: (020) 7387 2022
E-mail: political@croatianembassy.co.uk (Political)
economic@croatianembassy.co.uk (Economic Section)
cultural@croatianembassy.co.uk (Cultural Section)
consular-dept@croatianembassy.co.uk (Consular Department)
info-press@croatianembassy.co.uk (Information and Press Section)
amboffice@croatianembassy.co.uk (Office of Ambassador)

United States of America

2343 Massachusetts Avenue NW
Washington DC 20008
Tel: (202) 588 5899
Fax: (202) 588 8936
E-mail: webmaster@croatiaemb.org

Embassies in Croatia

Australia

Intercontinental Hotel, 6th Floor
Krsnjavoga 1
Zagreb
Tel: (385) (1) 489 1200
Fax: (385) (1) 483 1216

Belgium

Pantovchak 125 B1
10000 Zagreb
Email: Zagreb@diplobel.org
Tel: (385) (1) 4578 901, (385) (1) 4578 903
Fax: (385) (1) 4578 902

France

5 Schlosserove Stube – BP 466
10000 Zagreb
Tel: (385) (1) 455 77 67/68/69
Fax: (385) (1) 455 77 65

India

Boskoviceva 7A 10000
Zagreb
Tel: (385) (1) 487 3239, 487 3240, 487 3241
Fax: (385) (1) 481 7907
E-mail: embassy.india@zg.tel.hr

United Kingdom

Ul Ivana Lucica 4
Zagreb
Tel: (385) (1) 6009 100 (Switchboard)
E-mail: british.embassyzagreb@fco.gov.uk
commercial.section@zg.htnet.hr

United States of America

Andrije Hebranga 2
Zagreb 10000
Tel: (385) (1) 661 2200
Fax: (385) (1) 661 2373

Appendix 6

Contributor Contact Details

Croatia Airlines
Savska 41
10000 Zagreb
Tel: (385) (1) 6160 000
Fax: (385) (1) 6176 737
Sita: ZAGDDOU
E-mail: ivan.misetic@ croatiaairlines.hr

Croatian Privatization Fund (HFP or CFP)
Ivana Lucica 6
10000 Zagreb
Tel (385) (1) 4569 148
Fax (385) (1) 4569 140
Web site: www.hfp.hr
Contact: Mare Bulic-Mrkobrad, mare-bulic@hfp.tel.hr

Croatian Chamber of Economy (HGK)
Rooseveltov trg 2
10000 Zagreb
Tel: (385) (1) 4561 555
Fax: (385) (1) 4828 380
E-mail: hgk@hgk.hr
Contact: Ms SnjeZana Foschio-Bartol, Tel: (385) (1) 45 61 561,
sfoschio@hgk.hr

Deloitte & Touche Zagreb
Kaciceva 3b
10000 Zagreb
Tel: (385) (1) 4877 642
Fax: (385) (1) 4877 590
Contact: Visnja Bojanic, vbojanic@deloittece.com

Dr Josip Kregar
Pravni fakultet Zagreb
(School of Law Zagreb University)
Treg marsala Tita 3
HR 1000 Zagreb
Tel: (385) (1) 4804 422
Fax: (385) (1) 4802 421
E-mail: Josip.kregar@zg.tel.hr

Dr Velimir Srica
Tel: (385) (1) 2383 333, delfin-razvoj-managementa@zg.tel.hr
Foundation 2020
Contact: Professor P Turkovic
Tel: (385) (1) 2302 047
E-mail: petar@foundation2020.com

HEP
Contact: Mr Matkovic (HEP)
Tel: (385) (1) 6322 202
E-mail: Mihovil.Matkovic@hep.hr

Faculty of Agriculture, Zagreb University
PO Box 1
10002 Zagreb
Tel: (385) (1) 2393 777
Fax. (385) (1) 2315 300
E-mail: dekanat@agr.hr
Contact: Jasmina Havranek (Dean of the Faculty of Agriculture)

INA Oil Company
Avenija V Holijeva 10
10020 Zagreb
Tel: (385) (1) 6451 852
Fax: (385) (1) 6452 108
Contact: Ms Biserka Cimesa
E-mail: biserka.cimesa@ina.hr

Kaplast d.d.
Borlin Gaj 1
47000 Karlovac
Tel: (385) (4) 7451 146
Fax: (385) (4) 7451 142
E-mail: info@kaplast.hr
Web site: www.kaplast.hr
Contact: Mr Mario Dombos

Lowe Digitel
Babukiceva 3a
Zagreb 10000-HR
Contact: Ms Tina Mavar
Tel: (385) (1) 2359 140
Fax: (385) (1) 2319 411
GSM +385 98 227 501
E-mail: tina@digitel.hr

Markovic & Pliso Law Firm
Smiciklasova 21
10000 Zagreb
Tel: (385) (0) 1 4699 444
Fax: (385) (0) 1 4699 499
E-mail: markovic-pliso@zg.htnet.hr

Ministry of Craft and SMEs
Ksaver 200
10000 Zagreb
Tel: (385) (1) 4698 300
Fax: (385) (1) 4698 308
Web: http://www.momsp.hr

Ministry of European Integration
Grada Vukovara 62
10000 Zagreb
Tel: (385) (1) 4569 335, 4569 336
Fax: (385) (1) 6303 183
E-mail: info@mei.hr
Web: www.mei.hr
Contact: Ivana Grgic, spokeperson
Tel: 385 1 63.03.034, ivana.grgic@mei.hr

Ministry of Tourism
Grada Vukovara 78
10000 Zagreb
Tel: (385) (1) 6106 111, 6106 300
Fax: (385) (1) 6109 300
E-mail: ministarstvo-turizma@zg.tel.hr
Web: http://www.mint.hr

Ministry of Public Works, Building and Reconstruction
Vladimira Nazora 61
10000 Zagreb
Tel: (385) (1) 3784 500/3784 502/3784 520
Fax: (385) (1) 3784 550
Web: http://www.mjr.hr
E-mail: info@mjr.hr
Contact: Ivana Prohic, Tel: (385) (1) 3784 519, ivana.prohic@mjr.hr
Anita Klapan, Tel: (385) (1) 3784 553, anita.klapan@mjr.hr

Ministry of Environmental Protection and Regional Planning
Republike Austrije 20
10000 Zagreb
Tel: (385) (1) 3782 444, 3782 143, 3782 144
Fax: (385) (1) 3772 822, 3772 555
Web: http://www.mzopu.hr
Contact Ms Mirjana Papavala, Tel: (385) (1) 61 06 563,
mirjana.papavala@mzopu.hr

Office of Dr Zarko Primorac
Insenjerski biro – revizija
Heinzelova 4a
Zagreb 10000
Tel: (385) (1) 4600 808
Fax: (385) (1) 4650 797
Contact: Maja Tomasic, ured@ingrevizija.htnet.hr

Raiffeisen Bank Austria d.o.o Zagreb
Contact: Lidija Arbanas, Tel: (385) (1) 600 6900, lidija.arbanas@rba-
zagreb.raiffeisen.at

Zagreb Institute of Economics
Trg JF Kennedy 7
10000 Zagreb
Tel: (385) (1) 2335 700
Fax: (385) (1) 2335 165
Contact: Maruska Cenic, mcenic@eizg.hr, Andrea Mervar,
mervar@eizg.hr

Zagreb Insurance Company
Ozegoviceva 16
10000 Zagreb
Tel: (385) (1) 2392 995
Fax: (385) (1) 2392 992
Contact: Ksenija Kasalo, Tel: +385 (0)1 2392 965,
ksenija.kasalo@osiguranje-zagreb.hr

Index

Index of Advertisers